The Project Management Workshop

The Project Management Workshop

James Taylor

AMACOM
American Management Association

New York • Atlanta • Boston • Chicago • Kansas City • San Francisco • Washington, D. C.

Brussels • Mexico City • Tokyo • Toronto

Special discounts on bulk quantities of AMACOM books are available to corporations, professional associations, and other organizations. For details, contact Special Sales Department, AMACOM, a division of American Management Association, 1601 Broadway, New York, NY 10019.
Tel.: 212-903-8316. Fax: 212-903-8083.
Web Site: www.amanet.org

This publication is designed to provide accurate and authoritative information in regard to the subject matter covered. It is sold with the understanding that the publisher is not engaged in rendering legal, accounting, or other professional service. If legal advice or other expert assistance is required, the services of a competent professional person should be sought.

Library of Congress Cataloging-in-Publication Data
Taylor, James, 1937-
The project management workshop / James Taylor.
    p.cm.
Includes index.
ISBN 0-8144-7044-0
1. Industrial project management—Study and teaching. I. Title.

HD69.P75 T388 2000
658.4'04—dc21

00-042012

Printing number

10 9 8 7 6 5 4 3 2 1

This book is dedicated
to my wife and best friend
Karen Romano-Taylor.

Contents

———————————

Acknowledgments   ix

Module 1: Introduction   1

Module 2: The Project Selection Phase   17

Module 3: The Project Concept Phase   59

Module 4: The Project Development Phase   121

Module 5: The Project Implementation Phase   169

Module 6: The Project Close-Out Phase   231

       Slides   259
       Handouts   389
Index   451

Acknowledgments

_____

It would be arrogant of me to claim that this work is totally mine. It is the product of an accumulation of knowledge, skill, and experience of scores of people with whom I have worked for more than thirty years as a project manager and teacher.

I particularly want to thank the many students I have taught over the years. I am sure I learned as much from you as you did from me.

Introduction

_____

Project management is a specialized approach to managing business. However, there are still relatively few professional project managers in the world today. The Project Management Institute reported early in January 2000 that the number of certified project management professionals was just over fifteen thousand. That number is increasing rapidly, though, as more and more companies require their employees to participate in training courses to improve their project-management skills, with some stipulating that their employees become certified by the Project Management Institute before they can assume the title and work of project managers.

Not too many years ago, project managers got their training on the job. Anyone interested in becoming a project manager worked on a project team until a superior felt he or she was ready to manage a project. Only in the past fifteen years have any training courses specific to project management become available to companies interested in providing training for their employees. Those courses that were available focused on military defense contracts. Project management tools were thought to apply only to engineering projects.

Since the late 1980s and early 1990s, project management has grown into a separate, recognized career path. In fact, project managers today usually have a better understanding of how their organizations function than do their functional manager counterparts because of the breadth of knowledge required for managing projects. The first step to gaining this breadth of knowledge is formal training.

Why This Book

The Project Management Workshop is intended to provide the fundamentals of project management to new or relatively inexperienced project managers. It is designed so that an internal corporate trainer can conduct a two-day workshop to set the level for new project managers and to provide the foundation they will need to continue their learning journey. *The Project Management Workshop* also provides practical tools that the participants can begin using immediately.

A trainer who has a good background in project management will of course do well at teaching this course. However, it is not always practical or cost effective to hire an outside training company to get that level of expertise. Therefore, this book is written so that a trainer with moderate project-management skills can review the concepts and tools and be able to provide sound training to the participants. If you feel that your project-management skills need more support than is available in this book, I recommend that you obtain my book, *A Survival Guide for Project Managers*, also published by AMA-COM Books. It is a perfect companion to this course and provides greater detail on the major tools and concepts covered here.

Who Will Benefit from This Book

This book is written for the corporate trainer, or any trainer who needs guidance and help in structuring a fundamental project-management course. The book contains slides suitable for a two-day course along with exercises, training tips, handouts, and explanations of the theory covered in the course. A trainer can teach this course as it stands or use it to tailor a course to meet his or her organization's specific needs.

How This Book Is Organized

The book is organized to match a typical project-management life cycle. The particular model used for the book and the accompanying slides are shown in Exhibit 1. The Project Management Institute's standard project life cycle model has four phases: concept, development, implementation, and close-out. However, I have chosen to include an additional phase, project selection, at the beginning of the project. Many project managers are not involved in the project-selection process, but others are. In addition, project managers often have to provide the data used in selecting a project, so it is helpful to them if they understand the techniques that are being used. The trainer, however, may make the decision not to include this module for beginning project managers. You can do so with no detrimental effects to the rest of the course.

Each module includes:
*   A detailed explanation of content to help the trainer prepare for the lesson
*   An agenda with estimated times to keep the course on schedule
*   Slides with corresponding training notes
*   Common questions and answers to promote discussion
*   Training tips to help the trainer's delivery
*   Handouts

This book also features separate sections in the back for slides and overheads to facilitate photocopying.

A Final Word

Training is a joyful profession. I know that my years of training have been fulfilling and rewarding, and I am sure that those of you using this book feel the same way. I hope this book is of great benefit to you as your organization moves toward a project-management focus. My objective in writing the book was to provide you, the trainer, with as much information and as many tools as I could in a very short, concise way. The participants may not go away from the workshop knowing everything about project management, but they will know enough to begin making informed decisions and applying useful tools for a more effective project-management environment. The rest will come as they gain experience and knowledge.

Exhibit 1. Project Life Cycle Model				
Selection Activities	Concept Activities	Development Activities	Implementation Activities	Close-Out Process
—Perform financial analysis. —Analyze strategic projects. —Rank projects. —Choose projects to pursue.	—Gather data. —Analyze requirements. —Develop charter. —Develop WBS. —Organize project team. —Hold kickoff meeting.	—Refine WBS. —Perform network analysis. —Develop schedules. —Develop plans.	—Implement control process. —Control project progress with earned value.	—Perform scope verification. —Perform technical audit. —Perform financial audit. —Close out contract.

Agenda for Module 1: Introduction

8:30a.m.   Welcome to the Project Management Workshop   10 minutes

Workshop Objectives   6 minutes

Project Management Model   6 minutes

Workshop Agenda   5 minutes

Student Introductions   30 minutes

Total   57 minutes

Introduction to

The Project Management Workshop

Learning the Fundamentals
of
Project Management

Approximate time for module: 57 minutes

Welcome to *The Project Management Workshop*

Welcome to *The Project Management Workshop*

- **Emergency phone number**
- **Local emergency exit procedures**
- **Fax number**
- **Floor/facility layout**
- **Breaks**
- **Start and end expectations**
- **Attendance**
    - **Prerequisites**
    - **Maximum absence**

Start on time = End on time

1-1

Objective

- Welcome participants; discuss administrative information and course requirements.

Time: 10 minutes

Training Notes

- Put up Slide 1-1: Welcome to *The Project Management Workshop*.
- Greet participants and welcome them to *The Project Management Workshop*.
- Introduce yourself; provide your credentials for teaching project management.
- Discuss administration information and explain the ground rules for the course.
    —Review the break schedule. Talk about keeping to the schedule. Explain that you will give a break approximately every hour.

—Your role is to get the participants to become involved in the learning process. Therefore, it is imperative that you establish the expectation that this class is Socratic, that is, interactive. You will facilitate discussions, but it is important that participants are involved in the discussion.

—Set up times before and after the class to be available to the participants. Record on a flip chart the times you will be available for after-class discussions.

—Provide all necessary information regarding rest rooms, cafeterias, and coffee bars.

- Impress on the participants that the class will begin and end at times stated.

Workshop Objectives

Workshop Objectives

At the end of this workshop, you will be able to:

- **Define *project* and *program***

- **Describe the differences between project and functional management**

- **Apply financial techniques in comparing and selecting projects**

- **Develop a project charter**

- **Develop project requirements**

- **Describe the elements of a statement of work**

1-2

Objective

- Introduce the course objectives.

Time: 6 minutes

Training Notes

- Put up Slide 1-2: Workshop Objectives.
- Put up Slide 1-3: Workshop Objectives (*continued*).
- This course is intended to provide new project managers with the basic concepts and tools they need to manage a project successfully.
- The objectives on these two slides summarize these basic tools and provide the participants with an understanding of the material they will be covering during the workshop.

Workshop Objectives (*continued*)

- **Develop a Work Breakdown Structure**
- **Perform a network analysis**
- **Develop schedules using the Gantt chart**
- **Develop a risk management plan**
- **Develop and use a change management process**
- **Control project budgets and schedules using Earned Value**
- **Close a project**

1-3

Project Management Model

Project Management Model

LIFE-CYCLE PHASES OF A PROJECT

Selection	Concept	Development	Implementation	Close-out
Activities •Financial analysis •Analyze strategic goals •Rank projects •Choose projects to pursue	**Activities** •Gather data •Analyze re-quirements •Develop charter •Develop WBS •Organize project team •Kickoff meeting	**Activities** •Refine WBS •Perform net-work analysis •Develop sched-ules •Develop plans	**Activities** •Implement control process •Control project progress with earned value	**Activities** •Scope verification •Technical audit •Financial audit •Contract close-out

1-4

Objective

• Introduce participants to a model of a typical project life cycle.

Time: 6 minutes

Training Notes

• Put up Slide 1-4: Project Management Model.
• The four phases—Concept, Development, Implementation, and Close-out—make up a life cycle representative of most projects.
• Explain that the selection phase is usually not included in the life cycle because many companies don't regard a project as such until after the selection or decision to pursue the project has been made.

- This life-cycle model is used in this workshop because of the importance of the selection process and because project managers need to have an understanding of how the decisions were made about pursuing their project.
- Spend some time talking about the activities under each of the phases.
- Explain that project activities don't fall into neat categories such as those in this model, but if they can start thinking of the project phases and the typical activities they will encounter, then it is easier to learn which project management tools they can use in these activities.

Workshop Agenda

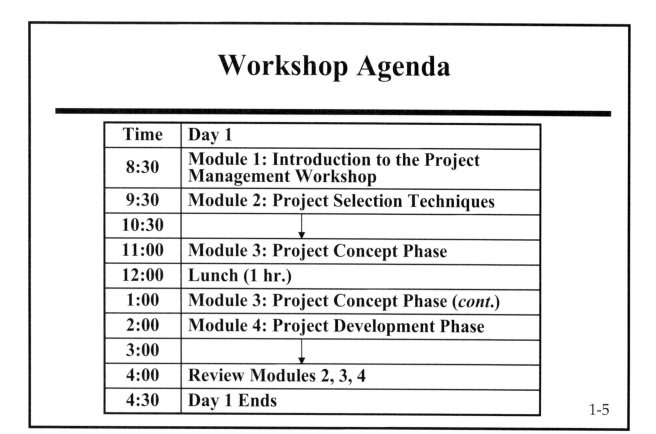

Objective

- Provide the participants with a plan of how the course will be taught and what the general approach will be.

Time: 5 minutes

Training Notes

- Put up Slide 1-5: Workshop Agenda.
- Put up Slide 1-6: Workshop Agenda (*continued*).
- Stress that this agenda is a plan. There may be some deviations from it to accommodate the needs of the group.
- Point out the times provided so that the participants will have a feel for how long each module is.

Workshop Agenda (*continued*)

Workshop Agenda (*continued*)

Time	Day 2
8:30	**Recap Day 1 Modules/Begin Case Study**
9:30	**Case Study**
10:30	
11:00	
12:00	**Lunch**
1:00	**Module 5: Project Implementation (*cont.*)**
2:00	**Module 6: Project Close-out**
3:00	**Module 7: Course Wrap-up**
4:00	**Day 2 Ends**
4:30	

1-6

Student Introductions

Student Introductions

- **Name**
- **Location**
- **Years in current organization**
- **Project and team member experience**
- **Objectives/expectations of the workshop**
- **What you do for fun**

1-7

Objective

- Give each person an opportunity to identify himself or herself and what his or her expectations are for the class.

Time: 30 minutes

Training Notes

- Put up Slide 1-7: Student Introductions.
- Tell the participants to limit their introductions to 1 minute.
- Ask each person to introduce himself or herself and to explain a little about his or her current job. Stress that you would like to hear about each person's duties, not just a job title . . . a title is not always descriptive.

- It is very important to find out how much project-team and project-management experience each participant has in order to ascertain the level of the group.
- Ask the participants if any of them have had any formal project-management training. If any of them have, ask them to share their experience with the group and to explain whether they are currently using any of the tools.
- Asking the participants what they do for fun is a way of breaking the ice with the group, particularly if they don't know each other. Some participants will reveal some interesting hobbies.

The Project

Selection Phase

The purpose of the project selection process is to rank the project choices according to the company's ability to pursue them and, ultimately, to choose the one(s) that offers the greatest chance of success.

The process of project selection is not usually considered to be a project phase, the argument being that it is not a project until a decision is made to pursue it. But as a trainer, you will find that participants routinely express their frustration about not knowing why or how a project is born. There are really four reasons that it is important to teach this section in a basic project management workshop. First, project managers have to manage the project. If they do not understand how or why the project came into being, how it fits into the company's strategic goals, how the budget was derived, or what the constraints and assumptions are, their task is much more difficult. Knowledge of the techniques applied in selecting their project will answer many of those questions. Second, some companies require the project manager to verify the worth of the project by performing benefit-to-cost or other analyses before authorizing him or her to start project work. If that is a requirement in your company, then it is imperative the project managers know how to apply and analyze the selection techniques. Third, project managers are often asked to supply data for selection analysis. An understanding of how the data are used improves the quality of the data. Fourth, the Project Management Institute requires an understanding of these techniques to become certified as a project management professional (PMP). If the long-range plan for your company is to encourage the pursuit of this certification, this module provides the information the participants need for those questions on the examination.

The Project Selection Phase Objectives

Projects begin in many ways. They may evolve as a means of meeting market or competitive pressures, satisfying regulatory or environmental requirements, upgrading office equipment and processes, or entering a new market. Whatever the reason for pursuing a particular project, it went through some kind of a selection process. Unfortunately, many companies do not determine which projects to pursue through a formalized or disciplined selection process. Project selection most often is the result of intuitive guesses or opinions by a few key personnel.

Because business today is highly competitive, companies are looking for better ways to choose projects having higher payoff potentials. Significant improvements to a company's bottom line are realized when a well-documented and formalized project selection process is established. The objectives for any selection process should be to:

1. Eliminate the "shotgun" approach to bidding. Many companies, especially smaller ones, tend to bid on every project that remotely resembles their core business. This practice costs a lot of money, and the win rate —that is, numbers of contracts compared to numbers of proposals submitted—tends to be very low. The principal reason is that no one examines the project closely enough to determine if it actually fits the company's strategic goals, if the company has the expertise, or if the company has the requisite resources to pursue it.

2. Provide the ability to make sound business decisions. With a formalized selection process, the company has a mechanism for choosing the projects to invest in with a higher degree of confidence in its ability to win the project or realize a positive payoff.

3. Provide a means for examining the company's capability, relative to expertise and resources, on a continuing basis. If each project is selected as a result of an examination of the benefits, costs, and capabilities, it will be clear where the company needs to focus its growth efforts.

4. Improve cash flow projections. A selection process includes techniques

that identify when and how much capital has to be expended as well as when the project is likely to start making a profit. Cash-flow and profit projections are especially important for small to mid-sized companies, which usually do not have excess cash on hand.

5. Involve project managers in the decision process. As mentioned earlier, project managers usually are not assigned to a project until after the decision has been made to pursue it. Even then, the project manager may not actually get involved with the project until it is time to start the planning process. A company that involves its project managers in the selection process helps the project manager understand the reasons for pursuing a project as well as the assumptions and constraints that were part of the decision.

Developing a formalized and disciplined selection process is not an objective of this workshop, but project managers should understand how their projects come into being and what the common techniques are for choosing one project over another.

Although the equations are not particularly difficult, an understanding of basic financial concepts is helpful in answering participants' questions. You should be prepared for resistance from your participants, particularly if they do not have either a financial or an engineering background. Many in your workshop session will look at the equations and immediately decide they are in over their heads. Although the selection techniques covered in the module are not difficult, some of them may seem daunting at first glance. However, with a little practice, you can handle the equations and answer any questions.

You can use this module separately from the basic project management workshop. Although every project manager should understand project selection techniques, it may be more important to you and your company that you first become proficient in the basic concepts and tools of managing projects. Besides, as stated at the beginning of the chapter, other company staff members, not including the project manager, usually decide which projects to pursue. If this is the practice at your company, it may be worthwhile considering a separate training session for those individuals. A separate session would ensure that those responsible for project selection are familiar with these techniques, and it would provide you with an opportunity to educate your company in the importance of a formalized and documented selection process and of including project managers in the process.

Content Notes: The Project Selection Module
The theory behind the selection techniques in this module is not particularly difficult, but you should be aware of some subtleties. All such sub-

tle points will be clearly identified so that you can emphasize them to your course participants.

Payback or Break-Even Point

Payback and break-even point are different terms for the same point in a project's life cycle, and they are used interchangeably. For convenience, we will use *payback* for this discussion.

The payback point is the moment at which a project becomes profitable, or, alternatively, it is the time required for the firm to recover its initial investment. A project cannot generate revenues until it is at least partially operational, and, therefore, initially the project generates only costs. At some point in the project's life cycle, though, some benefits will begin to accumulate, often before the project is completely finished. Suppose, for example, a company develops and installs a new management information system (MIS). During the first few weeks of the project, only costs are accumulated through the expenditures for labor, computers, and other equipment. But benefits begin to emerge as the new system starts coming on line. Even after the full system is operational, it still may be several months or even a few years before the benefits equal the costs of development, installation, and training. The payback period, then, is that point at which the benefits and costs are equal.

If the MIS system in the above example was estimated to cost a total of $100,000 and the yearly benefits are estimated to average $25,000, the payback period is four years. A word of caution—some companies use total or *gross* revenues for the project benefits number, whereas others use *net* revenues. Be sure the participants understand this point.

$$\text{Payback Period} = \frac{\$100,000}{\$25,000/\text{year}}$$

$$\text{Payback Period} = 4 \text{ years}$$

Senior management compares this payback number, 4 years, with the accepted criteria they have established. If 4 years is equal to or sooner than the established criteria, then the project is acceptable. Otherwise, the project is not pursued.

The advantages of the payback technique are that it is fast and easy. It is a quick way to assess future cash-flow projections. But the disadvantages are sufficient to warrant using the technique *only* as a quick assessment, not as the basis of business decisions.

Some companies use payback as a measure of risk. For instance, they assume that a shorter payback period is less risky than a longer one. This logic is flawed because the technique focuses on the short term, that is, it considers only what happens up to the point of breaking even. In other words, the net cash and it does not take into account the cost of money. Gambling in Las Vegas may have a shorter payback period than purchasing a U.S. government bond, but that does not mean the gaming tables in Las Vegas are less risky than T bills.

Return on Investment

The average return on investment (ROI) in a project is defined as average returns from the investment divided by the average investment in the project. Using the ROI criterion, the decision to invest in the project is made by comparing the ROI for the project with the firm's target return.

For example, suppose a company requires a rate of return of 55%, and the president wants the project manager to look at the prospective investment again with this criterion in mind. From previous calculations, the project manager determines that the cumulative net cash flows from the project are expected to be $11.9 million for the five years of the project's life. Hence, the *average* net cash flow is $11.9/5 = $2.38 million. Previous calculations also indicate that the average amount the firm will invest over the five-year period is $5.3 million. The ROI, then, is

$$ROI = 2.38/5.3$$
$$ROI = 45\%$$

Since this ROI is less than the firm's target return of 55%, the project is rejected, based solely on the basis of the ROI criterion.

You must be aware of two very important elements of the ROI technique. First, this technique uses *averages* of the benefits and costs over the anticipated life of the project. Second, the benefits are *net returns*. Many people make the mistake of assuming that the ROI can be calculated simply by inverting the payback period. But the benefits number used in the payback period calculation often stands for *gross returns*. Be sure you stress this point to the workshop participants.

Like the payback period, this technique is fast and easy to use, but it also has some disadvantages. First, it places too much emphasis on distant cash flows by assuming they are equivalent to current cash flows. Second, the ROI technique does not discount the cash flows.

Both the ROI and the payback period techniques are viable project selection tools. But they are best used as indicators of whether a project has the potential for the payoff the company is looking for. If the project clears either or both of these hurdles, then a more detailed analysis should be performed to determine the real value of the project to the company. Any of the following three selection techniques will provide the needed level of confidence in the project's worth.

Internal Rate of Return

The internal rate of return (IRR) is a special case of the net present value method that will be discussed next. Both these techniques discount the cash flows and, hence, offer a more realistic measure for determining the worth of a project or investment of any kind.

In the equation below, i is the IRR. This rate of return is the interest rate that equates the present value of the cash inflows to the present value of the cash outflows. Hence,

$$Pv = \sum_{t=0}^{n} \frac{Fv}{(1+i)^t}$$

or $\quad \sum_{t=0}^{n} \frac{Fv\ (Inflows)}{(1+i)^t} = \sum_{t=0}^{n} \frac{Fv\ (Outflows)}{(1+i)^t}$

and $\quad \sum_{t=0}^{n} \frac{Fv\ (Inflows)}{(1+i)^t} - \sum_{t=0}^{n} \frac{Fv\ (Outflows)}{(1+i)^t} = 0$

These formulas look much worse than they really are. They are commonly used for financial calculations, so any participant with a business or financial background will recognize and be able to use them. On the other hand, there are always some participants who have no previous experience with these equations, and it is important that you be able to explain how to interpret the equations and how to solve a simple example.

To teach the IRR technique, follow these steps:

1. Ask the participants if they recognize the present-value equation.
2. If any participants are unfamiliar with the equation, assure them that it looks worse than it is and that together you will work a simple problem to demonstrate how to interpret the equation.
3. Explain each of the terms:
    a. Pv is present value; that is, it is the value of money today.
    b. Fv is future value. It is the amount of money you expect to receive or to pay out.
    c. i is the internal rate of return, essentially rate or return.
    d. t is the time period
    e. Σ is the Greek letter sigma, meaning to sum all the cash inflows or out-flows as appropriate
    f. Use a simple example to demonstrate how to set up the equations.

Example: You have calculated that the costs and revenues for your project are as shown in the table. Determine the IRR for the project and compare it with the company's IRR of 25%. Would you recommend pursuing the project?

Year	Estimated Revenues	Estimated Costs
0	0	$4,000
1	$4,000	$3,000
2	$5,000	0

Solution: Pv (Inflows) – Pv (Outflows) is

$$\frac{0}{(1+i)^0} + \frac{4,000}{(1+i)^1} + \frac{5,000}{(1+i)^2} - \frac{4,000}{(1+i)^0} - \frac{3,000}{(1+i)^1} - \frac{0}{(1+i)^2} = 0$$

The first and last terms are equal to 0, since their numerators are 0. The fourth term is equal to 4,000, since its denominator is raised to the zero power (anything raised to the zero power is equal to 1 by definition). Therefore, the equation can be rewritten as

$$\frac{4,000}{(1+i)^1} + \frac{5,000}{(1+i)^2} - \frac{4,000}{1} - \frac{3,000}{(1+i)^1} = 0$$

Calculating IRR is cumbersome because it has to be done by trial and error. Since this equation cannot be solved for the one unknown, *i*, we must arbitrarily choose values for *i* until we find the one that makes the equation equal to 0. For example, suppose we start with 10%. Then the result is

$$\frac{4,000}{1.10} + \frac{5,000}{1.21} - \frac{4,000}{1} - \frac{3,000}{1.10} = 3,636.36 + 4,132.23 - 4,000 - 2,727.27 = 1,041.32$$

Our first choice, 10%, is obviously too low. If we try 20%, the result is

$$\frac{4,000}{1.20} + \frac{5,000}{1.44} - \frac{4,000}{1} - \frac{3,000}{1.20} = 3,333.33 + 3,472.22 - 4,000 - 2,500 = 305.55$$

The second choice, 20%, is also too low, but we are approaching 0 rapidly. Therefore, for the third choice, try 30%. Then we have

$$\frac{4,000}{1.3}+\frac{5,000}{1.69}-\frac{4,000}{1}-\frac{3,000}{1.3}=3,076.92+2,958.58-4,000-2,307.69=-272.19$$

If we develop a table of our results such as the one below, it is easy to see that the correct answer is halfway, or a little more, between 20 and 30%. One final iteration at 25% then results in

$$\frac{4,000}{1.25}+\frac{5,000}{1.56}-\frac{4,000}{1}-\frac{3,000}{1.25}=3,200.00+3,205.13-4,000-2,400.00=5.13$$

So the correct answer is about 25%. We can carry the math further to refine the number, but any answer within 5% is sufficient for an IRR analysis.

IRR Iterations	
Value of *i*	Equation Result
.10	1,041.32
.20	305.55
.30	−272.19
.25	5.13

This example is easy to demonstrate on a flip chart of white board, and it will facilitate an understanding of how to interpret and use the present value equations. The final analysis of these results is to compare the 25% IRR calculated for the example project with the company's cost of capital. If 25% is higher than the company's cost of capital, then the project should be pursued; otherwise, it should not be.

Net Present Value

Net present value (NPV) is the difference between the present value of the expected revenues and the present value of the expected costs. The equation was demonstrated with the IRR example, and the process is exactly the same except that the IRR is known. In other words, the company's IRR is used in the present-value equations to calculate both the revenue and cost present values. The NPV can be represented mathematically by

$$NPV = Pv \text{ (Inflows)} - Pv \text{ (Outflows)}$$

where inflows are the expected revenues and outflows are the expected costs of the project.

"Goodness" of a project is determined by whether NPV is positive, negative, or zero. Hence, if NPV is greater than 1, i.e., positive, then the project should be pursued according to the NPV analysis technique. If it is less than 1, then the project should not be pursued; if zero, the project is likely only to break even and not provide enough benefit to warrant pursuing it.

Benefit-to-Cost Ratio

The benefit-to-cost ratio that is most often used is

$$B/C = Pv \text{ (Inflows)}/Pv \text{ (Outflows)}$$

The procedure for determining the B/C is to calculate the present values of the revenues and costs as in the NPV analysis, but instead of subtracting the two, divide Pv (Inflows) by Pv (Outflows). This quotient is interpreted according to whether it is larger or smaller than 1.0. If B/C is greater than 1.0, then the project would be pursued; if less than 1.0, it would not be. If B/C is equal to 1.0, then it will break even.

Training Objectives for the Project Selection Module

The objectives for this module are to:

1. Allow the participants an opportunity to explore how their company currently selects projects and to describe a formalized and disciplined selection process.
2. Understand and demonstrate the most common techniques for selecting projects, how they are used, and the advantages and disadvantages of each method.
3. Prepare participants to be change agents within their organizational groups.

Summary

It is very important for project managers to know how to use various selection techniques. Most companies use one or more of the techniques covered in this chapter. However, many people do not understand that if used alone, some of the techniques may eliminate what otherwise would be excellent projects from a financial viewpoint. Each technique has its uses, and each will provide useful information as long as the limitations are clearly understood. Always use more than one technique to make business decisions that could affect a company's profit making and growth potential.

Agenda for Module 2: The Project Selection Phase

9:30   Objectives for Module 2   5 minutes

            Where We Are in the Process   3 minutes

            Project Selection Techniques   5 minutes

            Payback or Break-Even Point and Sample Calculation   12 minutes

            Return on Investment (ROI)   7 minutes

            Internal Rate of Return (IRR) and Sample Calculation   12 minutes

            Net Present Value and Sample Calculation   9 minutes

            Benefit to Cost (B/C) and Sample Calculation   10 minutes

            Exercise 2-1: Selection Techniques Exercise   30 minutes

            Key Messages—Module 2   3 minutes

            Total   96 minutes

Module 2: The Project Selection Phase

How Projects Are Selected

Approximate time for module: 1 hour and 36 minutes

Objectives for Module 2

Objectives for Module 2

At the end of this module you will be able to:

- Identify, define and apply various project selection techniques

- Describe the advantages and disadvantages of each selection technique

- Describe the use of project selection techniques

2-1

Objective
- Introduce module objectives.

Time: 5 minutes

Training Notes
- Put up Slide 2-1: Objectives for Module 2.
- This module is important because it introduces the participants to the most common techniques used for selecting projects to pursue.
- Many project managers are not involved in project selection decisions but are required to prepare or develop data that are used. An understanding of the techniques will improve the quality of the data that are developed.
- Understanding how decisions are made will provide the project manager

with a better understanding of the rationale for pursuing a project and what the assumptions and constraints are.

- Facilitate a discussion about the importance of having a formalized project selection process in place.
- Ask participants how projects come about in their company divisions or groups and how they are selected.
- Ask participants if they are ever involved in the project selection process and how they are involved.

 Training Tip: Start the session with a discussion about how projects are selected in the company and what the participants' experiences are with internal process. This approach will generate a lot of discussion about how important it is to have a formalized process with some good techniques for ranking the project choices.

Q Why aren't project managers included in the project selection process?

A Many times it is because the company doesn't consider something a project until a decision is made to pursue it. Of course, that creates problems for the project manager because he or she doesn't have the benefit of the decision-making process, that is, knowing who was for or against the project, what the assumptions and constraints were, and how the project fits into the company's strategic goals.

In some companies, the task of selecting projects is the responsibility of the business development group, with an approval from senior management. This process also bypasses the project managers. In either case, the company would benefit from the project managers' input because they have the technical expertise to assess the company's technical capabilities while it would make them knowledgeable about how the project to be pursued was selected.

Where We Are in the Process

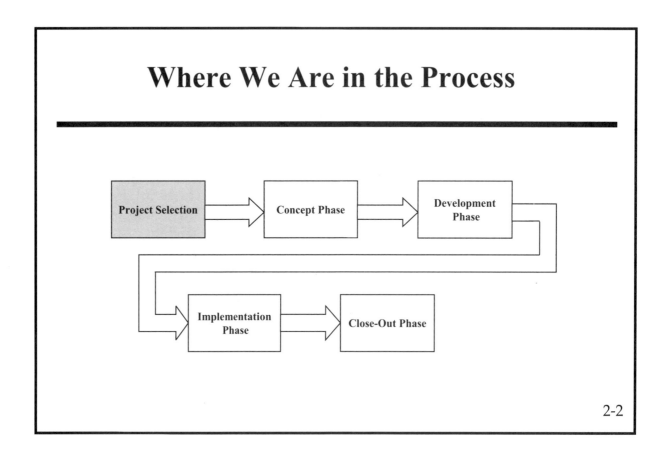

Where We Are in the Process

Objective
- Orient participants to the model for the course progression.

Time: 3 minutes

Training Notes
- Put up Slide 2-2: Where We Are in the Process.
- Tell the participants that this is the map we are using for the course progress.
- Review the general purpose of this phase.
- Ask participants what some of the activities are that they would expect to encounter during this phase.

Project Selection Techniques

Project Selection Techniques

There are several project selection techniques. The most commonly used are:

- Payback or break-even point

- Return on Investment (ROI)

- Internal Rate of Return (IRR)

- Net Present Value (NPV)

- Benefit to Cost Ratio (B/C)

2-3

Objective
- Introduce participants to the common project selection techniques.

Time: 5 minutes

Training Notes
- Put up Slide 2-3: Project Selection Techniques.
- These five selection tools are commonly used to determine the viability of a project.
- Ask participants if they are familiar with any of these techniques. Most will say that they are at least familiar with the payback period, ROI, and B/C. Some will be familiar with NPV. Most, unless they have a background in finance, won't be familiar with IRR.
- If any of the participants are familiar with some of these techniques, ask them how their business units use them.

- Tell participants that we will be going through each technique with an example so that everyone understands the elements of the technique and how it is used.
- Tell the participants that you are going to teach them several project-selection techniques, some of which are very simple, some of which are more complex but still much easier to use than first glance would indicate.

Reassure the participants that you will work through each technique with examples to demonstrate precisely how to use them, and that they will have an opportunity to demonstrate their understanding of the techniques by completing an exercise.

Q Is there one better selection technique than another?

A Any selection technique that accounts for the cost of money is more accurate than those that do not. But each technique is useful depending on how it is used and taking its limitations into consideration. The key is to use each technique as it was designed to be used, and not to rely on only one technique to determine whether a project is a good one to pursue.

Payback or Break-Even Point

Payback or Break-Even Point

One of the most commonly used "hurdle" rates today is the Payback or Break-Even Point:

Payback: The point in a project when revenues equal costs.

　How used:
　　• The payback period has to be equal to or less than target set by senior
　　　management. Often used as an early assessment of project viability.

　Advantages:
　　• Fast
　　• Simple

　Disadvantages:
　　• Assumes steady revenue stream
　　• Does not take into account the cost of money

2-4

Objectives
•　Explain the elements of the payback or break-even point.
•　Calculate the payback period.

Time: 12 minutes

Training Notes
•　Put up Slide 2-4: Payback or Break-Even Point.
•　The payback period technique is used often as a project-selection criterion.
　　It is particularly helpful for small companies because they need to control
　　their cash flow closely.
•　The payback technique uses estimated costs and revenues.
•　A major disadvantage of this method is that it focuses too heavily on early
　　cash flow, i.e., cash flow that occurs *prior* to the break-even point.
　　—Decisions made on the basis of early cash flow could exclude very prof-

itable projects if the major revenues aren't realized until after the break-even point.

—Decisions made without consideration of cash flows after the break-even point wouldn't reveal if profits die or costs escalate later in the project.

- Another disadvantage is that this method does not account for the cost of money. That is, it considers the value of money in two years to be the same as the value of money today.
- Demonstrate the method by going through the following slide.

Payback Period (*sample calculation*)

Payback Period (*sample calculation*)

The estimated cost of a project is $10,000,000. The project is expected to yield $2,000,000 per year. What is the Payback Period?

Solution:

Payback = total cost/yearly revenues
$$= 10,000,000/2,000,000$$
$$= 5 \text{ years}$$

2-5

- Put up Slide 2-5: Payback Period (*sample calculation*).
- Read the problem to the class very carefully.

 Training Tip: Read the instructor notes before the workshop to ensure that you are very familiar with each technique. Several additional examples are provided for your use at the end of the chapter. Put at least one and perhaps two of the examples on a white board or flip chart to demonstrate the techniques as you discuss them.

- The payback period is found by dividing the total costs expected over the life of the project by the estimated yearly revenues.
- Ask participants if they think this is a good project to pursue.
- Also, ask participants if they think their business unit of the company would consider a five-year payback period acceptable.

 Training Tip: Ask the participants often if they are following the explanation and if they have questions.

Return on Investment (ROI)

Return on Investment (ROI)

Return on Investment (ROI), another very commonly used selection technique, is a financial measure of how much profit is likely from invested costs.

How used: Average profits are divided by the average costs expected over the period of the project's life. Hurdle rate is set by the senior management; product ROI must equal or exceed the hurdle rate

Advantages:
- Used by most companies as one viability measure
- Easily understood and calculated

Disadvantages:
- Does not take into account cost of money

2-6

Objectives
- Define ROI and discuss its advantages and disadvantages.
- Demonstrate how to calculate ROI.

Time: 7 minutes

Training Notes
- Put up Slide 2-6: Return on Investment (ROI).
- ROI is another commonly used method to determine whether a project should be pursued.
- ROI is calculated by dividing the average *net* revenues (or profits) by the average costs expected over the project's life cycle.
- The corporation or group has a predetermined ROI level that is acceptable. Each project's ROI must be equal to or greater than this criterion before the project will be approved.

- ROI is calculated in various ways. The method shown here is perhaps the simplest.
- Ask the participants if their organizations have special methods of calculating ROI.
- Impress on the participants that the important thing to remember about ROI calculations is that they focus on the *expected net revenues*, not total revenues as in the payback-period method.
- Two disadvantages of this method are:
  —It does not take into account the cost of money.
  —It focuses too much on the later years of the project.

ROI (*sample calculation*)

ROI (*sample calculation*)

The average cost of a 6-year project is estimated to be $6,000,000 per year, and the estimated total returns are expected to be $12,000,000.
What is the ROI?

Solution:

The average return is 12 million/6 = $2 million per year

ROI = (Average Returns/Average Costs) x 100%
     = (2 M/6 M) x 100%
     = 33%

2-7

- Put up Slide 2-7: ROI (*sample calculation*).
- Tell participants to determine the average net revenues and the average costs of the project over its life cycle.
- To calculate the ROI, divide the average net revenues by the average costs.
- The ROI for the project must be equal to or greater than a corporate ROI hurdle rate to be acceptable.

Q Isn't there software available to perform these calculations? If so, why bother learning to do these by hand?

A All the commonly used spreadsheet software packages can quickly solve the project selection formulas. It is important, however, to learn how to solve these formulas by hand because if we do not understand how the formulas work, it is not possible to enter the data correctly into the spreadsheet. Once we understand how the formulas work, we will no longer need to struggle with solving the problems by hand.

Q Is there any other reason to learn how to solve these problems by hand?

A Yes! The Project Management Institute (PMI®[1]) believes that every professional project manager should understand these selection techniques, how they are solved, and the advantages and disadvantages of each. If the final objective of the participants is to be certified project management professionals (PMPs), then they must understand and be able to solve problems related to selection techniques. In particular, PMI often asks questions on present value, net present value, benefit-to-cost, and internal rate of return on the PMP certifying examination.

[1]PMI is a registered trademark of the Project Management Institute.

Internal Rate of Return (IRR)

Internal Rate of Return (IRR)

Internal Rate of Return (IRR) is used to compare against other strategic financial Goals. It is the interest rate that makes the present value of all revenues equal to the present value of all costs.

How used:
- Usually measured against the IRR of the organization but may be an arbitrarily set "hurdle rate"
- Used by most organizations to determine project viability

Advantages:
- Takes into account the cost of money

Disadvantages:
- Can't be directly calculated; must be iterated from tables or by spreadsheet software

2-8

Objectives

- Define the Internal Rate of Return (IRR) and its advantages and disadvantages.
- Demonstrate how to develop the data and set up the equations for the IRR calculation.
- Demonstrate the solution for the sample calculation.

Time: 12 minutes

Training Notes
- Put up Slide 2-8: Internal Rate of Return (IRR).
- The IRR is the interest rate at which the Present Value (PV) of all the revenues of the company or business unit is equal to the PV of all the costs of the company. That is, the PV of the revenues is set equal to the PV of the costs, and the internal rate of return is calculated to make the two sides of the equation equal. The IRR is also called the discount rate.

- Explain that many companies use IRR because it shows how a project compares with the company's cost of capital. The cost of capital rate is the discount rate that causes the NPV to equal zero (which occurs when the project is just earning the cost of capital). If the IRR for the project is larger than the company's cost of capital, then the project is acceptable. That is, it signals that the cost of capital for the company is less than the project's rate of return, and therefore the project will contribute to the company's profit.
- Point out that IRR cannot actually be calculated but rather is an iterative process. A guess is made for the IRR and each side of the equation is calculated. This process is repeated until a number is arrived at that makes the two sides equal.
- Explain that any spreadsheet software will perform the iteration and solve for the IRR.
- A primary advantage of this method is that it does take into account the cost of money. A disadvantage is that it can't be calculated directly and has to be iterated.

Q How does a project manager determine what the company's cost of capital rate is when assessing whether his or her project meets the company's criteria?

A Sometimes the rate arbitrarily set by senior management as a "hurdle rate," that is, a rate that must be matched or exceeded, or it is the actual cost of capital of the business group or the company. If the actual cost of capital is used, it will be calculated and provided by the comptroller or senior financial officer.

Preparing Data for an IRR Calculation

Preparing Data for an IRR Calculation

The IRR is much more accurate than the Payback or ROI methods because it accounts for the cost of money. It is used as a measure of a project's worth compared with the company's cost of capital rate.

Question: You have estimated the following revenues and costs for your project. If the corporate cost of capital is 18%, how does your project compare?

Years	Revenues	Costs
0	0	$10,000
1	$12,000	$10,000
2	$16,000	$10,000
3	$20,000	$15,000
4	$40,000	$15,000
5	$60,000	$20,000

(continued on next slide)

2-9

- Put up Slide 2-9: Preparing Data for an IRR Calculation.
- Determine what the expected revenues and costs for the project will be, for each year of its life.
- The most difficult part of determining the revenues and the costs for a project is identifying the hidden benefits or costs. As an example, it is sometimes difficult to quantify benefits of a new system. For example, if a new system is going to require fewer operators, it is not always clear what skill level or how many operators the system will actually require.
- The *opportunity costs* have to be considered when determining the total cost of a project. (To determine the opportunity costs, identify the revenues lost by not pursuing one project in favor of another; likewise, the costs not incurred by choosing one project over another will be added to the benefit column).
- The present value equation is used to set up cash inflows and outflows for each year (demonstrated on the next slide).

IRR Sample Calculation

IRR Sample Calculation

Solution: Use the equation

$$PV = \sum_{t=0}^{n} \frac{PV}{(1 + i)^t}$$

PV = present value of money
FV = future value of money
i = Internal rate of return
t = time period, i.e., 1st year, 2nd year
n = number of time periods

The PV of the revenues and costs are determined for the project's life cycle.

$$PV\ (Revenues) = \frac{12{,}000}{(1 + i)^1} + \frac{16{,}000}{(1 + i)^2} + \frac{20{,}000}{(1 + i)^3} + \frac{40{,}000}{(1 + i)^4} + \frac{60{,}000}{(1 + i)^5}$$

$$PV\ (Costs) = \frac{10{,}000}{(1 + i)^0} + \frac{10{,}000}{(1 + i)^1} + \frac{10{,}000}{(1 + i)^2} + \frac{15{,}000}{(1 + i)^3} + \frac{15{,}000}{(1 + i)^4} + \frac{20{,}000}{(1 + i)^5}$$

(continued on next slide) 2-10

- Put up Slide 2-10: IRR Sample Calculation.
- The best way to set up the problem is to draw a time line for the project and to indicate the costs as arrows pointing upward and revenues as arrows pointing downward as shown below.

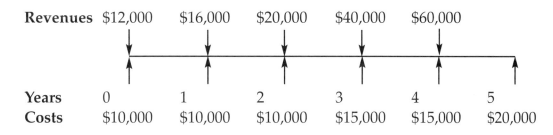

Revenues $12,000 $16,000 $20,000 $40,000 $60,000

Years 0   1   2   3   4   5

Costs $10,000 $10,000 $10,000 $15,000 $15,000 $20,000

- Once the equation is set up, as in the slide, a spreadsheet program should be used to calculate IRR.

IRR Sample Calculation (*continued*)

IRR Sample Calculation (*continued*)

Set the PV(Revenues) = PV(Costs)

$$\frac{12,000}{(1+i)^1} + \frac{16,000}{(1+i)^2} + \frac{20,000}{(1+i)^3} + \frac{40,000}{(1+i)^4} + \frac{60,000}{(1+i)^5} =$$

$$\frac{10,000}{(1+i)^0} + \frac{10,000}{(1+i)^1} + \frac{10,000}{(1+i)^2} + \frac{15,000}{(1+i)^3} + \frac{15,000}{(1+i)^4} + \frac{20,000}{(1+i)^5}$$

The computer iterates to determine value of *i* that makes the two sides of the equation equal. In this case,
$$i = 24\%$$

Project *i* (24%) > company cost of capital (18%). Therefore, pursue project.

2-11

- Put up Slide 2-11: IRR Sample Calculation (*continued*).
- If the IRR for the project is equal to or greater than the company cost of capital rate, then the project will be pursued.

Net Present Value

Net Present Value

Net Present Value is the difference between the Present Value of the project revenues and costs.

How used:
- Uses the corporate IRR or another interest rate index
- "Goodness" is measured by whether NPV is positive or negative
  - NPV > 1, revenues greater than costs
  - NPV < 1, revenues less than costs
  - NPV = 0, revenues and costs the same

Advantages:
- Takes into account the cost of money
- Very accurate compared to other methods

Disadvantages:
- Not easily understood by everyone
- Costs and revenues not always easy to quantify

2-12

Objectives
- Define net present value and discuss the advantages and disadvantages of the technique.
- Demonstrate how to set up and calculate the NPV.

Time: 9 minutes

Training Notes
- Put up Slide 2-12: Net Present Value.
- The net present value (NPV) is the present value of all the revenues less the present value of all the costs.
- A positive result indicates that the revenues are greater than the costs and, therefore, the project is worth pursuing.
- A negative result is the opposite and indicates the project is a losing proposition.

- A zero result shows that the project will break even.
- Point out that this technique takes into account the cost of money.
- Disadvantages:
  —NPV assumes that management can make detailed predictions of cash flows for future years.
  —The discount rate usually changes from one year to another.

Set Up Data Table for NPV

Set Up Data Table for NPV

Example: You have estimated the following revenues and costs for your project. If the corporate IRR is 18%, what is the Net Present Value of your project?

Years	Revenues	Costs
0	0	$10,000
1	$12,000	$10,000
2	$16,000	$10,000
3	$20,000	$15,000
4	$40,000	$15,000
5	$60,000	$20,000

2-13

- Put up Slide 2-13: Set Up Data Table for NPV.
- This table is the same as the previous example on IRR.
- The difference between this technique and the IRR technique is that the IRR for the company or business is used, rather than finding the IRR for the project. Then the PVs of all the revenues and costs are calculated (shown on the next two slides).

NPV Sample Calculation

NPV Sample Calculation

Solution: Use the formula for Present Value to determine PV of revenues and costs.

$$PV = \sum_{t=0}^{n} \frac{PV}{(1+i)^t}$$

$$PV(\text{Revenues}) = \frac{12{,}000}{(1+.18)^1} + \frac{16{,}000}{(1+.18)^2} + \frac{20{,}000}{(1+.18)^3} + \frac{40{,}000}{(1+.18)^4} + \frac{60{,}000}{(1+.18)^5}$$

$$= 10{,}169 + 11{,}491 + 12{,}173 + 20{,}632 + 26{,}227 = \boxed{80{,}691}$$

$$PV(\text{Costs}) = \frac{10{,}000}{(1+i)^0} + \frac{10{,}000}{(1+i)^1} + \frac{10{,}000}{(1+i)^2} + \frac{15{,}000}{(1+i)^3} + \frac{15{,}000}{(1+i)^4} + \frac{20{,}000}{(1+i)^5}$$

$$= 10{,}000 + 8{,}475 + 7{,}182 + 9{,}129 + 7{,}737 + 8{,}742 = \boxed{51{,}265}$$

2-14

(continued on next slide)

- Put up Slide 2-14: NPV Sample Calculation.
- Again, as in the IRR example, the PV for the revenues and the costs is calculated.
- The NPV is the difference between the PV of revenues and costs and can be represented by the following equation:

$$NPV = PV(\text{revenues}) - PV(\text{costs})$$

Solution to Sample NPV Calculation

Solution to Sample NPV Calculation

Net Present Value is the difference between the Present Value of the Revenues and Costs. Therefore,

$$NPV = PV \text{ (Revenues)} - PV \text{ (Costs)}$$
$$= 80,691 - 51,265$$
$$= 29,426$$

NPV is positive; pursue the project.

2-15

- Put up Slide 2-15: Solution to Sample NPV Calculation.
- If the NPV is a positive number, then the project is worth pursuing; if negative, do not pursue; if zero, the project will break even.
- The fact that the NPV is positive is not necessarily indicative of a good project. Decision makers also have to look at the size of the answer in relation to the other numbers. For instance, if the PV for the revenues and costs are 20,000 and 19,900 respectively, there is not a large enough difference between the two to justify pursuing the project. So whether the NPV is positive or negative provides a measure of how good the project is, but the size of the difference compared with the revenue and cost numbers is also a consideration.

Benefit to Cost (B/C)

Benefit to Cost (B/C)

Benefit to cost is a useful measure of the worth of a project because it provides a comparison of the relative difference between benefits and costs.

To calculate B/C, the Present Value (PV) of the project's benefits (Revenues) is divided by the (PV) of the project's costs.

Revenues and costs are estimated from historical data or comparisons with similar projects and their PVs are calculated.

B/C Interpretation:

B/C > 1; benefits greater than costs

B/C < 1; benefits less than costs

B/C = 1; break even (benefits and costs are equal)

2-16

Objectives
- Define benefit to cost (B/C) and describe how to interpret the analysis.
- Discuss the advantages and disadvantages of the B/C technique.
- Demonstrate how to set up and calculate the B/C.

Time: 10 minutes

Training Notes
- Put up Slide 2-16: Benefit to Cost (B/C).
- Benefit to cost utilizes the PV equations.
- To find the B/C ratio, simply calculate the PV of the revenues and the costs exactly as in the NPV technique.
- Divide the PV (costs) into the PV (revenues).

- If the B/C is greater than 1, then the project is worth pursuing; if less than 1, then the project should not be pursued. If the B/C is 1.0, then the project will break even.
- Ask participants how they can use the B/C to calculate the worst-case scenario. (If we assume all the costs of a project occur immediately and all the revenues are not received until the end of the project, then this will produce the worse-case scenario because the costs are not discounted and the revenues are discounted to the maximum. If the B/C is still greater than 1, then the project is good to pursue).

Advantages and Disadvantages of B/C

Advantages and Disadvantages of B/C

Advantages:
- Takes into account the cost of money
- Very accurate compared to other methods
- Easier to interpret ratios or percentages than pure numbers

Disadvantages:
- Not easily understood by everyone
- Costs and revenues not always easy to quantify

2-17

- Put up Slide 2-17: Advantages and Disadvantages of B/C.
- B/C ratio is very easy to interpret. Whereas a pure number may have meaning for the project manager, it will have less meaning for senior management. However, a B/C will be clear to everyone.
- The B/C ratio takes into account the cost of money.
- The benefits and costs of a project are not always easy to quantify and require more work to be accurate.

Set Up Data Table for B/C

Set Up Data Table for B/C

Question: You have estimated the following revenues and costs for your project. If the corporate IRR is 18%, what is the B/C ratio for your project?

Years	Revenues	Costs
0	0	$10,000
1	$12,000	$10,000
2	$16,000	$10,000
3	$20,000	$15,000
4	$40,000	$15,000
5	$60,000	$20,000

2-18

- Put up Slide 2-18: Set Up Data Table for B/C.
- This table is the same as those used in the IRR and NPV examples. In the B/C technique, the IRR of the company or business unit will be used.
- The next step is to set up the equations and solve for PV (revenues) and PV (costs).

B/C Sample Calculation

B/C Sample Calculation

Solution: The PV of the revenues and costs were calculated previously.

PV(Revenues) = $80,691

PV(Costs) = $51,265

B/C = 80,691/51,265
or B/C = 1.57

2-19

- Put up Slide 2-19: B/C Sample Calculation.
- As described in the definition, the B/C is simply the result of dividing the PV (revenues) by PV (costs).
- The B/C is preferred by management because a ratio is more meaningful than a pure number. In the example above, NPV is $29,426 but doesn't show that benefits are over 50% greater than costs, as does the B/C ratio.

Exercise 2-1: Selection Techniques Exercise

Selection Techniques Exercise

Using the data in the table, determine:
1. The net present value of the project
2. The B/C ratio
3. The payback period

Assume IRR is 10%.

Years	Revenues	Costs
0	0	$10,000
1	$10,000	$25,000
2	$30,000	$20,000
3	$60,000	$50,000
4	$100,000	$50,000
5	$100,000	$50,000

2-20

Objective
- Introduce participants to a practical exercise to learn how to calculate several selection techniques.

Time: 30 minutes

Training Notes
- Put up Slide 2-20: Selection Techniques Exercise.
- Tell the participants to work individually to solve these problems, but encourage them to discuss their answers with the other participants at their table.
- Tell them they will have 20 minutes for this exercise.
- Call time after 20 minutes and have one person from each table report their results.

- Record the answers on a flip chart and ensure that all participants calculated the same answer.
- Ask participants what their recommendations are for the project based on the results of the analyses.

Slide 2-20: Exercise 2-1 Solution

Using the data in the table, determine:
1. The net present value of the project
2. The B/C ratio
3. The payback period
Assume IRR is 10%

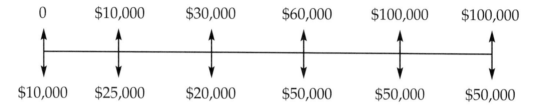

PV (revenues) = $10,000/(1 + .1)^1 + 30,000/(1 = .1)^2 + 60,000/(1 + .1)^3 +$
$\qquad 100,000/(1 + .1)^4 + 100,000/(1 + .1)^5$
$\qquad = 9,090.91 + 24,793.39 + 45, 078.89 + 68,301.35 + 62,073.25$
$\qquad = 209,337.79$

PV (costs) $\qquad = 10,000/(1 + .1)^0 + 25,000/(1 = .1)^1 + 20,000/(1 + .1)^2 +$
$\qquad 50,000/(1 + .1)^3 + 50,000/(1 + .1)^4 + 50,000/(1 + .1)^5$
$\qquad = 152,009.23$

1. NPV = PV (revenues) – PV (costs) = 209,337.79 – 152,009.23 = 57,328.56
2. B/C = 209,337.79/152,009.23 = 1.38
3. Payback = total costs/total revenues = 210,000/300,000 = .7 of a year, or 8.4 months

Key Messages—Module 2

Key Messages—Module 2

The key messages from this module are:

• Many project managers are involved in the project selection process or are asked for input into the analysis

• There are several techniques for determining a project's viability. The most common ones are:
  – Payback or break-even point
  – Return on Investment (ROI)
  – Internal Rate of Return (IRR)
  – Net Present Value (NPV)
  – Benefit to Cost Ratio (B/C)

2-21

Objective
• Summarize the module.

Time: 3 minutes

Training Notes
• Put up Slide 2-21: Key Messages—Module 2.
• Summarize the module and transition to the next module.
• Many project managers are involved in the project selection process or are asked for input into the analysis.
• There are several techniques for determining a project's viability. The most common ones are:
  —payback or break-even point
  —return on investment (ROI)
  —internal rate of return (IRR)
  —net present value (NPV)
  —benefit-to-cost ratio (B/C)

The
Project
Concept Phase

The Concept Phase is a data-gathering phase. If a project is the result of winning a competitive bid, a significant amount of information is available about the project. In fact, a proposal contains, among other things, a complete project-management plan. So the project manager, particularly if he or she helped prepare the proposal, is ready to begin work on the project immediately. But what happens if the project is not a result of a competitive bid and the project manager was not involved in any preproject selection or planning activities? How can the project manager hope to gather the necessary data to successfully begin and complete the project?

The Project Concept Phase Objectives

The project manager will have the task of collecting, analyzing, and organizing all the data available about the project. His or her objectives in this phase are to:

1. Determine what the project requirements are.
2. Determine who the key players are: the company, the customer, and any special-interest groups such as regulatory agencies.

3. Organize an initial team to help identify and interpret the requirements.

4. Prepare a high-level work breakdown structure (WBS).

5. Identify skill sets and resources.

6. Begin identifying the final members of the project team.

7. Identify as many risks as possible.

8. Prepare a network logic diagram if enough detailed information is available.

9. Develop as accurate a budget and schedule estimate as possible.

Often, the best a project manager can do at this stage is to identify some experienced persons for the initial team who can assist him or her in defining the requirements. Usually the group will consist of supervisory-level individuals who will not be working on the project as team members. It is important for the project manager to solicit this kind of help early in the project because these supervisors' experience will aid in identifying the requirements and the resources needed to accomplish the project. In addition, it is never a good idea for one person alone to try to identify all the requirements or tasks of a project because it is too easy to overlook a task. Besides, the project manager is not likely to possess enough expertise to know who in the functional groups will make good project team members.

The initial team can also be very helpful in developing the high-level WBS. Again, this is not something that should be attempted alone simply because it is so easy to overlook a task. If the project is similar enough to past projects, the initial team members will have a lot of suggestions about things that went well and things to avoid. A trainer should emphasize the importance of using experienced people for this initial planning effort because it is in this phase that the risk is highest. Although not much is at stake relative to capital investment at this point, the risk is high because the requirements are not fully developed and understood.

It is helpful to the project manager and initial team if they can develop a network logic diagram, such as project evaluation research technique (PERT) or precedence diagramming method because these tools define the project schedule duration. You as the trainer should emphasize that in order to yield information about the critical tasks in the projects, a network analysis uses the very lowest levels of the WBS. But at this stage of data gathering, all the tasks might not be identified. Therefore, a network analysis at a higher WBS level will have to suffice for rough schedule and budget estimates. A refined network analysis can be accomplished during the next phase of the project when the requirements have been better defined.

As the trainer, be sure to emphasize to your class that the project manager should be consulting with the customer during the process of identifying the requirements. The customer can be either internal or external, and the project need not be under contract. Either way, the project manager *must* consult with the customer or else the requirements cannot be properly identified. Likewise, the customer should provide a statement of work even if the customer is within the organization and the project is not the result of a contract. One of the major reasons for project failure is misinterpretation of statements of work, so it is critical that the project manager and the customer are in complete agreement about what the customer desires. All this requirements verification occurs during the concept phase so that during the next phase, the development phase, a project management plan, supporting plans, and analyses can be finalized for implementing or building the project.

Content Notes

The tools in this section are not difficult to master. The important thing is that if there is little project documentation to begin with, there is a significant risk that tasks will be overlooked. So the difficulty of this phase lies in determining the project requirements, which basically consists of data gathering. But that sounds much easier than it is! Gathering data is a function of perseverance and attention to detail, qualities that many of us don't have enough of. That is another reason for soliciting the aid of experienced people to help with this stage of the project. As the trainer, you can't emphasize the importance of this activity enough. Remind the participants that the major reasons for project failure is poorly defined or misinterpreted requirements.

Work Breakdown Structure

The WBS is perhaps the most useful project management tool. When done correctly, WBS is the basis for planning, scheduling, budgeting, and controlling the work of the project.

A WBS is a structured way of decomposing a project into its various components—hardware, software, services, documentation, labor, testing, delivery, and installation. In short, WBS is a formalized way of reducing the project into successively lower levels of greater detail.

The project decomposition should continue only to the level that is needed to identify the task or subtask as a work package, which is a natural subdivision of a cost account (cost center). The work package is where a job assignment can be made and is identifiable with a person, a job, or a budget number, and is where the actual project work is accomplished. The work package can occur anywhere below the first level, but usually occurs at the fourth or fifth level.

Levels refer to successively lower tiers of detail, beginning with the project name as the first level (see chart). A WBS rarely needs to be developed below the fifth level.

The indented WBS format is by far the most popular. Indeed, it's used by all project management software packages. What's more, it's required when specified in requests for proposals or requests for quotes. The following chart shows an indented WBS format with the levels and typical numbering system.

Number Element	Description	WBS Level
1.0	Project or Contract Name	1
1.1	Major Project Subsystem	2
1.1.1	Task	3
1.1.1.1	Subtask	4
1.1.1.1.1	Work Package	5
1.1.1.1.1.1	Components	6

Indented WBS Format With WBS Levels

The graphical format, which resembles an organizational chart, is especially helpful for those who prefer visual representations, but it requires a lot of space to develop, particularly with large, complex projects.

Level 1. The project or contract name is always at this level.

Level 2. Entries involving the major subsystems of the project, complete entities, or sections of the project are at this level. For example, the major subsystems of an automobile design project would include the engine, chassis, interior, and body.

Level 3. Each level 2 entry also can consist of one or more major task activities.

For example, if the level 2 subsystem is the engine, tasks might be the fan or carburetor, which are parts of the engine. These are designated as level 3 activities.

Level 4. Each level 3 activity can be decomposed into several more discrete entities, and so on, until the desired level of detail is achieved. For example, a subtask of the carburetor would be to design and build fuel jets. These level 3 subtasks are all entered into the WBS at level 4.

Level 5. Decomposing level 4 tasks usually brings us to a level where the actual work can be assigned: the work package. For example, one of the fuel-jet subtasks probably would be to design and build some kind of valve mechanism to control the jet flow. This is a discrete work package, which can be given to an individual or group. It is not necessary to go to level 5 to define a work package. Activities only need to be expanded to the level required to assign resources, that is, people and budgets. Indeed, some project managers might choose to define a work package at level 4 in this example. The idea is to define it to a level that the project manager feels comfortable with and can manage.

Level 6. This level deals with components such as screws, computer chips or other off-the-shelf items that are needed but are not usually tracked by the project manager.

Note that the first three WBS levels typically represent a management level with people managing, as opposed to doing, the work themselves. These are not usually the levels at which work is actually accomplished. The third level task usually represents a task-leader position—the person responsible for supervising the task.

The last three levels are where the work is actually done. An entry at each of these levels begins with an action word denoting what sort of work is accomplished. For example you might see "write," "develop," "perform," or "prepare."

Remember to tell the participants that the WBS is the very heart of project management, and that the entire project is built upon its framework.

The Project Charter

A project charter is a document that formally recognizes the existence of a project. It also is the vehicle by which the project manager is named and given the authority to proceed with the project.

The project charter can contain any information that the organization feels is pertinent, but at the minimum it should contain the following:

1. A brief summary of the project scope
2. The business or strategic goal that the project was undertaken to address
3. A description of the product
4. The name of the project manager
5. The functional areas supporting the project
6. A signature block for *all* internal stakeholders

Samples of a project charter outline and project charter are contained in the Forms section of this book and can be provided to the participants as handouts.

When the project is performed under contract, the signed contract serves as the project charter for the seller.

Stakeholder Analysis and Management

Stakeholder influence is the major reason a project succeeds or fails. I have often heard new project managers complain that they didn't receive the support they needed to deliver a project on time, on budget, or to the desired performance level. I later discovered they had overlooked a key stakeholder or didn't identify their stakeholders at all. Managing stakeholders requires planning, organizing, motivating, directing, and controlling in the same way a project is managed. In fact, stakeholder management can be thought of as a project within the project.

A stakeholder is anyone who has a vested interest in the project and—a word to the wise—it is also anyone who *thinks* he or she has an interest in the project. Typically, the stakeholders for most projects will include the project team members, functional managers, other corporate managers of business or financial groups, the customer, and the users. Look also to outside agencies for stakeholders especially if law or special-interests groups regulate your project.

There are always some organizational managers who don't fit the strict notion of vested interest but still feel they are stakeholders. The successful project manager will determine who these players are and include them in his or her stakeholder management plan. Usually, the unidentified stakeholders or would-be stakeholders can undermine a project before the project manager is even aware of a problem.

It is important to identify the project stakeholders, but it is absolutely critical that you discover their position, that is, whether they are for or against the project and why. A simple worksheet such as the one below is a great help. A copy of this worksheet is provided in the Handout section.

Stakeholder Analysis

Stakeholder Name	+	0	−	Reason for Position	Strengths & Weaknesses	Strategy

Using the worksheet, identify the stakeholders and check the appropriate column to indicate if they are for, neutral toward, or against the project. The next step is to determine the reason for their position and their strengths and weaknesses relative to their influence on the project. With this information, the project team can develop a strategy for moving the stakeholders to a positive position.

The following is a list of steps in the stakeholder management process. The steps for analyzing stakeholders should be a project team effort. Managing the process is the project manager's responsibility.

1. Identify stakeholders
2. Determine stakeholders' position on the project
3. Determine the stakeholders' agenda
4. Assess stakeholder strengths and weaknesses relative to their influence on the project

5. Identify strategy to move stakeholders to a positive position on the project
6. Predict stakeholder reaction to the strategy
7. Implement the stakeholder management strategy

Tell the participants that this list of actions is simple in concept but difficult to implement successfully unless they are politically aware of the corporate culture and possess effective interpersonal skills. It is imperative, however, for them to manage their stakeholders. Their project successes will improve significantly when they do.

Training Objectives for the Concept Phase Module

The training objectives for this module are to:

1. Impress the participants that they will often begin working on a project with little or no information, and the expectation from senior management is that the project manager's task is to develop the data needed.
2. Introduce the participants to the concept of gathering data relative to project requirements.
3. Teach the participants that they must learn to organize an experienced initial team to help with the requirements development and resource needs identification.
4. Introduce the participants to WBS development and its importance as a project tool.
5. Explain what a project charter is and encourage participants to introduce its use in their organizations.

Help foster the idea that they, the participants, are change agents and should start thinking about how they can make changes to their organizations' processes.

Summary

The concept phase of the project life cycle is a data-gathering phase. If the project results from an external contract, the information about it will be significant and usually very detailed. However, many projects originate within the organization and probably will have little or no documented data about their purpose, requirements, constraints, and assumptions, or anything else of value. Under these circumstances project managers really have their work cut out for them.

Organizing a team of experienced functional experts is the first task of the project manager. This initial team very likely will not be the final project team, but they can be valuable resources in developing a requirement's list and the WBS. Also, as the requirements are developed, this initial team can offer suggestions about the skill levels needed and who in the company is best able to accomplish the requisite tasks.

Stakeholder management is crucial for success, and the project manager must begin an aggressive campaign to win over any stakeholder who might have reservations about the project. So many project managers have had unsuccessful projects or even canceled projects because they failed to identify their stakeholders or didn't keep the stakeholders informed about project progress.

A major output of the concept phase is the project charter. The charter documents the existence of the project, names the project manager, and authorizes the project manager to begin work. It is important to the project manager to encourage his or her organization to use charters because having one makes negotiating for resources easier and helps eliminate issues arising because of project priority conflicts.

Agenda for Module 3: The Project Concept Phase

11:00	Objectives for Module 3	7 minutes
	Where We Are in the Process	3 minutes
	Activities in the Concept Phase	8 minutes
	Statement of Work (SOW)	25 minutes
	Collecting the Requirements	5 minutes
	Translating Requirements	10 minutes
	Initial Project Team	4 minutes
	Work Breakdown Structure (WBS)	20 minutes
	Stakeholders	8 minutes
	The Project Charter	8 minutes
	Kickoff Meetings	14 minutes
	Key Messages—Module 3	8 minutes
	Total	120 minutes

Module 3: The Project Concept Phase

Defining and Organizing the Project

Approximate time for module: 2 hours

Objectives for Module 3

Objectives for Module 3

At the end of this module you will be able to:

- Describe the elements of a Statement of Work (SOW)

- Explain how to interpret a SOW

- Identify and describe project requirements

- Describe a Work Breakdown Structure (WBS)

3-1

Objective
- Introduce module objectives.

Time: 7 minutes

Training Notes
- Put up Slide 3-1: Objectives for Module 3.
- This module is important because it introduces the concept of requirement identification, the statement of work (SOW) and the work breakdown structure (WBS).
- This phase is a data-gathering phase and is the time for the project manager to determine what the requirements are and what resources he or she will need for the project.

Training Tip: Introduce the module by telling the participants that they probably agree that most of the projects they work on started when someone assigned the project without providing much information about it (half the class will nod in agreement).

- Ask participants what types of activities they get involved with in their organizations during this period.
- Facilitate a discussion about the importance of a process for gathering and organizing information they will need to accomplish the task of identifying the project requirements.

Objectives for Module 3 (*continued*)

Objectives for Module 3 (*continued*)

- Develop a high level WBS

- List project stakeholders and develop strategies for obtaining their support

- Describe the use and structure of a Project Charter

- Understand the elements of and conduct a kickoff meeting

3-2

- Put up Slide 3-2: Objectives for Module 3 (*continued*).
- This is the phase in which a high-level WBS is developed.
- The major output of this phase is a project charter.
- Finally, the project kickoff meeting should occur at the end of this phase or very early in the next phase.

Where We Are in the Process

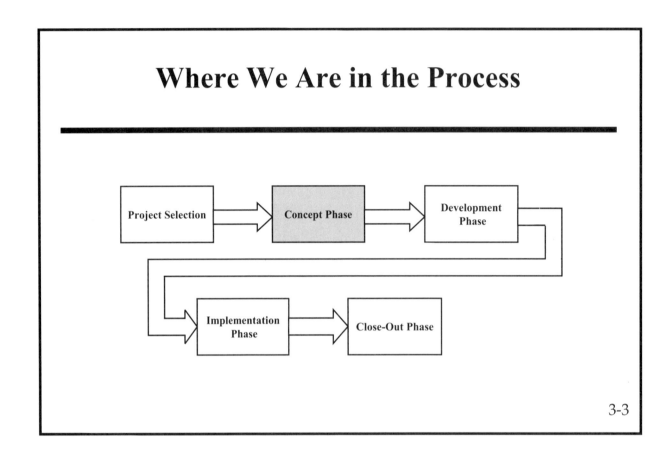

Objective
*   Orient participants to the model for the course progression

Time: 3 minutes

Training Notes
*   Put up Slide 3-3: Where We Are in the Process.
*   This is the map we are using for the course progress.
*   Review the general purpose of this phase.
*   Ask participants to name some of the activities that they typically encounter during this phase and ask whether they are aware of any kind of formalized process for their organization.

Activities in the Concept Phase

Activities in the Concept Phase

The project manager is chiefly concerned about understanding and organizing the project during this phase. The principal activities are:

- Interpreting the project requirements from:
  - Statement of Work (SOW)
  - Specifications
  - Contractual documents

- Developing a high level Work Breakdown Structure (WBS)

- Identifying project team skill requirements

- Providing input to the Project Charter

3-4

Objective
- Remind participants of the activities in this project phase.

Time: 8 minutes

Training Notes
- Put up Slide 3-4: Activities in the Concept Phase.
- The major activities of this phase are to define the project requirements, develop a high-level WBS and to start identifying the project resource requirements.
- The SOW is the document that outlines the scope of the project. It tells the project manager and the project team what they are required to do.
- When the definition and structure of a WBS is explained they will understand why the WBS is the single most important tool of the project manager.

- The concept phase is a data-gathering phase. It is the time in the project when the project manager is determining what the requirements are, where they came from, who is for and against the project, and what his or her resource requirements are.
- In order to understand the project and resource requirements better, the project manager will develop a high-level WBS, that is, identify the major components of the project deliverables.
- This is also the time when the project team starts to identify the stakeholders and a stakeholder management strategy.
- One of the major outputs of this phase is the project charter. The project charter is an internal organizational document that identifies the project manager and gives him or her the authority to begin the project. It also identifies the functional area responsibilities and which functional managers are to support the project.
- A kickoff meeting is an excellent communication tool and is the time to get buy-in from all the stakeholders. The project manager should chair the kickoff meeting. However, in many organizations a senior manager such as the VP of Business Development chairs the kickoff meeting.
- The kickoff meeting should occur sometime near the end of the concept phase and the beginning of the development phase, but the line delineating these phases is not clear cut. It just needs to be done as early as possible *after* enough information is available to provide meaningful explanations about the project scope, but not so late that it loses its effectiveness as a communication/buy-in forum.

Statement of Work

Statement of Work

The Statement of Work (SOW) is the principal document for transmitting the customer's project requirements. The characteristics of a SOW include:

- Written description of the project requirements

- High level schedule and milestones

- Occasionally a budget (usually for internal projects only)

- Acceptance criteria

3-5

Objectives
- Introduce statements of work (SOWs) and explain their use and importance.
- Introduce the information typically found in a SOW.
- Provide an outline for those involved in writing SOWs.
- Acquaint participants with the common problems associated with writing and interpreting SOWs.
- Provide guidelines for reading SOWs for project requirements.

Time: 25 minutes

Training Notes
- Put up Slide 3-5: Statement of Work.
- The SOW is the document that details the project requirements. Most organizations refer to it as the statement of work, but some call it the scope

statement. The term SOW is more common in the federal sector while the scope statement is more often used in the private sector. Regardless, it is the document that delineates the project requirements.

- Explain that the SOW can be thought of as a project specification. It describes:
  —what the project is about
  —what the deliverables are
  —who the key players are from both the customer and contractor sides
  —a high-level schedule
  —occasionally, a budgetary limitation.
- If the project was generated within the company, a SOW may not be available. Explain to participants that if there is no SOW, they need to talk with any stakeholder who might have had something to do with selecting the project. These stakeholders should at least be able to explain what the rationale was, the constraints, and assumptions, and, hopefully, how the project fits into the company's strategic goals (You may have to explain what a stakeholder is at this point).

Statement of Work (*continued*)

Statement of Work (*continued*)

- Key personnel in the customer organization

- Technical or performance specifications

- Scope change process

- Communication requirements

3-6

- Put up Slide 3-6: Statement of Work (*continued*).
- With the identification of key personnel, the SOW will also describe a communications plan. That is, it will specify the type and detail of various reports or reviews expected.
- The SOW will have, as an attachment, a separate specification if the project is for a product that is very complex, requiring detailed engineering drawings or designs from the customer.
- Emphasize to the participant that it is crucial to determine whether acceptance criteria are included in the SOW. Acceptance criteria tell the project team what has to be accomplished before the customer will formally accept the project.
- Explain that without acceptance criteria, the project could continue indefinitely because the project team may never be able to satisfy the customer.
- Ask participants who are involved with SOWs either in interpreting them or writing them.

- Explain that if the project is the result of a contract, that is, if the customer is from outside the organization, the customer should include in the SOW or other contract document a process for changing the project scope. Usually, the customer will state the change desired and ask the contractor for a proposal showing cost and schedule. The customer will then approve or reject the change. If the change is approved, the customer will issue a modification to the basic contract.
- Facilitate a discussion about the common mistakes in SOW writing or interpretation. Make sure these points are raised in the discussion:
  —Poorly stated requirements
  —Ambiguous language
  —Imprecise words or phrases

Q Who writes the SOW?

A The customer writes the SOW. If the project is an internal one, there will almost never be a SOW, although there should be. Many companies are large enough that one division or group "hires" another division or group to perform some of the work on a project. In this event, a SOW is absolutely required. Without a SOW, the requirements are not clearly defined. If there is no SOW, the project manager should insist on some sort of written statement detailing the requirements.

Q Would the project manager ever be asked to prepare a SOW for a customer?

A Yes, but only under the agreement that the project manager's company would not then be able to bid on the project described by the SOW. (To prepare a statement of work or other specification would provide the preparer with an unfair competitive advantage.)

SOW Outline

SOW Outline

A typical SOW will have the following outline:

Section Number	Section Heading
1.0	Introduction
2.0	Key Assumptions
3.0	Seller/Provider Responsibilities
4.0	Buyer/Customer Responsibilities
5.0	Estimated Schedule
6.0	Project Acceptance Criteria
7.0	Type of Contract and Payment Schedule
8.0	Additional Terms and Conditions
9.0	Miscellaneous
10.0	Appendixes

3-7

- Put up Slide 3-7: SOW Outline.
- Build on the last slide, when you asked participants if they had any experience with SOWs. If any of them have had some experience, ask them if this outline is similar to what they have seen or used. Ask them to discuss any differences in their organization's outline and this one.
- The headings of this outline are self-explanatory, but reemphasize the point about having clearly defined acceptance criteria in the SOW.
- If there are any additional or special contract clauses discussed or referred to in the SOW, project managers should have their contracts people interpret them.

Reasons that SOWs Are Misinterpreted

Reasons That SOWs Are Misinterpreted

Projects fail most often because the project requirements are not fully understood or they are misinterpreted. Reasons include:

- Poorly written SOWs

- Use of ambiguous words and phrases

- Conflicting requirements

- Lack of communication between customer and project manager

- Unreasonable requirements, particularly in schedules

3-8

- Put up Slide 3-8: Reasons That SOWs Are Misinterpreted.
- Writing a SOW is an art. SOWs require the ability to articulate clearly what the customer needs or requires.
- Go over each of the reasons in the slide for misinterpreting SOWs and ask participants if they can think of any other reasons.
- Discuss any problem areas in SOW interpretation that participants have seen or encountered.

Reading the SOW

Reading the SOW

Reading the SOW critically helps to focus on and identify the requirements. A disciplined process for reading the SOW will follow this pattern:

- Summarize the project background and general purpose

- Describe the project goals and objectives

- Relate the project goals and objectives to the organization's strategic goals

- List all "shall" statements

- Identify and list all assumptions and constraints

3-9

- Put up Slide 3-9: Reading the SOW.
- Read the SOW to determine the general goals and objectives of the project. Usually the SOW will have a summary paragraph or two to provide an overview of the project requirements. It is helpful to get this overview in mind because it provides a picture of the boundaries of the project.
- While reading the SOW, the project manager should begin comparing the project goals with the organization's goals. Often, the project will be outside the organization's core business or the requirements will include work that is not within the expertise of the company. If so, the reasons for pursuing the project need to be readdressed.
- In contract or directive documents, the verbs "shall" and "will" have special meaning. A "shall" statement is directive on the contractor or party interested in performing the project; in other words, you are legally bound by the contract to perform these tasks or provide these deliverables. Hence,

finding and listing the "shall" statements identifies the requirements of the project. On the other hand, "will" statements show intent on the part of the party requesting the project work.

"The contractor shall provide training manuals that allow the buyer's in-house trainers to prepare a cadre of instructors for the new training device" means that one of the deliverable requirements is a set of training manuals.

"The buyer will provide the contractor with data on student class size and training schedules so that he can design the training curriculum" means that the customer intends to provide the contractor with the data needed to design the training program.

- While reading the SOW, the project manager should identify and list all the assumptions and constraints. Usually they are not hard to find. For instance, the customer might state that "the training device must be delivered and operational no later than July 15, 2002." The date—July 15, 2002—is a schedule constraint. The customer might assume that the resources required to complete the project are going to be available when they are needed and that personnel will possess the requisite skill and experience levels.

Reading the SOW (*continued*)

Reading the SOW (*continued*)

- List all the project deliverables; data, services, hardware, software, documents
  - Decompose deliverables into component tasks
  - Identify required resources

- Gantt chart any imposed schedule dates or other key milestones

- List any risks

- Determine what the acceptance criteria are

3-10

- Put up Slide 3-10: Reading the SOW (*continued*).
- The next step is to list all project deliverables found in the SOW.
- Once a list of all the deliverables is completed, the project manager can begin to determine what tasks must be performed to accomplish the project and what skill sets are required for the job.
- Note in the SOW any imposed schedule dates or milestones that have to be met and to prepare a schedule of these events.
- Participants should begin to identify risks as early in the project as possible. Some risks will be obvious as the tasks are identified and the required resources are determined. Also, imposed schedule and milestone dates may constitute risk areas.
- The acceptance criteria is how the customer, internal or external, will determine whether the product or service meets his or her requirements. These criteria should be documented in the SOW or some other official correspondence before the project begins. Without acceptance criteria, the project may never come to completion.

Collecting the Requirements

Collecting the Requirements

Once the SOW has been thoroughly dissected, the requirements can be collected for interpretation and refining. They will be the:

- "Shall" statements

- Specific deliverables such as services, data, documentation, software, or hardware

- Tasks that are required to reach the customer's stated goals

- Ancillary tasks that support reaching the customer's goals, such as

    – Acquiring special equipment
    – Hiring specialists
- Reporting and communicating tasks to the customer and key internal personnel

3-11

Objective
- Summarize what participants need to do to document the requirements.

Time: 5 minutes

Training Notes
- Put up Slide 3-11: Collecting the Requirements.
- After you have thoroughly read the SOW and highlighted the "shall" statements, deliverables, schedule and milestone requirements, and so on, document each one carefully.
- Go through the SOW again carefully to ensure that all requirements are identified and that you list any additional actions the company has to take before or during the project. For instance, it might be required to hire more people if the company doesn't have adequate resources or expertise.

- The final action with SOW interpretation is to communicate the results to all the stakeholders and particularly with the customer.
- Once the SOW is interpreted and the requirements are documented, the project manager should discuss his or her interpretation with the customer to ensure that the interpretation mirrors the customer's desires. Documenting the requirements is most easily done using Handout 3-1 in the Handout packet. A completed sample is also provided with the handout.

REQUIREMENTS RECORD

PROJECT TITLE: **DATE:**

PROJECT MANAGER:

REQUIREMENT:

ASSUMPTIONS:

CONSTRAINTS:

REQUIRED RESOURCES:

FUNCTIONAL GROUPS PARTICIPATING:

REQUIREMENTS RECORD

PROJECT TITLE: The Jacksonville Company Management Information System

PROJECT MANAGER: Michael James   **DATE**: May 14, 2002

REQUIREMENT: A Management Information System (MIS) to support a corporate office consisting of fifty people. The MIS will produce forms, reports, data, and analyses specified by the Information Systems Department's needs analysis (MIS Needs Analysis, dated January 30, 2002). The MIS will be operational no later than April 1, 2003.

ASSUMPTIONS: The following assumptions have been made in determining the resource requirements for this project:
- Jack Smith will be assigned as the technical lead for the project
- Jean Jordan and Bill Williams will be available 50% of their time to support the project manager with clerical and financial assistance
- The IS department will complete their technology assessment by June 1, 2002
- This project has priority 1 status

CONSTRAINTS:
- Given the number of competing projects at Jacksonville, the schedule can be met only with complete functional area support of resources and materials
- A budget of $200,000 may be insufficient to support IS's technology recommendations

REQUIRED RESOURCES:
- Technical lead
- Two full-time programmers
- One part-time programmer
- Two design engineers
- One systems engineer

FUNCTIONAL GROUPS PARTICIPATING:
- Engineering
- Information Systems
- Software Development

Translating Requirements

Translating Requirements

Once the requirements are collected and generally understood, they can be interpreted and refined. The steps are:

1. List all the deliverables

2. Use an experienced initial team to help decompose and refine each of the task requirements

3. Develop a high level Work Breakdown Structure (WBS) for the project

4. Identify the resources that are needed to accomplish the task

5. Identify other project interdependencies

6. Identify risks because of project priorities and any constraints or assumptions that have been made

7. Develop strategies for completing the project

3-12

Objective
- Provide participants with guidelines for refining the project requirements and begin developing a work breakdown structure.

Time: 10 minutes

Training Notes
- Put up Slide 3-12: Translating Requirements.
- The participants, as project managers, should not try to decompose the project requirements into smaller tasks without the help of an experienced team. They will need to identify generally the task areas and then solicit the expertise from the functional areas likely to perform the tasks.

- Participants need to develop a high-level work breakdown structure so that resources, schedules, and budgets can be developed. (Note: The more detailed the SOW is, the more detailed the WBS can be at this stage of the project. If, for instance, the project resulted from a competitive bid, the SOW is likely to be very detailed. However, if the project is an internal one, there may be no documented SOW, and the project manager may have to work harder to identify the requirements.)

Initial Project Team

Initial Project Team

Initially, the project manager may be the only member of the project team. After analyzing the SOW, the project manager organizes an "initial" team to development requirements and identify team skills. Initial team members:

- Are usually experienced, even supervisory level

- May not be a part of the final team composition

- Provide expertise on SOW interpretation and WBS development

- Are knowledgeable about identifying skill sets and team composition/organization

3-13

Objective
- Teach participants that the project manager must form an initial or core team to help define the requirements and determine the skill sets and resources required for the project.

Time: 4 minutes

Training Notes
- Put up Slide 3-13: Initial Project Team.
- As project managers, the participants should not try to define the requirements without the help of functional experts.
- Early in the project, when requirements are still being defined, it is much better to have the help of an experienced team so that none of the tasks are overlooked.

- Form a team of experienced, usually supervisory-level, personnel to define the requirements and to identify the skills and resources needed to accomplish the project.
- Refer to Handout 3-2, Initial Project Team Analysis Worksheet, and explain that this worksheet is useful for identifying the initial cadre of people needed for the SOW interpretation and WBS development. The worksheet is straightforward, but you should spend a few minutes pointing out what goes in each column.
  —The left-hand column is for recording broad requirements. For example, there may be one requirement for some hardware design and another for some software development. These two requirements would be entered on separate lines.
  —Under the Functional Representatives columns, the project manager will first identify the area(s) of expertise needed to complete the requirements. Perhaps one area of expertise is design and another may be materials (materials in the sense that the hardware system will be subjected to high temperatures or have to withstand vibrations.)
  —Once the areas of expertise for each of the requirements are identified, then the project manager can identify individuals for the inital project team.
- This initial or core team may not be the final project team. They will, however, be able to identify who should be on the final team.

INITIAL PROJECT TEAM ANALYSIS WORKSHEET

PROJECT: _____

FUNCTIONAL REPRESENTATIVES

FUNCTIONAL REQUIREMENT DESCRIPTION	AREA	NAME	AREA	NAME	AREA	NAME	AREA	NAME	AREA	NAME

Work Breakdown Structure

Work Breakdown Structure

The Work Breakdown Structure (WBS) is the most important project management tool and is the basis for all other project management planning. It is a structured way of decomposing a project into its various components. The WBS:

- Reduces the project into successively lower levels of detail

- Provides a way of identifying tasks and task resources

- Provides a structure for estimating costs

- Provides a structure for identifying project skill sets

3-14

Objectives
- Introduce the participants to the work breakdown structure (WBS), its development, and its uses.
- Introduce the participants to the WBS formatting options.

Time: 20 minutes

Training Notes
- Put up Slide 3-14: Work Breakdown Structure.
- The WBS is the most important tool of project management because it completely defines the project requirements.
- Every other project management tool can be developed from a good WBS.
- The WBS is a decomposition of the project into smaller and smaller components until it is at the task level, i.e., the level where resources can be assigned.

- The Task Responsibility Worksheet is an excellent tool for identifying the task resources.
- One of the first uses of the WBS is that once the tasks are defined, a budget and schedule duration can be estimated.
- With the tasks identified, it is possible to identify the number of people and their skill and expertise levels needed to accomplish the task.

Work Breakdown Structure (*continued*)

Work Breakdown Structure (*continued*)

- Is used to develop network logic diagrams

- Is used to develop schedules

- Is used to identify risks

3-15

- Put up Slide 3-15: Work Breakdown Structure (*continued*).
- The next most important use of the WBS is to develop a network logic diagram.
- The process of developing a network diagram and analyzing it will be explained a little later in the course.
- The network diagram is necessary to determine the shortest duration of the project. Once this is determined, the schedule can be estimated.
- Point out that the WBS will also reveal risks in the project because project managers will begin to see project priority and resource conflicts when they analyze the task requirements.

WBS Formats

WBS Formats

The WBS can be represented in two ways:

1. Indented
   - Each lower level is indented as the project is decomposed
   - Resembles an outline format

2. Graphical or tree
   - Resembles a traditional organizational structure
   - Excellent for visual presentation of project tasks structure

3-16

- Put up Slide 3-16: WBS Formats.
- The WBS can be represented in either an indented form or a tree or graphical form.
- Ask participants if they are familiar with WBSs and if so, what form have they used.

Indented WBS

```
                        Indented WBS
────────────────────────────────────────────────────────────

        1.0  Project or Contract Name
             1.1  Major Project Subsystem A
                  1.1.1  Task 1
                            1.1.1.1  Subtask 1
                            1.1.1.2  Subtask 2
                  1.1.2  Task 2
                            1.1.2.1  Subtask 1
                            1.1.2.2  Subtask 2
             1.2  Major Project Subsystem B
                  1.2.1  Task 1
                  1.2.2  Task 2
                            1.2.2.1  Subtask 1
                            1.2.2.2  Subtask 2
                                       1.2.2.2.1  Work Package 1
                                                                        3-17
```

- Put up Slide 3-17: Indented WBS.
- Spend several minutes with this slide, explaining how the project is indented and numbered as it is decomposed into progressively smaller components.
- The numbering can be numeric, alphabetic, or a combination. The important thing is that the system is consistent.
- The first level is the project or contract name. Each indentation represents a successively lower level. For instance, 1.2.2 Task 2 is at the third level, 1.2.2.1 Subtask 1 is at the forth, and 1.2.2.2.1 Work Package 1 is at the fifth level.

Graphical WBS

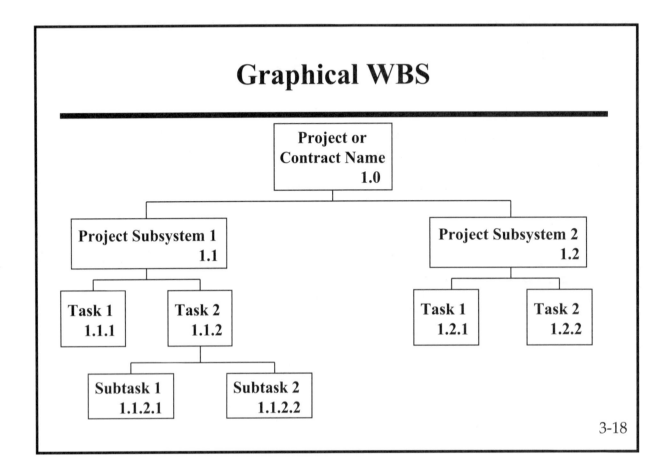

- Put up Slide 3-18: Graphical WBS.
- Point out that this is a representation of the same project shown on the previous slide, but here it is shown in a tree or graphical form.
- This is an excellent way to represent the WBS if participants are "visual." The problem with it is that it takes a lot of room if the project is complex with many components. Also, most project-management software packages don't currently support the graphical format. However, some add-on software programs do provide this capability.
- Determine the WBS levels from this graphic. (The project name is the first level; each line of activities below it represents a lower level in turn. The levels do not change regardless of whether the project is represented in a graphical or indented format.)

Developing High-Level WBS

Developing High-Level WBS

Initially, there may not be enough information or understanding of the requirements to develop a complete WBS. The first task is to develop at least a high level WBS so that:

- Major project deliverables can be identified

- Project scope parameters are clear

- General requirements are understood enough to identify major tasks

- Team member composition can be established

- Top level cost, schedule, and resource estimates can be developed/confirmed

3-19

- Put up Slide 3-19: Developing High-Level WBS.
- Now that the participants understand what a WBS looks like and generally how to develop one, go back to review the high-level WBS and the uses for it.
- Emphasize that the first thing the project manager should try to do is to identify at least the major deliverables and the resources required. The high-level WBS will allow him or her to do that. A high-level WBS will not extend below the third level.
- Depending upon the amount of detail provided by the customer, this step might not be required. That is, the more detailed the SOW, the more detailed the WBS can be initially.

Q What is the best way to develop a WBS?

A One person should not attempt to develop a WBS alone because of the risk of overlooking a task. It is best done by a team. Brainstorming the project requirements and tasks works well and quickly yields the data amount and detail needed. Also, the team should use the Post-it™ approach described in the section on concept phase content theory.

Stakeholders

Crucial to the project manager's success is the early identification and management of stakeholders.

Definition: A stakeholder is anyone with a vested interest in the project.
- Customer

- Sponsor

- Project team members

- Functional managers

3-20

Objective
- Define stakeholders and teach participants to analyze them.

Time: 8 minutes

Training Notes
- Put up Slide 3-20: Stakeholders.
- A stakeholder is anyone who has a vested interest in the project.
- Caution the participants about the importance of identifying those who *think* they have a vested interest in the project: often senior managers will think they are stakeholders, but they do not fit the strict interpretation of the term.

- Usually, stakeholders include the team, functional managers who support the project, the customer, the sponsor, and outside regulatory or special-interest groups.
- Ask the participants if they know who their stakeholders are on any of their projects.
- Ask the participants if they have had any problems on their projects because they didn't identify their stakeholders. (Occasionally, you will find at least one participant who didn't identify their stakeholders and was astonished to find their project canceled).

The Stakeholder Analysis Worksheet

The Stakeholder Analysis Worksheet

A stakeholder analysis includes identifying the stakeholder and determining how to sway them.

Stakeholder	+	0	−	Reason Against Project	Strengths & Weaknesses	Strategy

3-21

- Put up Slide 3-21: The Stakeholder Analysis Worksheet.
- This is a simple worksheet participants can develop to help in the stakeholder analysis process.
- A copy of this worksheet, Handout 3-3, is in their handout packet for later use.
- Go over each column in the worksheet to make sure participants understand what the columns mean.
- Ask participants whether they use any kind of stakeholder analysis.
- Facilitate a discussion about the importance of stakeholder analysis and how it might help the participants with their projects. Bring out the following points during the discussion:
  —A stakeholder is anyone who has a vested interest in the project.
  —Key stakeholders include the customer, user, project team, functional managers, and possibly regulatory agencies.

—Stakeholders can determine whether a project succeeds. If the stakeholder is against the project, he or she may not support the project with resources or might provide resources with inadequate skills and experience.

—It is important to move stakeholders from a negative viewpoint to at least a neutral one and, if possible, to a positive one.

Q Who are the stakeholders in most projects?

A Typically the stakeholders are the customer, the project team, the functional managers supporting the project, and some other group directors such as finance. The customer may not be the final user, in which case the user also will be a stakeholder. Occasionally, special-interest groups such as environmental groups or regulatory agencies have to be considered as stakeholders.

Q How can I analyze and manage my stakeholders?

A Use the stakeholder worksheet provided as a handout and identify the stakeholders. Determine whether they are for, neutral toward, or against the project; the reason for their position; their strengths and weaknesses relative to project influence; and what strategy you might use to move the stakeholders to a positive position on the project. Many times a stakeholder just wants to be kept informed about the project. So simply getting on his or her calendar once a month and providing a status update will satisfy the person.

Stakeholder Analysis

Stakeholder Name	+	0	–	Reason for Position	Strengths & Weaknesses	Strategy

The Project Charter

The Project Charter

The project charter is the major output of the Concept Phase of the project life cycle. It:

- Is an internal document signed by a senior executive who has functional authority over all the project's functional relationships

- Authorizes the project manager to begin work

- Is not a legal document

- Is a way to assign a project priority

- Is a way to obtain buy-in for the project

3-22

Objectives
- Define a project charter.
- Explain to participants how a project charter can make their projects more successful.
- Explain the major elements of a project charter.

Time: 8 minutes

Training Notes
- Put up Slide 3-22: The Project Charter.
- The project charter is an internal document that is issued by a senior manager who has overall functional responsibility for all the groups involved in the project.

- Spend some time on the project charter concept. A project charter can be a great help to the project manager because it is the document that the functional managers first agree to. Later, when the project manager is negotiating for resources or is having project priority problems, he or she can remind the functional manager of the commitment made in the charter.
- The charter is not a legal document; it is an internal one that usually is only a page or two long.
- The charter names the project manager and authorizes him or her to begin the project.
- The charter also names the functional groups that are expected to provide support to the project.

Major Elements of a Project Charter

Major Elements of a Project Charter

A project charter identifies the project manager and gives him or her the authority to start the project. The major elements of a project charter are:

- Project Scope—Provides a short summary of the project scope and the deliverables.

- Assignment—Announces the project manager by name, the name of the project, and the customer's name.

- Responsibilities—Specifies the project manager's responsibilities in delivering the project, and the functional groups responsibilities in supporting it.

- Authority—Outlines the project manager's authority limits.

- Priority—Assigns a priority to the project relative to the other projects in the organization.

3-23

- Put up Slide 3-23: Major Elements of a Project Charter.
- These are the minimum elements that should be in a project charter.
- It is very hard to get a project-priority system started in a company. Usually, all projects are considered equally important, but a priority system, can be of tremendous value to the project when the manager is negotiating for resources.
- Remind participants that a template for the project charter is provided as Handout 3-4. The handout also has a completed sample with it.

Q Does the project manager prepare the project charter?

A The senior executive who will sign it should prepare the project charter, and the project manager should contribute input as requested. In reality, the project manager usually prepares the charter for the senior executive's signature. The key point here is that the charter is issued under the signature of an executive who has functional responsibility for all the company resources who will work on the project. Otherwise, the charter lacks the necessary enforcement authority.

Q How long is the project charter?

A It usually is one to two pages long.

Q Is the project charter a legal document?

A No. It is an internal document that names the project manager and gives him or her the authority to proceed with the project. It also indicates that the functional managers will make every effort to support the project team.

Project Charter Outline

I.   Purpose (Scope statement)

II.   Project Establishment (Business reason
      for the project)

III. Project Manager Designation and Authority

IV.   Project Manager's Responsibility
      A. Support organization's responsibilities
      B. Project organization and structure
      C. Project team composition

V.   Project Initiation
      A. Formal project plan
      B. Approved budgets
      C. Approved plan

VI.   Project Personnel (By name if possible,
      but at least by skill area)
      A. Assignments to projects
      B. Reporting structure
      C. Performance appraisals

VII. Communication Plan

VIII. Definitions

IX.   Appendices

Sample Project Charter

Project Title: Project Management Control System (PMCS)   Date: April 7, 2000

Scope and Objectives: The Jacksonville Information Systems Company is undergoing rapid change and growth resulting in an urgent need for a more efficient use of capital funds and for managing our many projects. To this end, we are implementing a new project management control system that will satisfy both these needs and will enhance our project teams' ability to better focus on our customers' requirements.

General Objectives:
1. Enable better communication among project, group, and corporate management with regard to progress of major projects.
2. Enable senior management to more closely monitor progress of major projects.
3. Provide project personnel the capability to manage and control their projects.

Specific Objectives:
1. Reporting and Control System
   (a) For communication of project activity within and between groups and senior management
   (b) Initially for high-cost projects, then for "critical," then for all projects
2. Computer Support Systems
   (a) Survey with recommendations to determine the amount and cost of computer support
3. Procedures Manuals
   (a) Document procedures and policies
   (b) Preliminary manual available by end of year for operator and user training
4. Project Management Training Course
   (a) Provide basic project planning and control skills to personnel directly involved in project management
   (b) Follow-on courses to provide software, financial, and contracting skills needed by project managers

Defining Conditions, Constraints, and Assumptions: The PMCS must be operational on the last day of this year. The first phase of this project is a technical survey and a feasibility study with a go/no-go decision point at the conclusion of the study. Implementation of the PMCS will commence on July 1 if the recommendation is to proceed.

Project Organization: The key members of the project organization are:

Sponsor: Dr. Jack Malloney, VP of IS
Project Manager: Mr. James Martin
User Representatives: Ms. Jean Matthews and Mr. John Collier
Technical Lead: Mr. Sean O'Reilly

Team Members: To be nominated by functional managers based upon the project manager's skill set requirements and his recommendations. Functional managers will provide team members for the project duration and they will be 100% dedicated to the project.

Project Manager Authority and Responsibilities

1. Staffing—the project manager will determine the skill requirements for the PMCS project and provide them, along with specific team member names, by June 1 to the appropriate functional managers. The project manager is authorized to have one clerical person and one cost analysis to assist him. Because of other project priorities, the project team is limited to no more than 10 technical members without specific authority from the President.
2. Budget—the initial estimate of the project cost is $500,000. This budget cannot be exceeded without authority from the President and the Chief Financial Officer.
3. Communications—status reports will be provided to the President, CFO, and the Sponsor bi-monthly.
4. Planning/Tracking—this project will be tracked using our in-house project management software. An earned value analysis will be provided in every other status report beginning with the second report.
5. Change Control—the project manager is authorized to make project changes provided they do not exceed $5,000 in additional cost and do not impact the schedule. Otherwise, any changes will be made through the Configuration Change Control Board.
6. Document/System Access—the project manager is authorized access to any company document or system in the pursuit of this project completion.
7. The project manager will provide a project plan to the Sponsor no later than May 12. The project plan will include a description of the work, schedules, budget, spending plan, resource utilization charts, risk management plans, and a quality plan.

Support Requirements from Other Organizations:

The PMCS project has the top priority in The Jacksonville Information Systems Company. Functional groups will provide all support possible to the project manager. Where conflicts in personnel assignments occur, the President will resolve them.

Approvals:

VP Project Management_____
VP Information Systems _____
Chief Financial Officer _____
VP Human Resources _____
President _____

Kickoff Meetings

Kickoff Meetings

Kickoff meetings are excellent communication and team-building opportunities. The principal purpose is to get the project started on the right foot and should have all or most of the following objectives:

- Introduce team members to one another

- Establish working relationships and lines of communication

- Set team goals and objectives

- Review project status

3-24

Objectives
- Introduce kick-off meetings and their uses.
- Provide an agenda for the meeting.

Time: 14 minutes

Training Notes
- Put up Slide 3-24: Kickoff Meetings.
- Kickoff meetings are excellent communication forums.
- The kickoff meeting is the time to introduce all the team and the stake-holders.

- A kickoff meeting should occur near the end of the concept phase or near the beginning of the development phase.
- You should emphasize to the participants that the kickoff meeting is the time to get stakeholders to buy in. It is also an opportunity for the stakeholders to see who the team members are and to learn of the project's status. Hopefully the stakeholders will offer any suggestions about the technical approach or about project risks during the kickoff meeting.
- Waiting too long, that is, until everything is known about the project, diminishes the effectiveness of the meeting.
- The project manager should chair the kickoff meeting.

Kickoff Meetings (*continued*)

Kickoff Meetings (*continued*)

- Review project plans

- Identify project problem areas

- Establish individual and group responsibilities and accountabilities

- Obtain individual and group commitments

3-25

- Put up Slide 3-25: Kickoff Meetings (*continued*).
- The status of the project is reviewed and the stakeholders are given the opportunity to provide input about risks or the technical approach.
- Ask participants if they have kickoff meetings for their projects currently.
- Facilitate a discussion about the importance of kickoff meetings and how they can be more effective. Make these points during the discussion:
  —The primary purpose of the kickoff meeting is to get buy-in from all the stakeholders.
  —The kickoff meeting should be held as early as possible in the project.
  —The kickoff meeting should follow a predistributed agenda.
  —The begin and end times for the meeting must be enforced.
  —A kickoff meeting is an excellent communication tool and should be used to invite comments, suggestions, or any shared experiences relative to the project.

The Kickoff Meeting Agenda

The Kickoff Meeting Agenda

Kickoff meetings are important communication tools

1. Introductions
2. Vision
3. Scope and objectives
4. Risks, challenges, and project constraints
5. Project approach
6. Team members and project organization chart
7. Roles and responsibilities
8. Timeline
9. Major milestones
10. Process, standards, methods, and tools

3-26

- Put up Slides 3-26 and 3-27: The Kickoff Meeting Agenda.
- This is a generic agenda for a kickoff meeting.
- Explain again that the project manager should chair the meeting.
- The major purposes of the kickoff meeting are:
  —To communicate to all stakeholders the status of the project and the plans as they are currently understood
  —To obtain buy-in from the stakeholders
- Go over each item of the agenda with the class.
- Ask participants if they can think of any other items that should be included in the agenda.
- A copy of the agenda, Handout 3-5, is in the handout packet.
- Establish the roles and responsibilities of each team member using the Task Responsibility Matrix (Handout 3-6).

The Kickoff Meeting Agenda (*continued*)

11. Quality plan
12. Project management and schedule planning standards and guidelines
13. Centralized documentation storage facility
14. Time collection and project status requirements
15. Training schedule
16. Lessons learned from previous post-project reviews
17. Success factors
18. Project expectations and next steps
19. Unresolved issues, responsibility assignments, and target dates
20. Adjournment

3-27

Q Shouldn't the kickoff meeting take place just before the project is actually implemented?

A No. Many project managers take the view that because the kickoff meeting should "kick off" the project, it should be held just before the product build starts. Their rationale is that they don't really know everything about the project any earlier and so would not be able to answer all the stakeholder questions. But waiting until implementation negates the primary function of the kickoff meeting, namely to get buy-in from the stakeholders. A meeting at implementation might be appropriate, but then it would be a status meeting, not a kickoff meeting.

It is not required nor expected that all the project information will be available at the kickoff meeting. Of course, it is best to have all the answers, but the main objective is to provide at least a high-level summary of the project requirements and the status of the project team to that date. The stakeholders want to know what the project team is doing to define the project and to manage it.

Kickoff Meeting Agenda Format

1. Introductions

2. Vision

3. Scope and objectives

4. Risks, challenges, and project constraints

5. Project approach

6. Team members and project organization chart

7. Roles and responsibilities

8. Timeline

9. Major milestones

10. Process, standards, methods, and tools

11. Quality plan

12. Project management and schedule planning standards and guidelines

13. Centralized documentation storage facility

14. Time collection and project status requirements

15. Training schedule

16. Lessons learned from previous postproject reviews

17. Success factors

18. Project expectations and next steps

19. Unresolved issues, responsibility assignments, and target dates

20. Adjournment

TASK RESPONSIBILITY MATRIX

PROJECT: _____					
TASK ID(WBS #)	TASK DESCRIPTION	TEAM MEMBER RESPONSIBLE/TASK DURATION			

Legend: P = Primary
S = Supporting

Note: Write the name of the person responsible for the task and indicate whether they have a primary or supporting role.

Key Messages—Module 3

Key Messages—Module 3

- The SOW is the key document for transmitting the project requirements

- The SOW must be interpreted correctly to identify all the requirements

- The WBS is developed by an initial team once the requirements are identified

- The major output of the Concept Phase is the Project Charter

- The Project Charter identifies the project manager and gives him or her the authority to begin the project

- The kickoff meeting is critical for establishing communication channels and for team building

3-28

Objective
- Summarize the key points of Module 3.

Time: 8 minutes

Training Notes
- Put up Slide 3-28: Key Messages—Module 3.
- Go over each point on this slide and ensure that the participants have a good grasp of the major discussion items in this module.
- Ask participants if they have any questions about the module.
- Ask participants to discuss any of the tools or concepts covered in the module that will be of immediate benefit to them.
- Make a transition to the next module.

The Project Development Phase

The development phase, sometimes called the planning phase, is the time when the project is refined and all the preparations for implementing, monitoring, and controlling it are completed. It is also the phase during which the project team membership is determined, and negotiations for these individuals are completed.

It has been said that the plan is nothing, but planning is everything. Nowhere is that more true than in project management. The conceptual phase is important for defining the project scope, that is, the boundaries of the project, and the customer's specific requirements. But without the planning, the requirements can never be met. The activities of the planning process initiate the activities of the concept phase. There are a number of project management objectives to be satisfied in this phase. The first one is to finalize the project team membership.

The Project Development Phase Objectives

The project manager's first task in this phase is to determine who will form the project team and to negotiate for them. In many organizations, the makeup of the team is dictated either by the organizational structure or by a senior manager. This situation occurs often in functional organizational structures. In other organizational structures, such as matrix organizations or organizations with cross-functional teams, project managers are likely to find themselves negotiating for the needed resources. The initial team organized in the concept phase can make recommendations about the skill levels and team members. With these names and a signed project charter in hand, the project manager can finalize the team structure. Then the project manager and team together work at achieving the following objectives:

1. Complete or refine the WBS.
2. Develop a network analysis.
3. Analyze the project requirements and determine if the company's resources are adequate to accomplish them in the scheduled time.
4. Make make-or-buy decisions based on evaluation of requirements against the company's capability.
5. Conduct any required trade-off analyses.
6. Complete the technical approach design.
7. Write the project management plan and any ancillary plans.
8. Obtain sign-off on the project management plan from the stakeholders.

This workshop does not cover make-or-buy strategies and trade-off analyses techniques because of time limitations and the need to cover fundamental project-management concepts. However, it is probably worthwhile to mention these strategies and techniques to the participants. Most of them will have a concept of what you are talking about and probably even have been involved with a trade-off analysis.

The team and other functional-area experts should be asked to help refine the WBS and to determine the interdependencies of the tasks. Developing the network logic is not particularly hard, but it does require attention to detail and experience to determine whether one task depends on another task's results.

Content Notes

Most of the tools of this phase are tables, checklists, or formats, so they are simple to explain and to understand. The one exception is the network analysis.

Budget and Schedule Estimates

There are basically three techniques for estimating budgets and schedules. They are the rough order-of-magnitude (ROM), the top-down, and the bottom-up. The ROM is the least accurate method and is essentially an educated guess. It is usually done by one person and is only as good as that person's experience with a similar project and with estimating in general. However, this method does have its place. It is usually used as a measure of the organization's capacity for pursuing a particular project. For instance, if a company's revenues are $10 million a year and a ROM estimate of a potential project is $10 million, then it is not likely that the company will have the resources or experience to pursue the project successfully. Also, a ROM might be the best estimate a manager has at the beginning stages of defining a project. However, the ROM is good *only* for initial planning. It is not accurate enough for a planning figure and certainly not good enough to base a budget on.

The top-down estimate, sometimes called the analogous estimate, is significantly more accurate. It is based on some historical data, and comparisons with other similar projects are usually used to develop its costs. The one thing to be cautious about when using analogy, though, is to make sure the two projects are actually similar. The cost of building a road in Georgia during the summer is not the same as building the same size road in New York in the winter. One other disadvantage of this method is that you can easily overlook tasks that are required. One project might have some unique requirements that another one, despite similarities, does not have.

The most accurate method of all is the bottom-up or definitive estimate. It relies on estimates made at the lowest WBS level and is done by the people responsible for the task. Once the estimates are completed, the total cost of the project is the sum of the costs of all the tasks.

Network Analysis

There are actually three common types of networks: the precedence diagramming method (PDM), the project evaluation research (or review) technique (PERT), and the critical-path method. Because of time limitations, only the PDM is taught in this workshop. Also, the PDM is the network technique supported by project management software. Explain to the participants that as they grow in experience using the project management tools, they should investigate the other methods as well. They do have some benefits for any project manager.

The first step in the network analysis process is to construct a precedence table. I have included a simple one in the workshop for demonstration and the accompanying network. Consider the following table.

This precedence table is simple to construct. The first column is simply an identifier for each of the tasks so that we don't have to write the whole task description on the network. It is for convenience only. The team, and any func-

Identifier	Task Description	Precedent	Duration (in days)
A	1.1.1.2 Design subsystem	–	6
B	1.1.3 Build prototype	A	10
C	1.1.1.4 Test system	B	2
D	1.1.1.5 Ship system	C	1
E	1.1.1.6 Write training manual	B	4
F	1.1.1.7 Install system	D	3
G	1.1.1.8 Train students	E, F	6

tional experts available, helps determine the precedence column. We simply decide which tasks are dependent upon which other tasks and indicate their precedent tasks in this column. The duration column designates the time required to accomplish the task. Now we can construct the network.

If you examine the precedence diagram, the logic of drawing the network is clear. You just have to follow the precedence column and connect the nodes with the arrows. For instance, the precedence table says that A is not dependent on anything else. Hence, it is the starting node. B cannot begin until A is complete. So we draw the arrow from the finish of A to the beginning of B, and so on. Task G, though, cannot begin until *both* E and F are finished. Hence, we draw an arrow from the finish of E and the finish of F to the beginning of G. Notice that 28 is the duration of the project as determined by the forward pass. Therefore, we start with that number to complete the backward pass through the network. The two points in the network that cause some confusion occur at the beginning of Task G, where we have two arrows entering the node. When we are going through the network with the forward pass, the earliest start of a task is the earliest finish of the *largest* (i.e., latest) of the preceding tasks feeding it. Hence, the EF of Task F is the larger of Tasks F and G, so we choose the EF of Task F as the ES of Task G. Likewise, when we are doing the backward pass, a node that has two or more arrows backing into it, the *smallest* (i.e., earliest) of

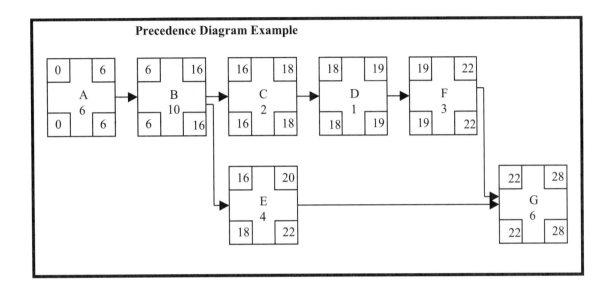

Precedence Diagram Example

the LS of the succeeding tasks feeding it determines the LF of the earlier task. For instance, Task B has Tasks C and E backing into it. The LS of Task E is 18, and the LS of Task C is 16. Hence, the LF of Task B must be 16.

The critical path is, by definition, the longest path through the network and the path with zero float. Path A-B-C-D-F-G has no float (defined by the equation LF – EF = 0), and so this is the critical path. Tell the participants that they will want to manage the tasks on the critical path very carefully because a slip in one of them affects the total schedule.

Project-Management Plan

The project-management plan is the major output of this phase. Most participants will tell you that they do not write management plans for internal projects. Of course, that is one of the major reasons they have problems getting the project completed on time and on budget. If a project results from a contract, then the proposal contains the management plan. But regardless of whether the project is internal or external to the company, a project management plan is necessary.

Exhibit 4-1 is a generic format that can be used with most projects. An external customer may have his or her own format that requires other information, but this format is inclusive enough for most projects that your participants manage.

The following paragraphs describe the contents of each of the plan headings.

Exhibit 4-1. Project Management Plan Format

I.   EXECUTIVE SUMMARY OR OVERVIEW
II. OBJECTIVES
III. GENERAL APPROACH
IV. CONTRACTUAL OBLIGATIONS
V.   SCHEDULES
VI. RESOURCES
    a. Project Budget(s)
       Cost Monitoring and Control Procedures
    b. Personnel
       Skills and Numbers
    c. Capital Equipment
VII. RISKS OR POTENTIAL PROBLEMS
VIII. EVALUATION METHODS

I. EXECUTIVE SUMMARY OR OVERVIEW

This is a short summary of the objectives and scope of the project. It is usually directed to the customer's top management—whether the customer is internal or external—or to the senior management of your organization. It contains a statement of the goals of the project, a brief explanation of the project's relationship to the firm's overall objectives, a description of the managerial structure that will be used for the project, and a list of the major milestones as a minimum. In short, this overview is a *brief* description of the entire project. The senior management should have an overall view of what the project is about after reading the executive summary.

II. OBJECTIVES

This section contains a more detailed statement of the general goals noted in the overview section. The statement should include profit and competitive aims as well as technical goals.

III. GENERAL APPROACH

This critical section of the plan includes a complete list and description of all reporting requirements, customer-supplied resources, liaison arrangement, advisory committees, project review and cancellation procedures, proprietary requirements, any specific management agreements—for example, use of sub-contractors—and the technical deliverables as well as their specifications and delivery schedule. Completeness is a necessity in this section. If in doubt about whether an item should be included or not, the wise planner will include it.

IV. CONTRACTUAL OBLIGATIONS

This section is the place for any special contract requirements. Not all projects will need this section. If the project is *not* a result of a competitive bid, for example, or if no vendors are involved, then you may not need this section. But you might want to consider using this section to list any agreements, verbal or written, that you as the project manager or your group have made with other groups or divisions of the organization.

V. SCHEDULES

This section outlines the various schedules and lists all milestone events. This section will contain the project master schedule and any other supporting schedules required, i.e., individual tasks, contractually required review meetings, test schedules, reports required, milestones. Gantt charts are used for these schedules. In addition, logic networks are developed to provide critical-path information. Gantt or logic networks can be attached as an appendix to the plan.

VI. RESOURCES

Cost

This section will contain your estimated budget. It will also include the WBS and as much task information as you have available.

Personnel

You should list the skill sets you need for the project along with an estimate of the number of people you will need. You should also list any consultants or other specialists you anticipate using.

Capital Equipment

This section is where you estimate any equipment, facilities, and rentals that you will need for the project. Occasionally, a project will include equipment provided by the customer. You can identify that equipment here as well.

VII. RISKS OR POTENTIAL PROBLEMS

It is crucial to anticipate as many potential difficulties as possible. One or more of the following is certain to occur during the project's lifetime: subcontractor default, technical failure, strikes, bad weather, critical sequences of tasks, tight deadlines, resource limitations, complex coordination requirements, insufficient authority in some areas, new complex or unfamiliar tasks, or a reordering of projects within the company or a reorganization of the company. The key in this section is to anticipate as many problems as possible before they occur and be prepared with alternative solutions.

VIII. EVALUATION METHODS

Every project should be evaluated against standards and by methods established at the project's inception. This section contains a brief description of the procedure to be followed in monitoring, collecting, storing, and evaluating the history of the project.

The development phase is where all the planning occurs. If the plans are weak, then the project will suffer and perhaps fail. Emphasize again and again the importance of planning.

Training Objectives for the Development Phase Module

The training objectives for this phase are to:

1. Teach participants the importance of relying on their team and other functional experts to help with project planing.
2. Teach participants how to develop and analyze a network.
3. Define critical path and float, and explain the importance of each.
4. Teach the basic concepts of a project management plan and provide participants with a plan format.

The development phase is a planning phase, so most participants will feel comfortable with the activities of the phase and the process for developing the final project management plan. The only difficult tool to master is the network analysis tool. You will have to spend time going over the steps in developing the precedence table and the network, and you will need to go through the analysis more than once. The example in the slides is designed so that you go through the analysis one small step at a time. Even so, it usually is a good idea to go through the analysis completely at least twice. You will find that participants don't have too much difficulty with the "forward pass" or the early schedule; it is the "backward pass" that is confusing for them. I have included one additional practice network problem in the handouts in case participants need additional practice.

Summary

The development phase of the project is where the project team membership is finalized, the final budget and schedule estimates are developed, and all the plans are written in anticipation of implementing the project. The major tools of this phase are the network analysis and the project plan format.

The network analysis is required because that is the tool that tells us what the duration of the project is given the resources we have available, the critical path, and whether any float is available.

The project-management plan is the document that establishes the baseline of the project and provides a measuring stick for assessing the project's progress, which will be the primary focus of the next phase, the implementation phase.

Agenda for Module 4: The Project Development Phase

1:00	Objectives for Module 4	6 minutes
	Where We Are in the Process	3 minutes
	Activities in the Development Phase	5 minutes
	Selecting the Project Team	5 minutes
	Estimating Budgets	16 minutes
	Network Analysis	15 minutes
	Early Schedule	12 minutes
	Late Schedule	11 minutes
	Project Duration, Float, and Critical Path	7 minutes
	Exercise 4-1	60 minutes
	Gantt Charts	5 minutes
	The Project Management Plan	10 minutes
2:18	Key Messages—Module 4	3 minutes
	Total	158 minutes

Module 4: The Project Development Phase

Planning the Project

Approximate time for module: 1 hour and 58 minutes

Objectives for Module 4

Objectives for Module 4

At the end of this module you will be able to:

- Develop project budget, schedule, and resource estimates from the WBS

- Develop a precedence table from the WBS

- Develop a network using the Precedence Diagramming Method (PDM)

- Develop a schedule using a Gantt chart

- Describe the elements of a project management plan

4-1

Objective
- Introduce module objectives.

Time: 6 minutes

Training Notes
- Put up Slide 4-1: Objectives for Module 4.
- Open the module by stating the importance of planning. It is easy to think of everyday projects that took much longer to accomplish than they should have or would have if we had done a little more planning. The example I use is some household project, such as changing a sink faucet, and the number of times we have to go to the hardware store because we didn't take the time to plan the job.

- This module is important because it discusses refining the WBS and using it to develop schedules, budgets, and resource requirements.
- This module also introduces another major project management tool, the network analysis.
- This is the phase in which the project requirements are refined, the WBS is completed, and all the plans are developed and written.
- Ask participants what type project planning they do in their organizations.
- Facilitate a discussion about the importance of planning. Bring out these points during the discussion:
    - Approximately half the project budget will be consumed before the project implementation phase.
    - Project managers often don't spend enough time planning because of the feeling of urgency to get the project started.
    - The more time spent on planning, the less rework has to be done.

Where We Are in the Process

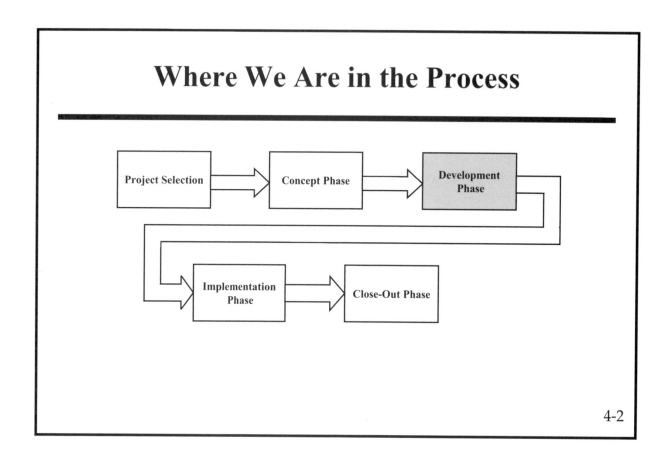

Where We Are in the Process

Project Selection → Concept Phase → Development Phase

Implementation Phase → Close-Out Phase

4-2

Objective
- Orient participants to the model for the course progression.

Time: 3 minutes

Training Notes
- Put up Slide 4-2: Where We Are in the Process.
- Remind the participants that this is the map we are using for the course progress.
- Review the general purpose of this phase.

Activities in the Development Phase

Activities in the Development Phase

The project manager is chiefly concerned about refining the requirements and developing the project plans during this phase. The principal activities are:

- Selecting and forming the project team

- Refining the requirements and clarifying the SOW

- Developing a complete WBS

- Developing budget, schedule, and resource estimates

- Developing a network analysis to determine critical tasks and the shortest time to complete the project

- Creating Gantt charts to describe the project schedules

- Performing a risk analysis

- Completing ancillary plans to support the project

4-3

Objective
- Remind participants of the activities in this project phase.

Time: 5 minutes

Training Notes
- Put up Slide 4-3: Activities in the Development Phase.
- The major activities in this project phase are to refine the WBS (which means the requirements are completely documented, understood, and agreed to by the customer and project manager), to develop a network logic diagram so that the project's duration can be determined, and to develop schedule and budget estimates.
- The project manager should identify members with key skills as he or she clarifies the requirements. With further WBS development to the task level, the project manager identifies the complete project team.

- With a complete project team identified the project manager can develop a task responsibility matrix, which identifies who is responsible for each WBS task. Handout 4-1 is an easy way to record these responsibilities.
- The WBS is the most important project-management tool. With it, all the other tools that are needed can be developed.
- Once the WBS is developed, the project manager can develop the network. This process is described in detail in this module.
- After the schedule is set, the master schedule, in the form of a Gantt chart, can be developed. Most participants are familiar with Gantt charts even if they don't know them by that name. Explain that a Gantt chart is simply a bar chart showing beginning and ending dates for a task/project.
- Most risks can be identified as the WBS is refined and the network analysis is completed.
- There usually are a number of other plans to be written besides the project management plan:
  —risk management plan
  —communications plan
  —logistics plan
  —quality plan
- Ask participants which of these activities they have been involved with. Ask them if their organizations typically prepare any of these plans.

Selecting the Project Team

Objective
- Explain the project team selection process.

Time: 5 Minutes

Training Notes
- Talk about selecting and obtaining the right skills and team members.

 Training Tip: You will find that many of the participants do not have the opportunity to choose team members. Teams often are formed by senior management or happen as a result of the organizational structure. These issues are a little beyond the bounds of this workshop, but they are worth mentioning and are usually of interest to the participants. Do not broach the subject, however, unless you have researched the various organizational structures and their advantages and disadvantages.

- Many times, though, a project manager has to negotiate for team members. Tell participants that if they do have to negotiate, they should:
  —Rely on the initial team to identify the proper skill sets and members.
  —Use the project charter to remind the functional managers of their commitment to the project.
- When negotiating for team members, a project manager should ask the functional manager for a person by name. Many inexperienced project managers make the mistake of going to the functional manager and just requesting a body. Unless a person is requested by name, the functional manager is likely to provide someone who happens not to be busy at the moment or someone who is less qualified than the project calls for. The functional manager may not be able to provide the particular person requested, but by making the request, the project manager has established the skill and experience level he or she wants.

Q What is the best way to approach a functional manager when negotiating for resources?

A I always go to a functional manager with three things in hand: a summary of the project requirements (the executive summary of the project management plan is excellent for this purpose), the project charter, and the names of the people I want for the project. Usually, functional managers are willing to support the project, but they have their own work to accomplish. So, if I can succinctly explain the project requirements and why I need particular people for the team, I'm more likely to get a sympathetic ear. I use the project charter only if there is an issue that the charter can address and resolve. I may not be able to get the people I want because they may already be assigned to other projects. But the functional manager will feel compelled to try to provide someone with at least comparable qualifications.

TASK RESPONSIBILITY MATRIX

PROJECT: _____					
TASK ID(WBS #)	TASK DESCRIPTION	TEAM MEMBER RESPONSIBLE/TASK DURATION			

Legend: P = Primary
S = Supporting

Note: Write the name of the person responsible for the task and indicate whether they have a primary or supporting role.

Estimating Budgets

Estimating Budgets

Project budgets are typically developed using one of the following methods:

- Rough order-of-magnitude (ROM)

- Top-down (analogous)

- Bottom-up (engineering or business)

4-4

Objective
- Introduce the participants to the most common techniques for estimating budgets: rough order-of-magnitude, top-down and bottom-up.

Time: 16 minutes

Training Notes
- Put up Slide 4-4: Estimating Budgets.
- There are basically three methods for budget estimating in use today. Of course, some software packages are used, particularly in certain industries, but the basis of all estimating techniques are these three or a combination of them.

- Each one of these techniques is discussed in detail in the next three slides.
- Ask participants if they ever get involved with estimating project costs.
- Ask them how costs are estimated in their organizations.

Q What is the best and most accurate way to estimate a project budget?

A The best and most accurate way to estimate the project budget is with the bottom-up or definitive technique. This technique is also called the engineering estimate. It is accomplished by going to the lowest level of the WBS and asking the person responsible for the task to estimate the task's duration and what materials are required to complete the task. Knowing the duration, simply apply the person(s)' labor rate for that period plus the cost of the materials to be consumed and you have the cost of the task. Each task is estimated in this fashion. The project cost is the sum of all the task costs.

Rough Order-of-Magnitude

Rough Order-of-Magnitude

Rough Order-of-Magnitude or ROM is the easiest and fastest estimating method, which provides an approximate figure for the project. It is useful as a general estimate of effort and:

- Is based on experience and some historical data, but is mostly based on intuition

- Gives a quick snapshot of the project costs or schedule

- Is usually done by one person

Disadvantages

- Is very inaccurate with estimates ranging between −25% and +75%

- It almost always sticks as the estimate when it is meant to provide an approximate guess for early planning purposes

4-5

- Put up Slide 4-5: Rough Order-of-Magnitude.
- The ROM is the least accurate of the estimating techniques. It is essentially an "educated guess."
- This technique has its place in project management. In fact, an ROM is the best figure available when a project is first considered as a potential target.
- Warn the participants that many times they may be asked to provide an ROM estimate for a task or a project, but it is important that any ROM be documented as an ROM. Otherwise, the figure they provide might stick as the budget figure. This kind of estimate easily can be 100% inaccurate.
- The ROM is most often used in the project selection phase or early in the concept phase, but it is not accurate enough for detailed planning.

Top-Down or Analogous Estimating

Top-Down or Analogous Estimating

Top-down estimating is based on historical data and comparisons with other similar projects.

- Based on comparisons with similar projects within the group or company

- Parametric models are often used to extrapolate data from one project to fit another

- Relatively quick estimate and useful for obtaining reasonably good estimates

- Most appropriate technique for top level planning and decision making

Disadvantages

- Accurate to within −10% and +25%

- Good enough for planning, but not good enough for a final estimate

4-6

- Put up Slide 4-6: Top-Down or Analogous Estimating.
- The top-down technique is considerably more accurate than the ROM.
- This method is based on some historical data and more corporate experience than the ROM is. Often analogies to past projects are used to determine the estimated cost. For example, if the company had a project last year that was similar to the current project, then the actual cost of the previous project, adjusted for inflation, might be used.
- Caution participants that if they are making an analogy to another project, they should make sure that the project or appropriate parts of the analogous project are actually similar. Otherwise, the estimate is no better than a ROM.

Bottom-Up or Definitive Estimating

Bottom-Up or Definitive Estimating

The bottom-up estimating method is the most accurate of the three methods.

- Based upon the lowest level of the WBS

- Estimates are determined with the person who performs the task

- The project cost is "rolled-up" from the lowest WBS level to the highest WBS level

- This technique is used to update estimates for the final project budget

Disadvantages

- Takes time

- Within −5% and +10% accurate

4-7

- Put up Slide 4-7: Bottom-Up or Definitive Estimating.
- This technique is the most accurate of the three techniques because it is derived from the work-package level of the WBS and requires costing each package.
- When using this technique, a project manager should go to the person who will actually be accomplishing the task and ask him or her how long it will take to do the task and what the cost will be.
- Warn participants that budgets and schedules are almost always underestimated. Ask them why this is so. (The biggest reason for underestimating budgets and schedules is that we don't account for risks. Also, the people making the estimates may not be trained or experienced).
- Ask participants if they have had projects that were underestimated and what the reasons were.

Network Analysis

Network Analysis

Network analysis is a scheduling tool developed from the WBS. It is used to:

- Show the interdependence of project tasks

- Determine the project duration

- Determine float or slack in a path

- Determine the project's critical path

- Expose risks

4-8

Objectives
- Introduce participants to the network analysis tool of project management.
- Explain how to develop a precedence table.
- Explain how to construct a network diagram.

Time: 15 minutes

Training Notes
- Put up Slide 4-8: Network Analysis.
- Networks, sometimes called logic diagrams, show the interdependencies of tasks within a project or graphically depict how each task is related to the others.
- Sometimes a task cannot be started until another one is completed because of some dependency. For instance, a design of a subsystem has to be com-

pleted before the subsystem can be built. In this case, the tasks are sequential.

- In other cases, two tasks might be independent of each other and can start at the same time. For example, a project that requires a piece of training equipment and a computer-based training system to support it. Building the training equipment and developing the computer-based training can be accomplished at the same time, or in parallel.
- From the network analysis, we can determine the critical path—float or slack—and the shortest time it takes to do the project.

 Training Tip: Go through the network analysis at least twice. The analysis is not difficult, but the backward pass is confusing to most participants.

Q Can a software program perform the network analysis?

A Yes. All project-management software programs can do the network analysis. However, it is imperative that you understand the network analysis because the software package analyzes the network from the data you enter. Unless you understand the analysis, your cannot direct the software program to analyze the network correctly.

Steps in Developing a Network

Steps in Developing a Network

Once the WBS is developed to the lowest desired level, the network can be developed and analyzed:

- The project team and other selected functional experts determine the interdependence of all the tasks

- Develop a precedence table after all task dependencies are established

- Construct the network

- Determine the duration, critical path, and float for each task

4-9

- Put up Slide 4-9: Steps in Developing a Network.
- The WBS is used to examine dependencies of tasks. That is, the project team or other functional experts will look at the work packages and determine how each task is related to every other task.
- The next step is to develop a precedence table, which is discussed on the next slide, so that the network can be drawn.
- After the precedence table is complete, the network can be constructed and the duration, critical path, and float can be determined.

Training Tip: Two points have to be emphasized strongly about going through the network analysis. First, work through the network and determine the early schedule. *Do not* try to determine the late schedule until the forward pass or early schedule process is finished. At least one person in every workshop group tries to determine both schedules at the same time. Second, the early schedule *must* be completed first because the final duration value of the early schedule is the starting value for determining the late schedule.

One of the several reasons for developing and analyzing the network is that a manager cannot make budget estimates without knowing the schedule. The network analysis provides the schedule duration given the resources available. If the duration is longer than the requirements dictate, more planning is needed to determine how to shorten the schedule. But once the duration is satisfactory, that number is used to estimate costs and to develop Gantt chart schedules.

Precedence Tables

Precedence Tables

A precedence table is necessary for developing networks or logic diagrams. They usually have the following form:

Task Identifier	WBS Element	Predecessor	Task Duration
a	Task 1	—	5
b	Task 2	—	4
c	Task 3	a	4
d	Task 4	b	4
e	Task 5	b	3
f	Task 6	c	4
g	Task 7	d	5
h	Task 8	e	8
i	Task 9	f,g,h	8
j	Task 10	e	8

4-10

- Put up Slide 4-10: Precedence Tables.
- The precedence table is easy to construct and is based on the WBS. Tell the participants that they should give each task an alphabetic identifier, as in column 1, for convenience. Writing the entire name of the task on the network makes the table too congested and messy.
- Once the tasks are listed and identifiers are assigned, then the team determines if any of the tasks are dependent on any other tasks.
- For instance, in the table above, tasks a and b are not dependent on each other and can therefore start at the same time. On the other hand, task c can not begin until task a is completed.
- The last column of the table shows duration of the tasks. These times to complete the task come from the task owners, that is, the people who will actually do the work on the task.

The Network Diagram

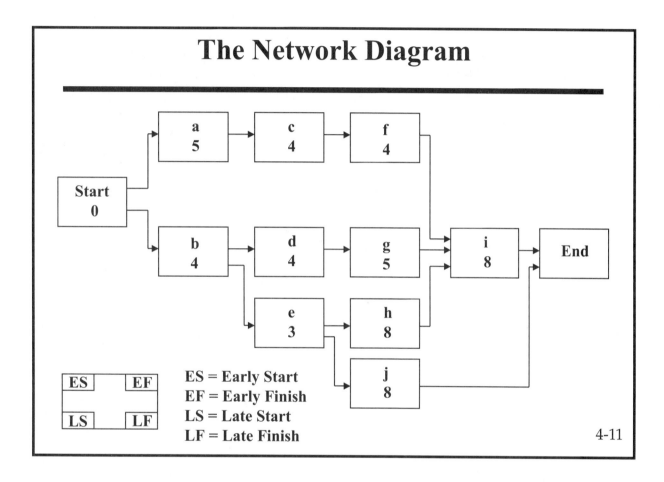

- Put up Slide 4-11: The Network Diagram.
- Refer back to the previous slide and point out to the participants that this network has indeed been constructed showing the interdependencies in the table.
- Explain that the squares are called nodes and that each represents a task. Point out that each node in the network has a task identifier and a number. The number is the duration from the table on the previous slide. The arrows show dependencies.
- A path describes a route from the start node to the end node. For example, Start-a-c-f-i-End is one path through the network.
- Ask participants to tell you what the other paths are (Start-b-d-g-i-End; Start-b-e-h-i-End; Start-b-e-j-End are the other paths).

- It is best to form the habit of creating a start node and an end node, as in the slide, to eliminate the problem of having dangling nodes.
- Emphasize that all nodes have to be connected to something.
- Point out the legend box on the slide. The top corners show the earliest beginning and ending times, and the bottom boxes show the latest beginning and ending times.

Early Schedule

Early Schedule

In analyzing the network, the early schedule is determined first.

- Begin at the project start node and determine the earliest possible time each task can begin and finish

- The "Early Finish" of each task in succession is determined by adding the task duration to its "Early Start"

- The "Early Start" of a task is the "Early Finish" of the preceding task

- The process of determining the early schedule is referred to as the "Forward Pass"

4-12

Objectives
- Introduce the concept of the earliest possible schedule.
- Explain how to determine the early start of a succeeding task when two or more arrows are entering the task.

Time: 12 minutes

Training Notes
- Put up Slide 4-12: Early Schedule.
- After constructing the network, the first step in network analysis is to determine the early schedule.
- We go from left to right through the network to determine the early schedule. The early schedule includes the earliest start and finish times of each task in the project.

- As will be more clearly seen on the following slide, the early start of a succeeding task is the early finish of the previous task.
- The earliest finish is the earliest start plus the duration time of the task.

Early Start

Early Start

When two or more arrows enter a task, the "Early Start" is the LARGEST of
the preceding task's "Early Finish"
Example:

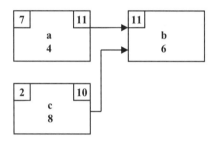

4-13

- Put up Slide 4-13: Early Start.
- When there is more than one arrow entering a task, as in the slide, the earliest start of that task is the *larger* of the early finish times of the preceding tasks.
- In the example of the slide, the earliest that task b can start is 11, which is the largest earliest finish times of tasks a and c.

Forward Pass: The Early Schedule

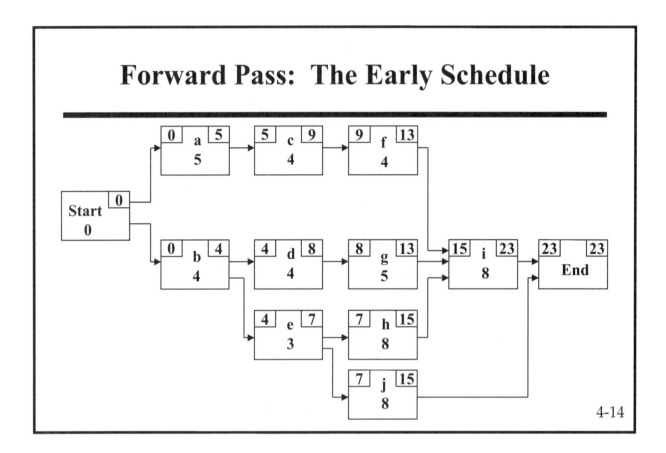

- Put up Slide 4-14: Forward Pass: The Early Schedule.
- This slide shows the early schedule for the project. Notice that the early start of each task is equal to the earliest finish of the preceding task, except for tasks i and End. Task i has three arrows entering it from tasks f, g, and h. The *largest* early finish time of those three tasks is task h. So task i cannot begin until 15, the latest early finish time of the three tasks. Also, task End cannot begin until task i is finished, since its latest finish time is greater than the finish time of task j.
- Twenty-three days (or whatever units are being used) is the duration of the project. Because of the interdependencies of the tasks, with the resources currently assigned, we cannot complete the project in fewer than 23 days.

Late Schedule

Late Schedule

The late schedule cannot be determined until after the early schedule is known.

- From the end of the project, work backwards through the network to determine the late schedule.

- Start with the duration determined by the Forward Pass as the beginning point

- The "Late Finish" of a task is the "Late Start" of the succeeding task

- The process of determining the late schedule is referred to as the Backward Pass.

4-15

Objective
- Teach participants how to determine the latest the project tasks can begin and end and still maintain the schedule.

Time: 11 minutes

Training Notes
- Put up Slide 4-15: Late Schedule.
- Determining the late schedule is not difficult, but it is confusing because we have to go backwards—from right to left—through the network.
- Emphasize that the starting point for determining the late schedule is the schedule duration time determined by the forward-pass process. In other words, we want to keep the same schedule but determine how late we can start or end a task without negatively affecting the schedule time.

Late Finish

Late Finish

When two or more arrows back into a task, the "Late Finish" is the SMALLEST
of the succeeding task's "Late Start"
- Example:

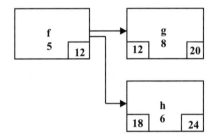

4-16

- Put up Slide 4-16: Late Finish.
- When going backwards in the network, the latest a task can finish is the late start of the succeeding task except when two or more arrows BACK into the task, as shown in the slide.
- The latest finish for task f is the SMALLEST of late start times of the two succeeding tasks. Hence the latest task f can finish is 12.
- The logic is very clear. If, in the example of Slide 4-16, we are using task f's late schedule, then it finishes at the twelfth day because tasks g and h can not start before f finishes. If we had chosen 18, the late start of task h, to be the late finish of task f, task g would be starting 6 days before task f finished, and that would violate the network logic.

Backward Pass: The Late Schedule

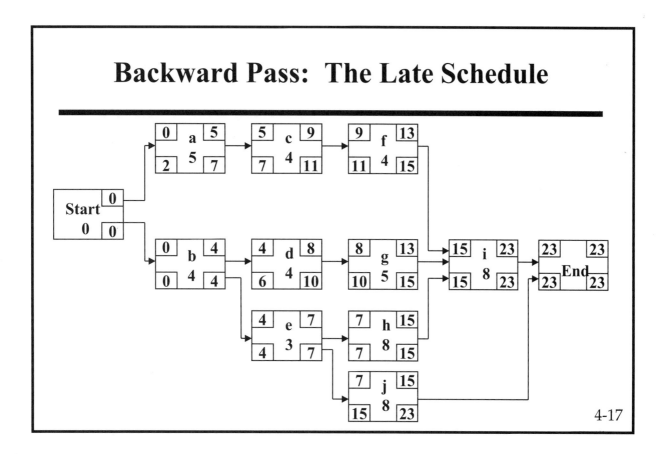

- Put up Slide 4-17: Backward Pass: The Late Schedule.
- This slide shows the completed schedules for the network. Again, the early schedule is in the top boxes of the nodes and the late schedule is in the bottom boxes.
- Note that the latest finish for the project is the same as the earliest finish. In other words, we start the backward pass with the same duration as was determined by the forward pass, namely 23 in this example.
- Point out that task i has a latest finish of 23, which is the latest start of task End. Likewise, task j has a latest finish of 23.
- Point out that task e has two arrows backing into it, one from task h and the other from task j. In the backward-pass process, we take the smaller of the possibilities, so the latest finish for task e is 7.

Project Duration, Float, and Critical Path

Project Duration, Float, and Critical Path

Three important pieces of information derived from network analyses are the duration, amount of float or slack in each path, and the project's critical path.

- Project duration: The shortest required time to complete the project.

- Float: The amount of time the start of a task can be delayed without impacting the schedule.

    Float = Latest Start – Earliest Start or Latest Finish – Earliest Finish

- Critical Path: The longest path through the network or the path with zero float. This path identifies the tasks that have to be managed closely so that no slips to the schedule occur.

4-18

Objectives
- Define duration, float, and the critical path.
- Demonstrate how to show the critical path on a network diagram.

Time: 7 minutes

Training Notes
- Put up Slide 4-18: Project Duration, Float, and Critical Path.
- Duration of a project is the earliest that the project can be finished. In our example, it is 23 days. Another way of looking at it is that the duration is the shortest time through the network.
- Float is defined as the difference between the late finish and the early finish of a task. It is also the difference between the late start and the early start of the task.

- "Float" and "slack" are the same thing.
- Critical path has two characteristics that distinguishes it from any other path in the network: it is the longest path through the network, and it is the path that has zero float on it. Hence the term "critical path." It is critical because if any task on that path slips, then the whole schedule slips.
- Project managers must manage the tasks on the critical path very closely.

The Critical Path

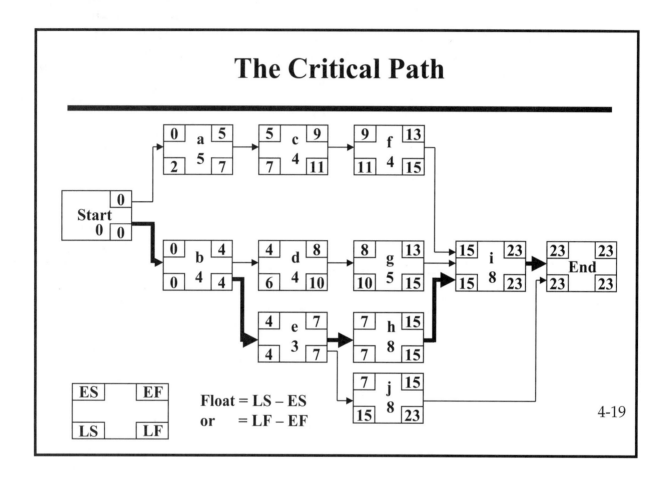

- Put up Slide 4-19: The Critical Path.
- The critical path for our example is Start-b-e-h-i-End because none of these tasks have any float.
- The critical path is usually shown in red or with heavy arrows, as in the slide.

Exercise 4-1

Exercise 4-1

Using the information from the precedence table, construct a Network Diagram and answer the following questions:

1. **What is the project duration?**
2. **What is the critical path?**
3. **How much float is in Task ....?**

Task Identifier	WBS Element	Predecessor	Task Duration
a	Task 1	—	5
b	Task 2	—	6
c	Task 3	a	2
d	Task 4	a,b	5
e	Task 5	b	4
f	Task 6	c,d,e	4

4-20

Objective
- Provide the participants with an opportunity to practice drawing a network diagram from a precedence table and to analyze it.

Time: 60 minutes

Training Notes
- Put up Slide 4–20: Exercise 4–1.
- This precedence table provides the participants with all they need to draw the network.
- Participants should work individually. Allow 40 minutes to construct and analyze the network.

- You will have to circulate around the room to help some of the participants. Usually, very few people have problems with the forward pass process; it is the backward pass that is confusing.
- After 20 minutes, call time and ask the participants to answer the questions in the exercise. Work through the exercise if anyone was unable to analyze it completely.

Gantt Charts

Gantt Charts

Gantt charts are developed after the network analysis is completed. They are used for:

- Showing beginning and ending points for each of the project tasks

- Graphically depicting project progress against the project baseline

- Communicating project progress to stakeholders

4-21

Objective
- Introduce participants to the use of Gantt charts for showing project schedules.

Time: 5 minutes

Training Notes
- Put up Slide 4-21: Gantt Charts.
- The Gantt chart is a bar chart that shows the beginning and ending points of tasks in a project.
- The Gantt chart is an excellent communications tool because it is easy to interpret and graphically depicts the project's progress.

Sample Gantt Chart

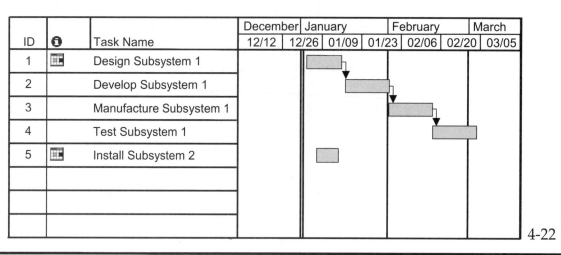

Slide 4-22

- Put up Slide 4-22: Sample Gantt Chart.
- This is an example of a Gantt chart constructed with Microsoft Project, a project-management software package.

The Project-Management Plan

The Project Management Plan

Once the schedule, budget, and resource estimates are completed, the project plan can be finalized. A format that will fit most projects will have these elements:

    I. Executive Summary
    II. Project Requirements and Objectives
    III. General Methodology or Technical Approach
    IV. Contractual Requirements
    V. Schedules
    VI. Resource Requirements
        A. Equipment
        B. Materials
        C. People
    VII. Potential Risks
    VIII. Performance Evaluations

Appendices
    Project Charter
    Supporting plans
    Drawings
    Specifications

4-23

Objective
- Introduce the participants to a project-management plan format.

Time: 10 minutes

Training Notes
- Put up Slide 4-23: The Project-Management Plan.
- Once the network analysis is completed, the schedules can be drawn up and the budget estimates can be completed.
- The next step is to prepare the project-management plan.
- A copy of this format is provided as Handout 4-2.

- Go through each element of the management plan to make sure the participants understand the type of information that is required in the plan.
- Tell the participants that they should write a project-management plan regardless of whether it is an internal or external project. You will find that many participants do not write management plans for internal projects. Yet they will readily admit that their projects do not run as smoothly as they should. Ask them if they can now surmise the reason(s) their projects have trouble.

Q How do you prepare the project management plan?

A I use the plan format headings and prepare a series of files for each one. Then I begin to record everything I know about each of the headings. It doesn't take long for me to discover what I don't know, and what I need to concentrate on.

PROJECT MANAGEMENT PLAN FORMAT

I.   Executive Summary

II.   Project Requirements and Objectives

III.   General Methodology or Technical Approach

IV.   Contractual Requirements

V.   Schedules

VI.   Resource Requirements
        A. Equipment
        B. Materials
        C. People

VII.   Potential Risks

VIII.   Performance Evaluations

Appendices
        Project Charter
        Supporting plans
        Drawings
        Specifications

Key Messages—Module 4

Key Messages—Module 4

The key messages of this module are:

- There are three primary methods for estimating budgets, resources, and schedules. They are:
    - ROM
    - Top-down
    - Bottom-up

- The precedence diagramming method is a critical analysis tool. It provides the following information:
    - Project duration
    - Critical path
    - Float in each task

- The Gantt chart is a bar chart showing the beginning and ending of each task

- The project plan can be finalized once the budget, schedule, and resource estimates are completed

4-24

Objective
- Summarize the key points of the module.

Time: 3 minutes

Training Notes
- Put up Slide 4-24: Key Messages—Module 4.
- Go over each point on this slide and ensure the participants have a good grasp of the major discussion items in this module.
- Ask participants if they have any questions about the module.
- Ask participants to discuss any of the tools or concepts covered in the module that will be of immediate benefit to them.
- Make a transition to the next module.

The Project Implementation Phase

The implementation phase is the monitoring and control phase of the project. If we have defined the project requirements and planned thoroughly, this phase should run smoothly. Organizations that support the planning process spend as much as 50% of their project budget by the time the project is implemented.

The risk management discussion is included in this phase because it fits the design of the workshop better. However, you should make clear to the participants that the risk plan is written along with the project management plan. Therefore, the risk analysis should be completed by the time the project is implemented. Even so, it is not totally out of place to include the risk analysis and risk plan in this phase because risk has to be assessed at every phase of the project.

The activities of the implementation phase focus on tracking the progress of the project and reporting this progress to the stakeholders. However, the project manager and his or her team have to accomplish several other objectives to support this effort.

The Implementation Phase Objectives

The objective of this phase is to teach the participants about:

1. Change-management process
2. Risk identification
3. Risk ranking
4. Risk-management plan format
5. Tracking a project using earned value

Risk analysis is best done with the team. It is too easy to overlook a task or risk event when you are trying to identify potential risks. Risk planning is one thing that project teams generally do not do well. You, the trainer, should be aware of this and emphasize to the participants how important the risk process is.

The risk-management plan format is straightforward and should offer no real challenges to explain.

Earned value is an easy analysis to perform but a hard concept to grasp. You should master the concept before you try to teach it because under the very best circumstances, some participants have a very hard time understanding the terms used in the analysis.

Trainers generally are adept at explaining difficult concepts. This module will challenge your ability to do so. The concepts dealing with risk would not be particularly difficult to explain if it were not for the fact that most participants will not have had any real experience with risk identification, analysis, and planning. Even so, they tend to grasp the discussion on risk intellectually with little trouble, but you may find that some of the participants have difficulty realizing the importance or impact of risk to their projects. Therefore, you will need to work through this section of the slides carefully, impressing on the group just how poor a job most project teams do with risk planning and how dire the results of inadequate risk planning can be.

Content Theory for the Implementation Phase

The three major discussion topics in this module are change control, risk, and earned value. None is particularly hard but earned value in particular requires the trainer to patiently explain the concepts more than once.

Change Control

Change control is required in a project to eliminate scope creep and to ensure that the customer and other stakeholders are aware of any changes to the original scope. The control system and control process should be clearly documented in the SOW and in the project-management plan. The configuration control board (CCB) is an ad hoc group of three to five functional experts who are responsible for considering change requests submitted through the project manager. The project manager presents the requests to the CCB along with a reason for the request and the impact to the project's budget and schedule. If the CCB decides the change request is beneficial to the project, they will make a recommendation to the customer along with a proposal outlining the benefits and costs. The customer decides whether to pursue the requested change or not. If he or she decides to go ahead, then a formal modification to the contract is written and communicated back to the selling organization. The change is made and the stakeholders are notified. This change process is clearly shown in Exhibit 5-1 and in the module slides covering this section.

Risk Identification and Analysis

Risk identification is best accomplished with a brainstorming session. Of course, if the participants have access to historical data in terms of lessons learned, then they can identify risk events that occurred on previous, similar projects.

Once the risk events are identified, it is important to filter them to determine whether they really do constitute a risk to the project and when they are likely to occur. If the risk is short term, then it has to be dealt with immediately. If not, then it can be dealt with at the appropriate time. That does not mean that one should wait until the risk event occurs to address it. It means that consideration of whether the risk is short or long term is one of the factors in ranking risks.

The comparative risk-ranking table is a simple-to-use tool that quickly provides a priority list. There are several ways to fill in the table, but the easiest way is shown in the example in Exhibit 5-2. Start at the top with the Task A column and go down the column considering each of the risks in turn. If Task A is more important, in terms of its impact on the project, than Task B, then assign a 1 to Task A. Write "A = 1" in the box for BA. If Task C is more important than Task A, then assign a 1 to Task C. Write "C = 1" in the box for CA. Continue until every task has been compared against every other task. Add the 1s for each task. The result is shown in Exhibit 5-3.

This tool is fast and easy to use particularly if the project is a team effort.

Earned Value

Earned value developed as a concept in the fall of 1968. The Department of Defense (DOD) had difficulty tracking its projects' progress because every con-

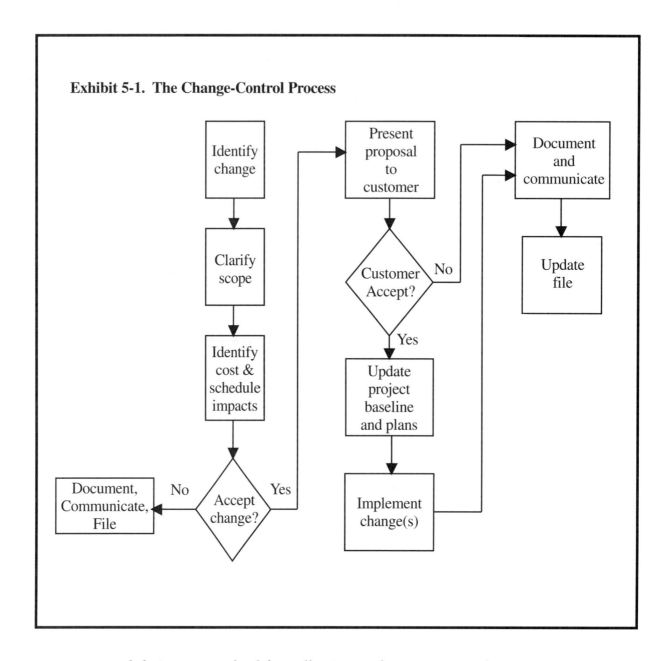

Exhibit 5-1. The Change-Control Process

tractor used their own method for collecting and representing data, in particular financial and schedule data. The earned-value concept grew out of this effort to establish a standard way of representing these data. Since then, earned value has become the standard not only for the DOD, but for the private sector as well.

Three terms have to be mastered before the concept of earned value can be understood or taught. These terms are budgeted cost of work scheduled (BCWS), actual cost of work scheduled (ACWS), and budgeted cost of work performed (BCWP).

Exhibit 5-2. Comparative Risk Ranking Example

A	A	B	C	D	E	F	G
B	A = 1						
C	C = 1	C = 1					
D	A = 1	B = 1	D = 1				
E	E = 1	E = 1	C = 1	D = 1			
F	A = 1	B = 1	F = 1	F = 1	F = 1		
G	G = 1	B = 1	C = 1	D = 1	G = 1	F = 1	

Exhibit 5-3. Risk-Ranking Table

Task C = 4
Task F = 4
Task A = 3
Task B = 3
Task D = 3
Task E = 2
Task G = 2

BCWS

BCWS is the amount of money estimated for the project costs. It is not a new term—it is what we have previously referred to as the budget—but it has been renamed. Actually, the name makes perfect sense because we are referring to the estimate for the amount of work we plan or schedule to do. This budget is estimated from the WBS at the work-package level and summed to get the total cost of the project. The budget is usually shown as a cumulative curve.

ACWP

ACWP also is not a new term. It is the actual amount of money that is spent on a task of the project. We usually refer to this term as the "actuals" and collect them from time sheets, i.e., labor costs and invoices. The actual cost of a task has nothing to do with the estimated cost. That is, our estimate may be accurate or not, but the cost is whatever we have to spend to accomplish the work.

BCWP

BCWP is a new term to the project management field. It is also known as the "earned-value" term because it is the amount of work we have actually accomplished against the planned work. People new to this concept easily confuse this term with ACWP. But ACWP represents the amount of money *actually spent* on the work completed; BCWP represents the amount of money *budgeted* for the work that has been completed.

BCWP is a percentage of the BCWS figure. In other words, what we really are trying to do is to determine what percentage of work *planned* has been accomplished. The percent of the planned budget accomplished is the BCWP, or the amount we have earned. For example, suppose we estimated that the cost of a task is $1,000, but at our scheduled finish date, we are only 80% complete. The BCWS, the amount planned to be accomplished, is $1,000; but the BCWP, the amount actually accomplished, is $800 (BCWS x 80% = 1,000 x .8 = $800). In other words we have only earned $800 of the amount we had planned to earn on that date.

Once the concept of these three terms is understood, the analysis is very simple. Exhibit 5-4 is a table that lists the analysis formulas and is useful as a handy reference. The same table is provided as a handout to the participants for their reference also.

The earned value example in this module works through all the steps of this analysis. You should be prepared to go through this example more than once to make sure the participants understand how it works.

Exhibit 5-4. Table of Earned Value Formulas

Use This Formula	To Calculate
CV = BCWP – ACWP	Cost Variance
SV = BCWP – BCWS	Schedule Variance
CPI = BCWP/ACWP	Cost Performance Index
SPI = BCWP/BCWS	Schedule Performance Index
EAC = BAC/CPI	Estimate at Completion
ETC = EAC – ACWP	Estimate to Complete

Where: BCWP is the amount of work accomplished against the amount planned.

BCWP = BCWS x % of work completed

Training Objectives of the Implementation Phase

The training objectives of this phase are:

1. To provide the participants with a basic understanding of risk identification, risk ranking, and risk planning.
2. To teach participants the earned value concept and how to track a project using the earned value analysis.

There are not as many objectives in this phase as in the others, but the concepts tend to be more difficult to grasp. Once the concepts are clear, however, the analysis is very simple.

Summary

The implementation phase is the monitoring, tracking, and controlling phase of the project. The major tool used for this purpose is earned value. The Department of Defense developed earned value in 1968, but it is now accepted worldwide as the standard method for tracking project progress.

The major difficulty in understanding the earned-value concept is the earned-value term itself, or BCWP, which is actually a schedule term. That is, we are measuring the amount of work actually accomplished compared with what was scheduled to be accomplished. That is why this tool is so useful—it measures how we are doing on the project from both a budget and a schedule perspective.

Agenda for Module 5: The Project Implementation Phase

Objectives for Module 5	5 minutes
Where We Are in the Process	3 minutes
Activities in the Implementation Phase	4 minutes
Goals of the Change-Control System	8 minutes
Risk Analysis	4 minutes
Types of Risk	4 minutes
Risk Assessment Methods	27 minutes
Prioritizing Risks	6 minutes
A Risk Management Plan Format	14 minutes
Earned Value	10 minutes
Cost and Schedule Variance and Sample Calculation	10 minutes
Cost and Schedule Performance Indices	9 minutes
Estimate at Completion (EAC)	9 minutes
Estimate to Complete (ETC)	5 minutes
Exercise 5-1	10 minutes
Exercise 5-2	20 minutes
Key Messages—Module 5	8 minutes
Total	156 minutes

Module 5: The Project Implementation Phase

Monitoring and Controlling the Project

Approximate time for module: 2 hours 36 minutes

Objectives for Module 5

Objectives for Module 5

At the end of this module you will be able to:

- Develop a change management process

- Identify and prioritize project risks

- Develop a risk management plan

- Employ "earned value" concepts and formulas to track project progress

5-1

Objective
- Introduce module objectives.

Time: 5 minutes

Training Notes
- Put up Slide 5-1: Objectives for Module 5.
- This module addresses how to implement, monitor, and track a project.
- If the planning has been thorough and detailed, then the project should run relatively smoothly.
- The major project management tool for this phase is earned value.
- Earned value is a concept that has been accepted worldwide as the standard method for measuring project progress.
- Also during this phase, you will learn about risk and risk management.

- Finally, in this phase, we will put into place a change management process to manage any changes that occur to the project, both from the customer and from internal sources.
- Ask participants how project progress is currently tracked in their organizations.
- Facilitate a discussion about how important it is to have a formal, documented change process. Bring these points into the discussion:
  —Ask how changes are made in projects in the participants' organizations. If a participant states that his or her company doesn't have a formal process, ask him or her to describe any problems this situation causes.
  —The project should be the point of contact for all change requests or recommendations.
  —Most companies have a configuration change board (CCB) to consider change requests.

Where We Are in the Process

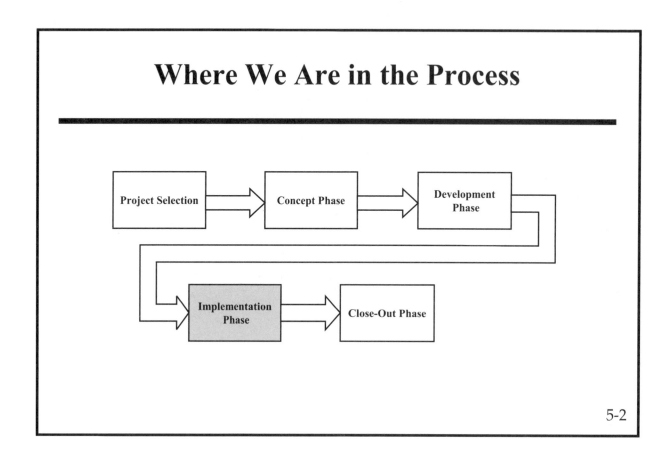

Objective
• Orient participants to the model for the course progression.

Time: 3 minutes

Training Notes
• Put up Slide 5-2: Where We Are in the Process.
• Remind the participants that this is the map we are using for the course progress.
• Review the general purpose of this phase.
• Ask participants to name some of the activities that they typically encounter during this phase and ask whether they are aware of any kind of formalized process for this phase in their organization.

Activities in the Implementation Phase

Activities in the Implementation Phase

The project manager is chiefly concerned about monitoring and controlling the project relative to the project baseline during this phase. The principal activities are:

- Setting up the project organization

- Securing the required resources

- Setting up and executing the work packages

- Directing, monitoring, and controlling the project

5-3

Objective
- Remind participants of the activities in this project phase.

Time: 4 minutes

Training Notes
- Put up Slide 5-3: Activities in the Implementation Phase.
- This module focuses on monitoring, tracking, and controlling the project.
- Planning for resources and building the project team were accomplished during the development phase. In this phase, all the planning will be put into action.
- Ask participants how their work is currently implemented. In other words, do they have some system of work-order execution?

Goals of the Change-Control System

Goals of the Change-Control System

A well developed and documented change-control process is crucial to project management success. Change-control systems should:

- Continually identify changes, actual or proposed, as they occur

- Reveal the consequences of the proposed changes in terms of cost and schedule impacts

- Permit managerial analysis, investigation of alternatives, and an acceptance or rejection checkpoint

- Communicate changes to all stakeholders

- Insure that changes are implemented

5-4

Objective
- Introduce participants to change control and change-control processes.

Time: 8 minutes

Training Notes
- Put up Slide 5-4: Goals of the Change-Control System.
- Explain that one of the project manager's major tasks is controlling change in the project.
- Ask participants if they know what "scope creep" means. (Scope creep occurs when the customer asks for relatively small changes in the project scope without a formal change to the original scope.)
- Ask participants if they are familiar with the change process in their organizations or projects.

Q Does the project manager have the authority to make changes to the scope of the project?

A Some organizations assign the project manager a level of authority for accepting change requests. This does not mean that the project manager can arbitrarily make the changes. It means that he or she can make recommendations for changes to the customer without first consulting senior management, provided the request is for a change that does not affect the budget or schedule more than a preset amount. Otherwise, the change requests are passed through the project manager to a configuration control board (CCB) for resolution (see the discussion on CCB in the content theory section for more details on the CCB).

The Change-Control Process

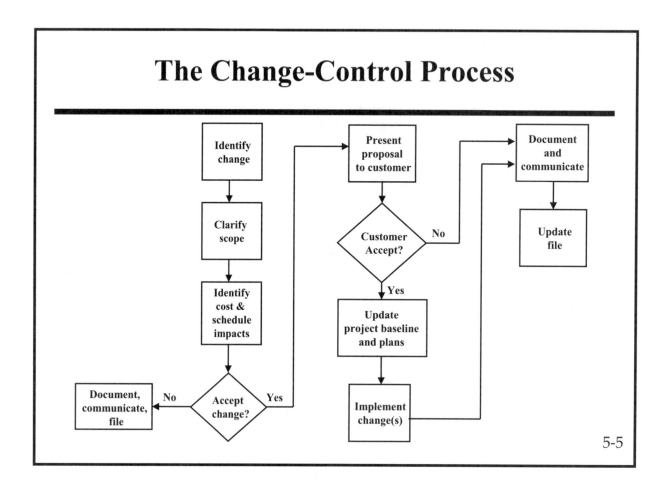

- Put up Slide 5-5: The Change-Control Process.
- This slide is a graphical picture of the previous slide and shows the process clearly.
- Go through each step of this graphic and explain the process.
- Anyone—team members, stakeholders, the customer, or outside sources— can recommend a change.
- Any recommended change should go to the project manager.
- The configuration control board (CCB) is an ad hoc group of three to five functional experts. They are responsible for considering change requests submitted through the project manager.
- When the CCB approves of a change request, it makes a formal presentation to the customer that details the benefits and costs of the proposed change.

- The project manager determines whether the recommended change is within scope or not and determines the impact, relative to cost and schedule, if the change is accepted.
- A proposal is prepared for the customer. If the customer agrees with the change, then a formal contract modification is issued.

Why Risk Analysis?

Why Risk Analysis?

The main objectives of a risk analysis are:

- Timeliness: A risk analysis must identify issues before they occur

- Priorities: Because of insufficient time or resources, a risk analysis must help assign realistic priorities

- Aggregation: The risk analysis must help aggregate all the individual risks into a measure of overall project risk

- Decision support: The risk analysis must produce information in a form that supports the decision makers

5-6

Objective
- Present the objectives of risk analysis to the participants.

Time: 4 minutes

Training Notes
- Put up Slide 5-6: Why Risk Analysis?
- Risk analyses occur throughout the project. During project planning, managers will have developed a risk plan.
- Although the project should run smoothly, invariably something always goes wrong. Talk about risk and how important it is to plan for risk and to develop contingency plans. We usually react to risk events, instead of forestalling them. The objective of risk planning is to allow us to be proactive.
- The beginning of the implementation phase is the time to review the risk

plan and to determine whether they can now identify other risks that were not identified in the planning stages.

• This slide outlines what a risk analysis accomplishes.

Q Who in the project organization is responsible for risk management?

A The project manager is responsible for risk management. Some organizations have tried to establish a "risk office" so that certain individuals are charged with managing risks for all projects. However, I do not recommend this approach because only the project manager can be aware of all the activities of his or her project at any given time. A third person outside the organization is likely to overlook or be unaware of a risk event until it occurs. In addition, the project manager is responsible for the success of the project. He or she must be given the authority to deal with risk events. Often the project manager assigns responsibility for tracking risks to a project-team member so that risk events are monitored by more than one person, but ultimately, the project manager is responsible for managing the risk if the event occurs.

Types of Risk

Types of Risk

There are two kinds of risk in a project. They are:

1. Business risks: Potential for loss but also an opportunity for gain
   - Example 1: Customer expands the project scope.
   - Example 2: A project task requires use or development of new technology. Successful completion of the development opens a new market to the company.

2. Pure or insurable risks: Potential only for loss
   - Example 1: Company is located in an area susceptible to hurricanes.
   - Example 2: Company has no expertise required by one of the project tasks.

5-7

Objective
- Define the two types of project risks.

Time: 4 minutes

Training Notes
- Put up Slide 5-7: Types of Risk.
- There are two types of risk: business risk, which has potential for both gain and loss, and pure or insurable risk, which has potential only for loss.
- Project managers should only try to manage the business type of risk. The pure risks are passed to someone else.
- Ask participants how risks can be passed to someone else (by buying insurance against fire, hurricanes, or work stoppages; by hiring a consult-

ant or another company to be responsible for part of a project if your company does not have the expertise).

- To identify all of the projects risks, the project manager should use the team and any other functional experts available to participate in a risk brainstorming session. This method generates a large amount of data in a short period. It also has the advantage of tapping the experiences of many people. As with any brainstorming session, the risks are categorized and filtered to develop a final list of the potential events. It is also important to designate whether the identified risk is short term or long term. If short term, then the risk has to be dealt with immediately; if long term, it can be moved to a "watch list" for later action.

- Risks generally impart either quality or performance, budget, or schedule and often impart all three. A worksheet is provided on Handout 5-1 that can be used to aid in identifying, assessing, and documenting potential risks.

RISK ASSESSMENT CHART

PROJECT PARAMETER	POTENTIAL PROBLEM	WHEN AND HOW IT COULD OCCUR	ALTERNATIVE ACTION
Quality			
Budget			
Schedule			

Risk Assessment Methods

Risk Assessment Methods

Methods for assessing risks fall into three broad groups:

1. Issue-based methods

2. Scoring techniques

3. Quantitative techniques

5-8

Objective
- Acquaint participants with the different ways of assessing risks and their advantages and disadvantages.

Time: 27 minutes

Training Notes
- Put up Slide 5-8: Risk Assessment Methods.
- Several different methods or techniques can be used in risk assessment. Each of these techniques is discussed in detail in the following slides.
- Ask participants if they can describe how risk assessment is accomplished in their organizations.

Risk Classifications for Issue-Based Risk Assessment

Risk Classifications for
Issue-Based Risk Assessment

Issue-based methods usually start with the assertion that all risks can be classified under a set of headings, such as:

- Commercial

- Technical

- Programmatic

- Resource availability

- Project priorities

5-9

- Put up Slide 5-9: Risk Classifications for Issue-Based Risk Assessment.
- People who use an issue-based approach to risk assessment think that all risks can be collected under specific categories.
- This type of assessment depends on checklists that are useful in identifying project risks and can be used to good advantage.
- Like most things, this technique has advantages and disadvantages.

Advantages and Disadvantages of Issue-Based Risk Assessment

Advantages and Disadvantages of Issue-Based Risk Assessment

Advantages

- Provides a checklist, which helps in remembering to look at all project elements
- Checklists provide access to the experience of others

Disadvantages

- Checklists tend to be seen as exhaustive, giving a sense of false security
- Checklists don't help provide an overall level of risk in a project nor do they help determine realistic budget and schedule estimates

5-10

- Put up Slide 5-10: Advantages and Disadvantages of Issue-Based Risk Assessment.
- This method uses checklists, which is good, because checklists help people to remember to look at the various areas of the project. Also, checklists provide access to the experience of others because they are usually developed with input from all the functional groups.
- The major disadvantage to using checklists is that people tend to view them as being exhaustive, and so they consider only the items on the checklist.

Scoring Techniques

Scoring Techniques

Scoring techniques are natural extensions of checklists. They:

- Are based on a questionnaire

- Provide a checklist approach as memory joggers

- Ask for a numerical rating of a factor if it appears in the task or project

- Provide for a way to assess the overall project riskiness by adding the risk assessment points

5-11

- Put up Slide 5-11: Scoring Techniques.
- This approach combines a checklist with a numerical scoring system. It is an improvement over the pure issue-based approach because it does offer a way to quantify risk.
- This approach also provides a way to assess the overall project riskiness, whereas the issue-based approach does not.

Advantages and Disadvantages of Scoring Techniques

Advantages and Disadvantages of Scoring Techniques

Advantages

- Combine the checklist approach with a numerical rating of the task riskiness
- Provide a way to measure overall project riskiness
- Valuable because they highlight separate issues and indicate which are the most important

Disadvantages

- Arbitrary scoring measures often are difficult to interpret
- Don't provide a clear insight into the risk's impact if it occurs
- The relationship between individual risks in a project and the risk to the whole project is more complicated than simple addition

5-12

- Put up Slide 5-12: Advantages and Disadvantages of Scoring Techniques.
- This technique is very useful because it combines the checklist with a numerical assessment. It also provides a measure of the overall riskiness of the project.
- The problem with using a scoring system is that the measurements may be arbitrary and therefore difficult to interpret.
- Using this method makes it a very complicated task to relate one risk to the risk potential to the overall project, principally because of the arbitrariness of the numbering schemes used.

Quantitative Techniques

Quantitative Techniques

Quantitative techniques are designed to identify the risk event and to determine the impact to the project if the event occurs. Quantitative techniques:

- Are based on the planning structures project managers use, i.e., cost breakdowns and schedules

- Identify the risk event

- Determine a probability of likelihood of occurrence

- Provide a way to prioritize the risks relative to the overall impact to the project

- Provide a basis for decision making

5-13

- Put up Slide 5-13: Quantitative Techiques.
- This technique is generally better than the other methods, if some arbitrariness is involved in its use.
- There are two important points to remember about this technique:
  —This technique identifies the risk event based on the project's planning structure.
  —A probability of occurrence is determined, which provides a way to rank the risks relative to the overall project risks.
- Management decisions are generally better when they are made on the basis of a quantitative technique.

Advantages and Disadvantages of Quantitative Techniques

Advantages and Disadvantages of Quantitative Techniques

Advantages

- – Provide a measure of the impact of a risk event on a project
- – Provide a mechanism for decision making
- – Easier to rank

Disadvantages

- – Probabilities are not always easy to assign
- – Using probabilities requires an understanding of how to apply "expected value" theory

5-14

- Put up Slide 5-14: Advantages and Disadvantages of Quantitative Techniques.
- It is much easier to rank risks and make project decisions using this technique.
- The major difficulty with this technique is that it is very hard to quantify accurately the probabilities of occurrence. Often a small change in a probability figure causes large changes in the results, so that a business decision may be tainted.
- See the theory content for a more complete explanation of "expected value." Simply stated, EV is the sum of the different potential outcomes of an event's happening multiplied by the amount of potential gain or loss of each event. For example, depending on the marketing strategy used, there is a 25% probability that profits from a product will be $50,000; a 50% probability of their being $80,000; and 25% of their being $40,000. What is the expected value of the most likely amount of profits? It is unlikely that

either one of the above situations will occur exactly. It is more likely to be a "weighted average" of these three, which is actually what EV is. To determine the number, multiply each probability times its corresponding amount of profits and sum the results. Hence:

$$EV = (.25 \times 50{,}000) + (.5 \times 80{,}000) + (.25 \times 40{,}000)$$
$$= 12{,}500 + 40{,}000 + 10{,}000$$
$$= 62{,}500$$

Ranking Risks

Ranking Risks

Once the risks are identified, they can be prioritized. An easy-to-use technique involves comparing each identified risk with every other risk to determine which has the greatest impact on the project.

A	A	B	C	D	E	F	G
B							
C							
D							
E							
F							
G							

5-15

Objective
- Introduce participants to a method for ranking risks.

Time: 6 Minutes

Training Notes
- Put up Slide 5-15: Ranking Risks.
- This method is called a comparative risk-ranking method because it is used to assess the importance, relative to risk impact, of each risk measured against every other risk in the project.
- Explain that the steps in using this method are to:

—Identify the risks (usually by brainstorming with the project team and other functional personnel).

—List the risks down the left side and across the top of the worksheet. Tell participants that a blank worksheet is provided as a handout for their use in their organizations.

—Explain that they do not need to list the risks in any particular order at this point. However, it is important that the order be the same down the left column and across the top.

—Starting with the first risk on the list (risk A in our example) compare this risk with every other risk. If, for instance, the team agrees that risk A is more important than risk B, write "A = 1" in the square where the risk B row intersects with the risk A column. Continue down the list, then repeat the process with risk B, risk C, and so on until each risk is compared against every other risk. In each intersecting row and column, indicate which risk is most important by assigning it a 1. When the list is exhausted, add all the 1s for each of the risks. The risk that has the most 1s is the most important risk, with the risk having the next-highest number of 1s being the next most important, and so on.

- Project managers must rank all the identified risks but should try to manage only the top ten. The rest of the risks are kept on a "watch list" and added to the top-ten list as the project progresses and the higher risks are disposed of.

- A copy of this worksheet, Handout 5-2, is in the handout packet.

Comparative Risk Ranking Worksheet

A	A	B	C	D	E	F	G
B							
C							
D							
E							
F							
G							

Six Major Sections of a Risk-Management Plan

Six Major Sections of a Risk-Management Plan

---

1. Project summary and system description

2. Approach to risk management

3. Application issues and problems

4. Other relevant plans

5. Conclusions and recommendations

6. Approvals

5-16

Objectives
- Introduce the participants to the risk-management plan.

Time: 14 minutes

Training Notes
- Put up Slide 5-16: Six Major Sections of a Risk-Management Plan.
- Risk-management plans are written during the planning stage of a project and are usually a part of or appendices to the project-management plan.
- The risk-management plan identifies the risks and explains how the project manager plans to manage these risks, what the impact will be should the risks occur, and how this plan relates to other plans.

- All plans in a project are related to all other plans. For instance, the risk-management plan may have listed as a risk the possibility of not having the right number of people or the right skills during a critical part of the project. If that situation actually occurs, then the resource-loading plan and the technical approach would be affected, as well as schedule and budget spending.

A Risk-Management Plan Format—Part 1

A Risk-Management Plan Format—Part 1

I. Project summary and description
    1.1 Project summary
         1.1.1 Project and organizational objectives
         1.1.2 Operational and technical characteristics
         1.1.3 Key functions
    1.2 Project description
         1.2.1 Requirements
         1.2.2 Schedule
         1.2.3 Special contractual requirements

II. Approach to Risk Management
    2.1 Definitions
         2.1.1 Technical risk
         2.1.2 Programmatic risk
         2.1.3 Supportability risk
         2.1.4 Cost risk
         2.1.5 Schedule risk
    2.2 Risk assessment methods overview
         2.2.1 Techniques applied
         2.2.2 Implementation of assessment results   *(continued on next slide)*

5-17

- Put up Slide 5-17: A Risk-Management Plan Format—Part 1.
- This format is self-explanatory. Go through each heading and ask participants if they can think of any other heading that should be included.
- Participants have a handout, Handout 5-3, detailing the plan format in their handout packets.

A Risk-Management Plan Format—Part 2

A Risk-Management Plan Format—Part 2

III. Application
    3.1 Risk Assessment
        3.1.1 Risk identification
        3.1.2 Risk quantification
        3.1.3 Risk prioritization
    3.2 Risk response development
    3.3 Risk response control
        3.3.1 Control evaluation
        3.3.2 Risk documentation

IV. Other relevant plans

V. Conclusions and Recommendations

VI. Approvals

5-18

- Put up Slide 5-18: A Risk-Management Plan Format—Part 2.
- Ask participants if their organizations use printed guidelines or formats such as this one.

A Risk-Management Plan Format

I. Project summary and description
    1.1 Project summary
        1.1.1 Project and organizational objectives
        1.1.2 Operational and technical characteristics
        1.1.3 Key functions
    1.2 Project description
        1.2.1 Requirements
        1.2.2 Schedule
        1.2.3 Special contractual requirements

II. Approach to Risk Management
    2.1 Definitions
        2.1.1 Technical risk
        2.1.2 Programmatic risk
        2.1.3 Supportability risk
        2.1.4 Cost risk
        2.1.5 Schedule risk
    2.2 Risk assessment methods overview
        2.2.1 Techniques applied
        2.2.2 Implementation of assessment results

III. Application
    3.1 Risk Assessment
        3.1.1 Risk identification
        3.1.2 Risk quantification
        3.1.3 Risk prioritization
    3.2 Risk response development
    3.3 Risk response control
        3.3.1 Control evaluation
        3.3.2 Risk documentation

IV. Other relevant plans

V. Conclusions and Recommendations

VI. Approvals

Important Earned-Value Terms

Important Earned-Value Terms

Earned value is the accepted technique for monitoring and tracking project progress. The concept of earned value revolves around these three measures:

BCWS: Budgeted Cost of Work Scheduled
- BCWS is the cumulative budget for the project.

ACWP: Actual Cost of Work Performed
- The cumulative costs actually expended during the project's life cycle.

BCWP: Budgeted Cost of Work Performed (Also called "Earned Value")
- The percentage of work actually performed measured against the budget for work scheduled or planned to be completed.

5-19

Objective
- Introduce participants to the major project-management tool—earned value—and to explain how it is used to track project progress.

Time: 10 minutes

Training Notes
- Put up Slide 5-19: Important Earned-Value Terms.
- The earned-value concept is accepted worldwide as the standard tool for tracking project progress. It measures not only progress against the budget, but also progress against the schedule.
- This tool was developed by the Department of Defense because of the difficulty it was having tracking progress on a program that had scores

of subcontractors using different data-collecting and data-presentation techniques.

- Even though earned value originated in the federal sector, the private sector has adopted it as well because it provides a way to track the costs and the schedule of a project and shows a relationship between the two.
- The following three terms have to be mastered in order to understand and use earned value. The analysis is not difficult, but the concept is sometimes hard to grasp.
  - —Budgeted cost of work scheduled (BSWS) is the cumulative budget for the project.
  - —Actual cost of work performed (ACWP) is the cumulative costs actually expended during the project's life cycle.
  - —Budgeted cost of work performed (BCWP) is the percentage of work actually performed measured against the budget for work scheduled or planned to be completed. BCWP is also known as earned value.
- BCWS and ACWP actually are not new concepts. They are simply new names for the estimated budget and the actual costs.
- The new term, BCWP, is a new way of looking at schedule impacts. BCWP assigns a dollar figure to the schedule or to what is actually accomplished against the plan.

$$BCWP = BCWS \text{ x percent complete}$$

- BCWP is called the earned-value term because it represents the amount that has been accomplished or earned against what was planned to be accomplished.

 Training Tip: Be sure to understand the section on content theory about earned value because it is difficult to explain to participants just what this term represents.

- After going through the earned value concept, talk through the concept, terms, and formulas using a flip chart. Then, as a review, pick up with the slides and go back through the concept, terms, and formulas again. This approach seems to clarify the concept of earned value well and quickly. Handout 5-4 is a handy reference for the most important formulas.
- Lead into the section on earned value by discussing earlier methods for tracking (actual costs versus budget), which didn't give us any insight about how we were doing on the schedule.

Q How are risks accounted for in the budget?

A Risk events, to the extent possible, must be identified and an estimate of their cost should be included in the budget. The cleanest way to do this is to make contingency plans with a contingency budget estimate. To keep the project on track, the project manager sets the contingency reserve aside for use when risk events occur. It is important to remember that the contingency reserve is not for use when the project slips or the team underestimates the costs; it is used for risk events only.

Q Who is responsible for collecting earned value data?

A If the organization is supported by a management cost-control system, the earned value data will be collected and reported by the accounting department. However, many companies do not have such a system, so the project manager or a project team member may have to collect the data. Project-management software packages all have the capability to collect and analyze these data.

Earned Value Formulas

To Calculate	Use This Formula
Cost Variance	CV = BCWP – ACWP
Schedule Variance	SV = BCWP – BCWS
Cost Performance Index	CPI = BCWP/ACWP
Schedule Performance Index	SPI = BCWP/BCWS
Estimate at Completion	EAC = BAC/CPI
Estimate to Complete	ETC = EAC – ACWP

BCWP (budgeted cost of work performed) is the amount of work accomplished against the amount planned.

BCWP = BCWS x % of work completed

BCWS (budgeted cost of work scheduled) is the planned or estimated cost estimate of the task/project, i.e., the budgeted amount.

ACWP (actual cost of work performed) is the actual amount spent on the task/project.

Cost and Schedule Variance

Cost and Schedule Variance

Cost and schedule variance are the two primary measures of the project progress. They can be determined by:

- Cost Variance (CV)

    CV = BCWP – ACWP

- Schedule Variance (SV)

    SV = BCWP – BCWS

    If CV/SV = 0; then project is on track
    If CV/SV = +; then project is under budget and ahead of schedule
    If CV/SV = –; then project is over budget and behind schedule

5-20

Objective
- Explain how to interpret earned-value analyses.

Time: 10 minutes

Training Notes
- Put up Slide 5-20: Cost and Schedule Variance.
- Once participants understand the concept of the earned value, the analysis is straightforward.
- These formulas are important to earned-value analysis because they provide information about whether the project is on budget and on schedule. A table of the formulas is provided as a handout for the participants' reference.

- The formulas for CV and SV yield a positive or negative numeric value. If the value is positive, then the project is under budget and ahead of schedule; if negative, then the project is over budget and behind schedule.
- It is common to have a negative cost variance (i.e., to be over budget) but to have a positive schedule variance. This means that although you have overspent at that point, you are ahead of schedule. So the project is not necessarily in trouble. It may mean that you were able to begin some tasks sooner than planned.
- Point out that the breakthrough leading to this technique was the realization that schedule can be represented in terms of dollars. Or, stated another way, BCWP is the sum of budgets for completed work and the completed portions of open work. Therefore, BCWP is a dollar measure of progress toward completing the work, or a schedule of how the work is progressing. Hence, a positive dollar figure for SV means the work is ahead of schedule. Point out that some people find it difficult to relate schedule to dollars, and that is why the schedule performance index (SPI) is helpful: It depicts schedule progress in terms of percentage (refer to Slide 5-22).

Sample Calculation for Cost and Schedule Variance

Sample Calculation for Cost and Schedule Variance

Example: You planned to be finished with Task A today. The scheduled cost of the task was $1,000. You have actually spent $900 to date but you are only 90% complete. What are the cost and schedule variances for Task A?

Solution: BCWS = $1,000 (Planned or scheduled cost of the task to date)
ACWP = $900 (Actual cost expended)
BCWP = BCWS x 90% = 1,000 x .90 = $900 (amount of work performed compared with amount scheduled)

$$CV = BCWP - ACWP$$
$$= 900 - 900$$
$$= 0$$
$$SV = BCWP - BCWS$$
$$= 900 - 1,000$$
$$= -100$$

Task is on budget but behind schedule.

5-21

- Put up Slide 5-21: Sample Calculation for Cost and Schedule Variance.
- This is a typical scenario that you can use to demonstrate how earned-value analysis works.
- The slide is self-explanatory, but you should go through each step to make sure all the participants understand the concept.

Cost and Schedule Performance Indices

Cost and Schedule Performance Indices

Two indices that are useful for communicating progress status are the Cost Performance Index and the Schedule Performance Index. They are determined by:

Cost Performance Index—The cost efficiency factor representing the relationship between the actual costs expended and the value of the physical work performed.

CPI = BCWP/ACWP

Schedule Performance Index—The planned schedule efficiency factor representing the relationship between the value of the initial planned schedule and the value of the physical work performed.

SPI = BCWP/BCWS

If CPI and SPI = 1, then the project is on budget and on schedule

        < 1, then the project is over budget and behind schedule

        > 1, then the project is under budget and ahead of schedule

5-22

Objectives
- Define cost and schedule performance indices and explain how they are used in tracking project progress.
- Demonstrate how to calculate CPI and SPI.

Time: 9 minutes

Training Notes
- Put up Slide 5-22: Cost and Schedule Performance Indices.
- The cost and schedule indices are very useful communication tools.

- Cost and schedule variances have meaning to the project managers analyzing project progress, but they have less impact on senior managers, who are not so close to the project.
- CPI and SPI provide the same information as CV and SV— whether the project is on budget and schedule—but in a decimal format. For instance, a CPI of .75 means that for every dollar spent, you are earning 75 cents. This is a much more meaningful measure and is very good for use in status reports.
- To interpret CPI and SPI: if they are equal to 1, then the project is on budget and schedule; if less than 1, then the project is over budget and behind schedule; if greater than 1, then the project is under budget and ahead of schedule.

Sample Calculations for CPI and SPI

Sample Calculations for CPI and SPI

Example: The BCWS for a task is $1,000, the ACWP is $900, and the BCWP is $900. What are the CPI and SPI for this task?

$$CPI = BCWP/ACWP$$
$$= 900/900$$
$$= 1.00$$

$$SPI = BCWP/BCWS$$
$$= 900/1,000$$
$$= .90$$

Project is on budget but behind schedule.

5-23

- Put up Slide 5-23: Sample Calculations for CPI and SPI.
- This slide is self-explanatory. The same terms are used as with the CV and SV calculations, but here they are divided.

Estimate at Completion

Estimate at Completion

The estimate at completion (EAC) is a projection of the final costs of work at project completion.

EAC = BAC/CPI

The project manager should recalculate the EAC each time project progress is measured.

Budget at completion (BAC) - Original estimate of completed project costs.

CPI = Cost Performance Index

5-24

Objectives
* Demonstrate how to calculate a new estimate for the required budget at completion.

Time: 9 minutes

Training Notes
* Put up Slide 5-24: Estimate at Completion.
* Every time a report on the status of the project is made, the project manager should determine whether the original budget is going to be sufficient for the project.
* BAC is the Budget at Completion, or the cumulative total estimated cost of the project.
* To determine if that estimate still holds, a new estimate at completion is calculated as shown in the slide.

- If CPI is smaller than 1, then the new EAC will be greater than the original estimate. Likewise, if CPI is greater than 1, the new EAC will be less than the original estimate.
- The BAC is used only the first time the analysis is performed. At every succeeding analysis, the latest calculated EAC should be used. This is because CPI is computed using the latest *actual* cost information, which means that each time the new EAC is calculated, it should be more accurate as the project progresses.
- Point out that if it becomes obvious to the project manager that the original BAC estimate was flawed, then it is better to reestimate the remaining work than to use the EAC formula.
- The status at a point in the task or project's life is an indication of what is likely to happen in the future *if* the project manager makes no changes. The purpose of tracking progress is to determine if changes in management tactics, resources, or skill levels need to be made. For example, if the project is a little over budget or a little behind schedule, it might be because too few people are working on a task or because they don't have the requisite skills and experience. It is the project manager's job to determine why the problem exists and to make adjustments so that the trend doesn't continue.

Sample EAC Calculation

Sample EAC Calculation

Example: The original estimate of the project costs is $100,000. If the BCWP for the project to date is $8,000 and the ACWP is $9,300, what is the new EAC for the project?

Solution: CPI = BCWP/ACWP
                    = 8,000/9,300
                    = .86

EAC = BAC/CPI
        = 100,000/.86
        = 116,279.07

(Note: This will be the amount needed if no changes are made to the way the project is currently being managed.)

5-25

- Put up Slide 5-25: Sample EAC Calculation.
- Go through each step of the calculation to be sure all participants understand the calculations.
- Emphasize the fact that the EAC is now what the project will cost unless changes are made in the way the project is currently being managed.

Estimate to Complete

Estimate to Complete

Estimate to complete (ETC) or the amount of money needed to fund the project to completion is calculated by:

$$ETC = EAC - ACWP$$

5-26

Objective
- Demonstrate how to calculate the amount of money needed to progress from the current status point to the end of the project.

Time: 5 minutes

Training Notes
- Put up Slide 5-26: Estimate to Complete.
- The estimate to complete (ETC) is a useful calculation because it tells the project manager how much money he or she will need to complete the project.
- This estimate is especially useful in small companies because it provides an estimate of cash-flow requirements for the project's remaining life.

Sample ETC Calculation

Sample ETC Calculation

Example: If the estimate to complete for a project is $116,279.07 and the actual expenditures to date are $9,300, what is the estimate to complete the project?

Solution: ETC = EAC – ACWP

= 116,279.07 – 9,300

= 106,979.07

5-27

- Put up Slide 5-27: Sample ETC Calculation.
- Go through each step of the calculation with the participants.
- Emphasize that many companies want to know this number because they have to plan for cash-flow requirements.

Exercise 5-1

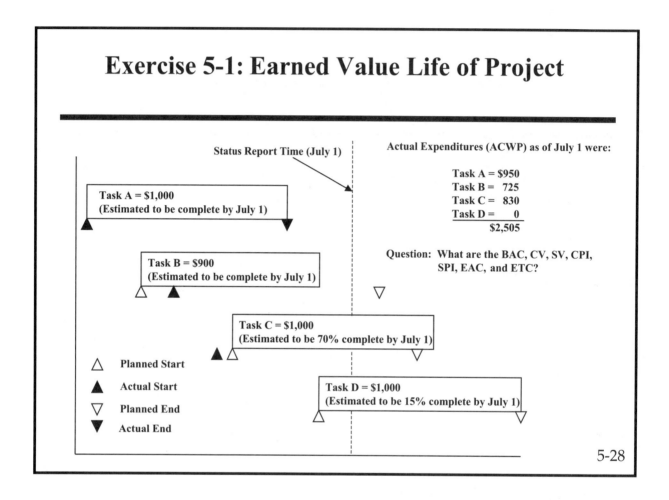

Exercise 5-1: Earned Value Life of Project

Status Report Time (July 1)

Actual Expenditures (ACWP) as of July 1 were:

Task A = $950
Task B = 725
Task C = 830
Task D =   0
          $2,505

Task A = $1,000
(Estimated to be complete by July 1)

Question: What are the BAC, CV, SV, CPI,
SPI, EAC, and ETC?

Task B = $900
(Estimated to be complete by July 1)

Task C = $1,000
(Estimated to be 70% complete by July 1)

△ Planned Start

▲ Actual Start

▽ Planned End

▼ Actual End

Task D = $1,000
(Estimated to be 15% complete by July 1)

5-28

Objective
- Provide an example of how to calculate earned value and perform an earned value analysis over a project's life (as opposed to a task).

Time: 10 minutes

Training Notes
- Put up Slide 5-28: Exercise 5-1. There is a handout, Handout 5-5, in the handout packet.
- Explain to participants how to add up the total BCWS and BCWP amounts (see the theory content for a full explanation of this analysis).
- From Slide 5-29, show them what the analysis yields.

- Be sure to explain that ACWP has absolutely nothing to do with BCWS and BCWP. Whereas BCWP is a percentage of BCWS, ACWP is not related to either of these amounts. ACWP is the amount that the project manager has spent on the project; he or she gets that information from the accounting department. The amount actually spent comes from labor wages and invoices from subcontractors and vendors.
- Work through every step of this example to be sure the participants understand the concept and the analysis.
- Ask participants to complete the exercise by calculating BAC, CV, SV, CPI, SPI, EAC, and ETC.

Exercise 5-1

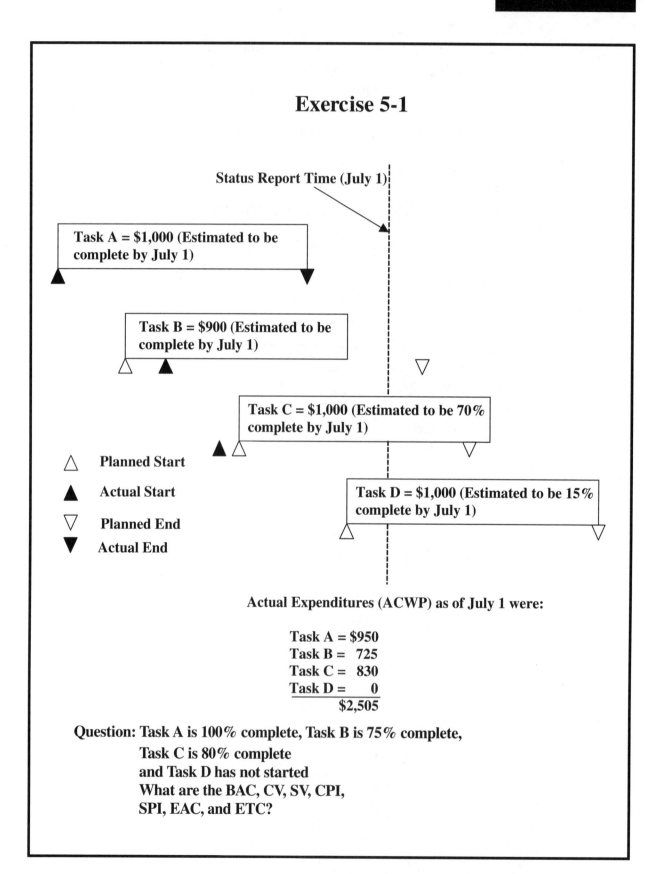

Status Report Time (July 1)

Task A = $1,000 (Estimated to be complete by July 1)

Task B = $900 (Estimated to be complete by July 1)

Task C = $1,000 (Estimated to be 70% complete by July 1)

Task D = $1,000 (Estimated to be 15% complete by July 1)

△ **Planned Start**

▲ **Actual Start**

▽ **Planned End**

▼ **Actual End**

Actual Expenditures (ACWP) as of July 1 were:

Task A = $950
Task B =   725
Task C =   830
Task D =   0
          $2,505

Question: Task A is 100% complete, Task B is 75% complete,
Task C is 80% complete
and Task D has not started
What are the BAC, CV, SV, CPI,
SPI, EAC, and ETC?

Earned Value Sample Solution

Earned Value Sample Solution

Solution:

1. BAC = Task A cost + Task B cost + Task C cost + Task D cost
    = 1,000 + 900 + 1,000 + 1,000 = $3,900
2. CV = BCWP – ACWP = 2,475 – 2,505 = –30
3. SV = BCWP – BCWS = 2,475 – 2,750 = –275
4. CPI = BCWP/ACWP = 2,475/2,505 = .99
5. SPI = BCWP/BCWS = 2,475/2,750 = .90
6. EAC = BAC/CPI = 3,900/.99 = 3,939.39
7. ETC = EAC – ACWP = 3,939.39 – 2,505 = 1,434.39

5-29

As of 1 July:

BCWS:	A =	$1,000	(Expected to be complete: 1,000 x 100% = 1,000)
	B =	900	(Expected to be complete: 900 x 100% = 900)
	C =	700	(Expected to be 70% complete: 1,000 x 70% + 700)
	D =	150	(Expected to be 15% complete: 1,000 x 15% = 150)
		$2,750	
BCWP:	A =	$1,000	(Was complete: 1,000 x 100% = 1,000)
	B =	675	(Was only 75% complete: 900 x 75% = 675)
	C =	800	(Was only 80% complete: 1,000 80% = 800)
	D =	0	(Task D has not started) 1,000 x 0% = 0)
		$2,475	

Exercise 5-2

Exercise 5-2

You are working on a project that was estimated to be completed on May 5 for a cost of $150,000. Today is May 9 and the project is 85% complete. You have spent $145,000. Answer the following questions:

1. What is the BAC for this project?

2. What is the BCWS, BCWP, and ACWP for the project?

3. What is the CV?

4. What is the SV?

5. What is the CPI and the SPI?

6. What is the new EAC?

7. What is the ETC?

5-30

Objective
- Provide the participants with practice in calculating and analyzing earned value.

Time: 20 minutes

Training Notes
- Put up Slide 5-30: Exercise 5-2. They should use Handout 5-6 in the handout package.
- Participants have 20 minutes for this exercise. Ask them to work individually, but if they finish early, they can check their answers with others at their table.
- After 20 minutes, call time and go through each of the questions and answers. If participants have problems with any part of the exercise, go back to the appropriate slides and review them.

Exercise 5-2

You are working on a project that was estimated to be completed on May 5 for a cost of $150,000. Today is May 9 and the project is 85% complete. You have spent $145,000. Answer the following questions.

1. What is the BAC for this project?

2. What are the BCWS, BCWP, and ACWP for the project?

3. What is the CV?

4. What is the SV?

5. What are the CPI and the SPI?

6. What is the new EAC?

7. What is the ETC?

Key Messages—Module 5

Key Messages—Module 5

The key messages of this module are:

- A well-structured and documented change-control system is crucial for project success

- Risk analysis begins with the interpretation of the SOW and continues throughout the project's life cycle

- There are two kinds of risk:
  - Business risk
  - Pure or insurable risk

- A risk management plan is required to be proactive rather than reactive to risks

(*continued on next slide*)

5-31

Objective
- Summarize the key points of the module.

Time: 8 minutes

Training Notes
- Put up Slides 5-31 and 5-32: Key Messages—Module 5.
- Go over each point on this slide and ensure the participants have a good grasp of the major discussion items in this module.
- Ask participants if they have any questions about the module.
- Ask participants to discuss any of the tools or concepts covered in the module that will be of immediate benefit to them.
- Make a transition to the next module.

Key Messages—Module 5 (*continued*)

- Earned value is a concept that has been universally accepted as the best way to monitor and control project progress

- There are three basic definitions associated with earned value that have to be understood before the concept can be used:
  - Budgeted cost of work scheduled (BCWS)
  - Actual cost of work performed (ACWP)
  - Budgeted cost of work performed (BCWP)

- BCWP is known as the "earned-value" term

5-32

The

Project

Close-Out Phase

The project close-out phase is often the most difficult one to complete. There is enormous pressure on the project team to move on to other projects. Not only that, but also many senior managers do not support the activities of this phase because of the internal competition to start new projects. So project managers often struggle at project's end to provide the customer with the final product.

The project manager has to focus on this phase with as much, if not more, intensity as he or she did on the other phases. The planning for close-out should begin at the very start of the project. It is a good idea to develop a WBS of close-out activities. A generic close-out WBS is shown in Exhibit 6-1 and is provided in the Forms section as a handout. The close-out WBS is actually a checklist of action items required to close out the project. However, since most of us are "visual," the WBS format works better than the checklist format.

Teaching the activities of this phase is straightforward, with no particularly difficult tools to learn. Some forms are provided to aid in teaching as well as to provide the participants with handy references when they go back to their organizations. Part of your job as the trainer is to instill in the participants the urge to be change agents so that they will start encouraging their organizations to begin using these tools and concepts.

Project Close-Out Phase Objectives

The major objective of this phase is to provide the customer with the product or service he or she contracted for, and to do it on time and under budget. Other supporting objectives include:

1. Conducting a technical and financial audit to determine if the project scope requirements are met.
2. Delivering the product and obtain formal customer acceptance.
3. Completing the administrative requirements of the project.
4. Conducting a lessons-learned session of the project.
5. Closing the facility if required and returning any customer provided equipment.
6. Providing performance evaluations of the project team to their functional managers.
7. Closing the project and contract files.

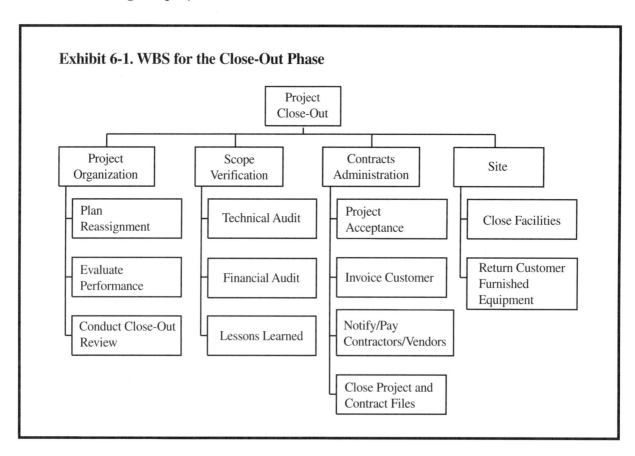

Exhibit 6-1. WBS for the Close-Out Phase

Many companies do not support close-out activities as strongly as they should. In fact, I have heard colleagues refer to the close-out phase as the "forgotten phase." Unfortunately, this is often true. The project managers taking this workshop should be encouraged to help their organizations implement formalized close-out procedures. It will make their projects end much more successfully and increase their chances of obtaining more contracts from a happy customer.

The beauty of this phase is that almost without exception, all your participants will be familiar with how *not* to go about closing a project. That is nothing to be happy about, but it sets the level for the entire group, and you will find them eager to learn how the process should work. Take advantage of this situation and allow the participants as much time as is available to talk about their experiences and about how they would like the process to work.

I find the best way to teach this module is to ask more questions of the participants than usual, and I usually ask a lot of questions. But what I find is that the close-out activities tend to be more noticeable to observers than some of the other phase activities. Participants new to the project-management environment—even those who have never served on a project team—are aware of problems with project close-out. That is because close-out is the moment when it becomes very obvious throughout an organization if a project is not going to be delivered on time or if the customer is unhappy with the result.

This phase is very important. You should emphasize how difficult it is to conclude a project successfully and encourage the participants to be better prepared the next time they are a project manager or team member.

It is not unusual for participants to have more questions during this module than the other modules. This module has more to do with corporate culture than with applying project-management tools: Closing out a project doesn't get the corporate support that starting a project does. The corporate mindset is to start as many projects as possible, then to assume that closing them will occur naturally.

Content Theory for the Close-Out Phase

Exhibit 6-1 is an excellent checklist of close-out activities. Encourage the participants to use it and refer to it as a guideline for talking about the activities.

The key activity of the close-out phase is to provide the product to the customer and obtain formal acceptance. To accomplish this, the project manager and team have to conduct a scope verification to ensure that all the project requirements have been met. Scope verification involves both a technical audit and a financial audit. Once the audits are complete, an audit report should be written and delivered to the stakeholders. A high-level audit report format is

---

Exhibit 6-2. Final Project Audit Format

I. Executive Summary
II. Introduction
III. Project Review
IV. Planning Effectiveness
V. Project Management Effectiveness
VI. Effectiveness of Technical Solution
VII. Project Deliverables
VIII. Quality
IX. Schedule
X. Finances
XI. Resources Utilization
XII. Individual Team Member Assessment and Recommendations (submit as separate, confidential report)
XIII. Lessons Learned
XIV. Recommendations

---

shown in Exhibit 6-2, with an expanded format provided in the Forms section as a handout. Notice that this format lists all the close-out activities and is the major tool of this phase. It can serve as a checklist for the project manager.

Focus on the difficulties the participants can expect during this phase, particularly the problem of keeping the project team focused. This phase requires an abundance of interpersonal skills to resolve conflicts, negotiate with functional managers, and close the project with the customer. If time permits, you should talk about interpersonal and leadership skills and relate them to the close-out activities.

Training Objectives of the Close-Out Module
Your objectives for this module are to:
1. Provide the participants with an opportunity to assess how their organization addresses project close-out.
2. Teach the participants a process for closing a project.
3. Provide some forms and checklists that will aid the close-out process.
4. Assess the value of the workshop to the participants.

Summary

The close-out phase can be the most difficult phase in the project's life cycle. The team members are anxious about finding new projects to work on, and functional managers are anxious to reassign their people to start other projects. However, the project manager has to complete the tasks and obtain customer approval for the project.

A major tool in the close-out phase is the audit report format, which contains all the activity requirements of this phase. The project team must perform a technical and a financial audit to ensure that the project requirements have been met. Once these audits are complete, the audit report is written and provided to all the stakeholders.

Agenda for Module 6: The Project Close-Out Phase

Objectives for Module 6	3 minutes
Where We Are in the Process	1 minute
Plan, Schedule, and Monitor Activities	10 minutes
The Project Audit	12 minutes
Project Close-Out Checklist	5 minutes
Key Messages—Module 6	10 minutes
Total	41 Minutes

Module 6: The Project Close-Out Phase

Bringing the Project to a Successful Conclusion

Approximate time for module: 41 minutes

Objectives for Module 6

Objectives for Module 6

At the end of this module you will be able to:

- Describe the project termination, or close-out process

- Determine and describe the project team's activities in completing the project requirements

- Describe the audit activities required to complete the project

- Describe and use a project close-out checklist

6-1

Objective
- Introduce unit objectives.

Time: 3 minutes

Training Notes
- Put up Slide 6-1: Objectives for Module 6.
- The close-out phase of a project is often the most difficult phase of the project.
- Ask participants to explain why this phase can be so difficult. Some of the reasons are:
  —The project manager is faced with the task of wrapping up the project and finishing on schedule.
  —Team members are interested in finding a new project to work on.

—Functional managers are pulling team members off the project so that they can be assigned to new projects.

—Conflicts within the team may lead to members' desire to move on to another team.

- Impress on the participants that this is a very important phase and that the project manager is responsible for completing several important tasks.

Where We Are in the Process

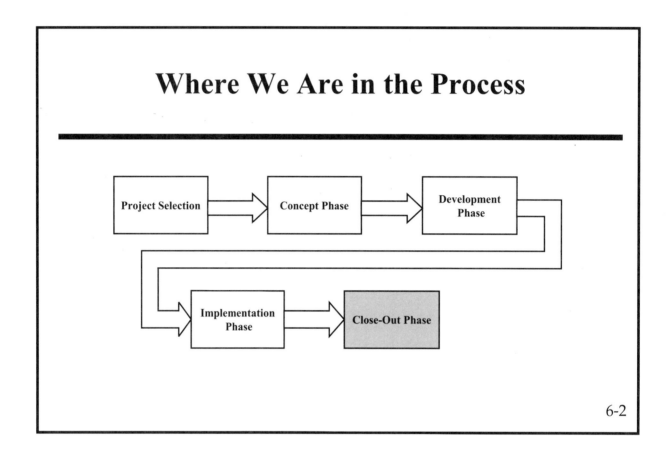

Objective
- Orient the participants and remind them where we are in the project's life cycle.

Time: 1 minute

Training Notes
- Put up Slide 6-2: Where We Are in the Process.
- Remind the participants that this is the map of our progress through the project's life cycle.
- Close-out is the last phase of the project.
- Impress on the participants that this phase is often the most difficult phase of the project.

Plan, Schedule, and Monitor Activities

Plan, Schedule, and Monitor Activities

The project close-out phase is often the most difficult phase of the project's life cycle. To successfully close the project, the project manager must:

Plan, schedule, and monitor completion activities:

- Obtain and approve termination plans and schedules

- Prepare and coordinate termination plans and schedules

- Plan for reassignment of project team members and transfer resources to other projects

- Monitor termination activities and completion of all contractual agreements

- Monitor the disposition of any surplus materials or customer-supplied equipment

6-3

Objective
- Introduce participants to the activities that a project manager typically encounters in this phase of the project's life cycle.

Time: 10 minutes

Training Notes
- Put up Slide 6-3: Plan, Schedule, and Monitor Activities.
- Stress that project managers have a very difficult time during the close-out phase because of the requirements to close the project administratively and technically. Often, the project manager's requirements don't coincide with functional management's agenda.
- Ask the participants when planning for the close-out should begin. (Planning for close-out has to begin at the start of the project.)

- Ask participants about their experiences with close-out and if they have experienced any difficulties with this phase of a project. One common response here is that someone has had a project that he or she couldn't get the customer to accept.
- Explain that looking at the WBS for close-out is helpful because it depicts the close-out activities in a graphical format. Since most of us are "visual," this format is easier to understand and remember than the typical checklist format. See Handout 6-1 in the handout packet.
- Discuss each point of the slide and ask participants if they can think of any other activities required of the project manager during this phase.

Q What can I do to ensure my project team stays focused through the end of the project?

A There are several things the project manager can do to keep the team focused. First, push for a project charter at the beginning of the project. All the functional managers who are supporting the project sign this document, and it is very nice, as a project manager, to be able to bring out the project charter to remind the functional managers of their commitment. This action often precludes the problem of functional managers reassigning their people before the project is completed. Second, much of the project manager's success depends on his or her leadership capabilities. If the project manager starts the project with the attitude that the project continues through close-out, and he or she gets that message across to all project team members from the beginning of the project, then their chances of success increase. Third, project close-out planning begins at the start of the project. Using a tool such as the WBS for close-out, and inculcating this notion into the project team's thinking early, will pay dividends when the actual close-out process begins. The WBS for close-out is developed in the same way a project WBS is developed. It is a representation of the close-out phase activities on a task level. That is, each task of close-out is identified and task responsibility is assigned. The close-out WBS is used instead of a checklist because it is easier to read and remember. In addition, developing a WBS for the phase activities, rather than using a canned checklist, results in a more accurate representation of the activities required to complete the project. Finally, the most senior management must support the idea that the close-out process is as important as the other project phases, if not more important. Project managers must begin by encouraging senior management to support this phase as strongly as the other phases and to implement guidelines and procedures for the close-out process.

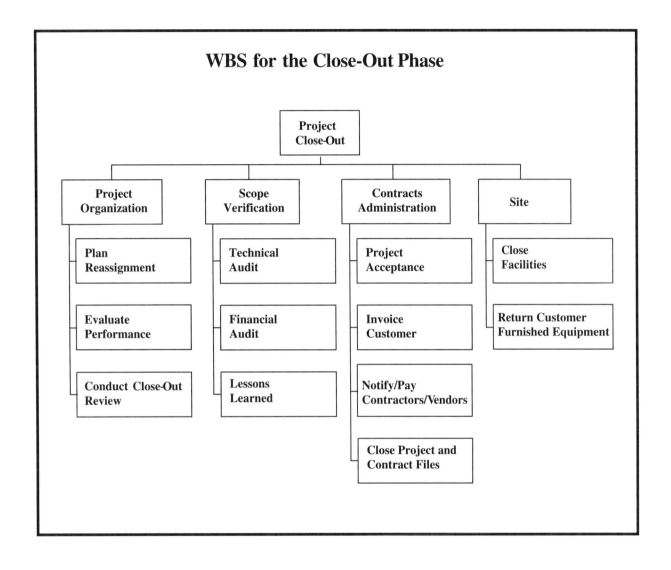

WBS for the Close-Out Phase

Project Close-Out

- **Project Organization**
  - Plan Reassignment
  - Evaluate Performance
  - Conduct Close-Out Review
- **Scope Verification**
  - Technical Audit
  - Financial Audit
  - Lessons Learned
- **Contracts Administration**
  - Project Acceptance
  - Invoice Customer
  - Notify/Pay Contractors/Vendors
  - Close Project and Contract Files
- **Site**
  - Close Facilities
  - Return Customer Furnished Equipment

Administrative Activities

Administrative Activities

Complete administrative close-out activities:

- Close work orders and subcontracted work completion

- Notify all stakeholders of project completion

- Close project office and any other project facilities

- Close project books

- Archive project files and records

6-4

- Put up Slide 6-4: Administrative Activities.
- Ask participants if they ever get involved with these activities. Ask them to share their experiences with the class.
- Stress the importance of doing a "lessons-learned" session with the project team.
- Ask participants how often their company or group does a real lessons-learned session and documents the results (very few companies do a good job of recording and archiving lessons learned).
- Stress the importance of a lessons-learned session as well as documenting and archiving the results.

Q How important is the lessons learned session?

A It is ironic that all the information is available at the project's close to do a thorough and accurate lessons-learned session: status reports, reports on issues and how they were resolved, financial reports, change actions, and on and on. All that really is required for a session is to pull the pertinent data together and present them in a form that other project managers can use. The lessons learned are important because they directly affect future business. The primary purpose of a lessons-learned library is access to records that show such things as:

1. How close were the budget and schedule estimates?
2. Why were our estimates too low or high?
3. What risks did we encounter that we hadn't planned for?
4. How well did we anticipate the project risks?
5. Which corporate processes worked well to support the project and which ones did not work?
6. How can we make our estimating and planning processes more accurate for future projects?

Customer Acceptance, Obligation, and Payment Activities

Customer Acceptance, Obligation, and Payment Activities

- Ensure deliverables are completed and accepted by customer

- Communicate to the customer completion of all contractual items

- Ensure all contract obligations and documentation are complete

- Transmit formal payment request to the customer

- Monitor customer payment and collection of payments

6-5

- Put up Slide 6-5: Customer Acceptance, Obligation, and Payment Activities.
- Stress that the project manager's major task is to obtain the customer's acceptance of the product. This requirement applies whether the customer is external or internal.
- This is when the project manager and project team conducts scope verification. Scope verification involves examining the project results against the original scope requirements.

Q If I have an external customer and that customer refuses to accept the project product even though the project team demonstrates compliance with the acceptance criteria, what can I do to close the project? What is my next step?

A It is rare that a customer won't accept a product if it clearly meets the acceptance criteria of the SOW. However, it does happen! The project manager first tries to determine what the customer is *really* looking for. Then the project manager determines if the product the customer was expecting met the scope of the contract. Occasionally, the customer has envisioned a totally different result from what is provided. In that case, the customer's image of the product is different from the project manager's image of the requirements.

The project manager is bound to resolve the differences in opinion about what is acceptable. Often, it is a matter of semantics. But occasionally, a customer tries to get more than was agreed to in the beginning. Also, especially in the federal business arena, the customer contact changes during the project, and the new contact may not interpret the original requirements in the way that his or her predecessor did. This problem can usually be resolved by meeting with the new contact and by revisiting the original agreement. If the problem is still unresolved after the project manager has exhausted all the avenues and used all the interpersonal skills available, the only recourse is to refer it to the next-higher authority. What usually happens is that the next-higher authority of the selling organization meets with the next-higher authority of the buying organization and the problem is resolved. In short, the best thing to do is to ensure that the criteria in the original SOW are very clear, concise, and strong.

Project Audit Format

Project Audit Format—Part 1

The project manager and team must perform an audit of the project to ensure all the requirements are met and that the financial records are complete. A typical final audit format report includes:

I. Executive summary
II. Introduction
III. Project Review
    A. Project objectives
    B. Method or approach
IV. Effectiveness of Planning
V. Effectiveness of Project Management
VI. Effectiveness of Technical Solution
VII. Project Deliverables
    A. Description
    B. Assessment against requirements
VIII. Quality
    A. Standards used
    B. Measurement
    C. Assessment against requirements

6-6

Objectives
- Provide participants with a format for a project audit.

Time: 12 minutes

Training Notes
- Put up Slide 6-6: Project Audit Format.
- Participants can use Handout 6-2 (see page 252) as a checklist for preparing their project audit format.
- Two audits have to be completed during the close-out phase: the technical and the financial audits.

- Technical audits determine whether the scope requirements—that is, the technical and administrative requirements—have been met.
- This is a generic format for conducting a project audit. It includes the technical as well as the financial considerations.
- Ask participants if they can think of any other elements of a project audit format that should be included in the format.
- Go through each element of the format and ensure the participants have no questions about it.

Project Audit—Part 2

Project Audit—Part 2

    IX. Schedule
        A. Delays
            1. Reasons
            2. Recovery actions
        B. Assessment against plan
    X.   Finances
        A. Problems
            1. Reasons
            2. Recovery actions
        B. Assessment against plan
    XI. Resource Utilization
        A. Effectiveness
        B. Problems
            1. Reasons
            2. Recovery actions
    XII. Lessons Learned
    XIII. Individual Team-Member Assessment and Recommendations
        (submit as separate confidential report)
    XIV.   Recommendations

Module 6 - Project Closeout

6-7

- Put up Slide 6-7: Project Audit—Part 2.
- Point out the lessons-learned section and ask participants if their companies or groups do a lessons-learned session after each project. (Most companies do a poor job of lessons-learned analysis and an even poorer job of archiving the results for future use.)
- Stress the importance of lessons learned. The major reasons for doing a lessons-learned analysis are to:
  —Determine how accurate the budget and schedule estimates were.
  —Collect risk and issue-resolution data.
  —Develop more efficient processes.

—Assess how well the project was managed

—Assess how efficiently and effectively the resources were used.

* Facilitate a discussion about how this audit format might be useful to the participants in the future.

Project Audit Format

The project manager and team must perform an audit of the project to ensure that all the requirements are met and that the financial records are complete. A typical final audit format report includes:

I.   Executive summary
II.   Introduction
III.   Project Review
    A. Project objectives
    B. Method or approach
IV.   Effectiveness of Planning
V.   Effectiveness of Project Management
VI.   Effectiveness of Technical Solutions
VII.   Project Deliverables
    A. Description
    B. Assessment against requirements
VIII. Quality
    A. Standards used
    B. Measurement
    C. Assessment against requirements
IX.   Schedule
    A. Delays
       1. Reasons
       2. Recovery actions
    B. Assessment against plan
X.   Finances
    A. Problems
       1. Reasons
       2. Recovery actions
    B. Assessment against plan
XI.   Resource Utilization
    A. Effectiveness
    B. Problems
       1. Reasons
       2. Recovery actions
XII.   Lessons Learned
XIII. Individual Team-Member Assessment and Recommendations (submit as separate confidential report)
XIV.   Recommendations

Project Close-Out Checklist

Project Close-Out Checklist

- ☐ Prepare a close-out plan
- ☐ Verify scope
  - – Contractual obligations
  - – Administrative obligations
  - – WBS (tasks and deliverables)
- ☐ Obtain customer acceptance of deliverables
- ☐ Document and archive files and records
- ☐ Document lessons learned
- ☐ Reassign resources
- ☐ Notify all stakeholders of project completion
- ☐ Celebrate success

6-8

Objective
- Acquaint participants with the close-out activities and to provide a checklist to facilitate the close-out process.

Time: 5 minutes

Training Notes
- Put up Slide 6-8: Project Close-Out Checklist. This checklist appears in the handout packet as Handout 6-3.
- Ask participants when they should start planning for close-out. (Planning for close-out begins as soon as the project is approved and the project manager is assigned.)
- Project managers have responsibility for obtaining customer acceptance of the project deliverables.

Training Tip: Note: This is a good time to stress to the participants the importance of ensuring that acceptance criteria are included in the original statement of work. Without acceptance criteria in place, it is difficult to close out the project.

- There will be two distinct sets of project records if the project is the result of an outside contract. One set of records deals with contractual activities and the other deals with project business. Both sets of records have to be updated and archived at project's end.
- Stress once again the importance of documenting and archiving lessons learned.
- Ask participants if their organizations have a formalized process for closing out their projects.

Q I have a project that never seems to end. Why can't I get this project closed?

A The reason most projects don't close smoothly is that there were no acceptance criteria in the SOW. In the future, participants should be sure that acceptance criteria are clearly stated in the SOW if it is an external contract or in some memorandum of agreement if it is an internal project.

Project Close-Out Checklist

❏ Prepare a close-out plan

❏ Verify scope

- Contractual obligations

- Administrative obligations

- WBS (tasks and deliverables)

❏ Obtain customer acceptance of deliverables

❏ Document and archive files and records

❏ Document lessons learned

❏ Reassign resources

❏ Notify all stakeholders of project completion

❏ Celebrate success

Key Messages—Module 6

Key Messages—Module 6

The key messages of this module are:

- The close-out phase is often the most difficult phase in a project

- The project manager has to complete numerous activities relating to
  - Technical and operational issues
  - Administrative issues
  - Customer approval and acceptance

- A formal project audit is necessary to ensure that all project requirements are complete

- The project manager and team should use a close-out checklist through the close-out process

6-9

Objective
- Summarize the module.

Time: 10 minutes

Training Notes
- Put up Slide 6-9: Key Messages—Module 6.
- Summarize the close-out procedure and remind participants they have the audit format and close-out checklist available as handouts.
- Summarize the course. Go back to the participants' expectations, which you listed on a flip chart at the beginning of the course. Go over each one and verify that all their expectations have been met.
- Look also at the course objectives and verify with the participants that the course objectives were met.

- Ask participants to discuss which aspects of the course they think will be most beneficial to them.
- Ask participants to discuss what they intend to do to improve themselves and their work environment to become more project-management oriented.
- Ask participants to spend a few minutes completing the course assessments, Handout 6-4, in their handout packets. Explain that the assessment exercise has three objectives:
  —It is an opportunity for the participants to think about their level of knowledge about project-management tools and concepts before they started the workshop.
  —It provides a means for the participants to assess whether the workshop has increased their knowledge about project management.
  —Finally, it is a way for participants to assess the benefits of their increased knowledge. In other words, it is a way for them to determine if the workshop is teaching practical and usable tools.
- Point out that any additional comments about the workshop length and amount of detail, or about whether other topics should be covered, will be helpful.

COURSE ASSESSMENT

Course Title: _____   Date: _____

For each of the five areas covered by the course, indicate:

   — How much you knew about the areas before the course.

   — How much you know now about the area.

   — How valuable you think having the knowledge/skill in the area will be to you.

Assign a rating of 0 to 9 for each of the three questions, using the scale below.

0	1 2 3	4 5 6	7 8 9
Nothing/No Value	A Little	Some	A Lot

KNEW BEFORE	KNOW NOW	COURSE AREA	VALUE
		1. Project Selection Techniques — Payback Period — ROI — IRR — NPV — Benefit to Cost	
		2. Project Concept Phase — Defining Requirements — WBS — Project Charter	
		3. Project Development Phase — Network Analysis — Project Management Plan	
		4. Project Implementation Phase — Risk Management — Earned Value	
		5. Project Close-Out — Close-Out Procedures — Project Audits — Lessons Learned	

Slides

_____

Introduction to

The Project Management Workshop

Learning the Fundamentals

of

Project Management

Welcome to *The Project Management Workshop*

- Emergency phone number

- Local emergency exit procedures

- Fax number

- Floor/facility layout

- Breaks

- Start and end expectations

- Attendance

  - Prerequisites

  - Maximum absence

Start on time = End on time

Workshop Objectives

At the end of this workshop, you will be able to:

- Define *project* and *program*

- Describe the differences between project and functional management

- Apply financial techniques in comparing and selecting projects

- Develop a project charter

- Develop project requirements

- Describe the elements of a statement of work

Workshop Objectives (*continued*)

- Develop a Work Breakdown Structure

- Perform a network analysis

- Develop schedules using the Gantt chart

- Develop a risk management plan

- Develop and use a change management process

- Control project budgets and schedules using Earned Value

- Close a project

Project Management Model

LIFE-CYCLE PHASES OF A PROJECT

Selection	Concept	Development	Implementation	Close-out
Activities •Financial analysis •Analyze strategic goals •Rank projects •Choose projects to pursue	**Activities** •Gather data •Analyze re-quirements •Develop charter •Develop WBS •Organize project team •Kickoff meeting	**Activities** •Refine WBS •Perform net-work analysis •Develop sched-ules •Develop plans	**Activities** •Implement control process •Control project progress with earned value	**Activities** •Scope verification •Technical audit •Financial audit •Contract close-out

Workshop Agenda

Time	Day 1
8:30	**Module 1: Introduction to the Project Management Workshop**
9:30	**Module 2: Project Selection Techniques**
10:30	
11:00	**Module 3: Project Concept Phase**
12:00	**Lunch (1 hr.)**
1:00	**Module 3: Project Concept Phase (*cont.*)**
2:00	**Module 4: Project Development Phase**
3:00	
4:00	**Review Modules 2, 3, 4**
4:30	**Day 1 Ends**

Workshop Agenda (continued)

Time	Day 2
8:30	Recap Day 1 Modules/Begin Case Study
9:30	Case Study
10:30	
11:00	
12:00	Lunch
1:00	Module 5: Project Implementation (*cont.*)
2:00	Module 6: Project Close-out
3:00	Module 7: Course Wrap-up
4:00	Day 2 Ends
4:30	

Student Introductions

- Name
- Location
- Years in current organization
- Project and team member experience
- Objectives/expectations of the workshop
- What you do for fun

Module 2: The Project Selection Phase

How Projects Are Selected

Objectives for Module 2

At the end of this module you will be able to:

- Identify, define and apply various project selection techniques

- Describe the advantages and disadvantages of each selection technique

- Describe the use of project selection techniques

Where We Are in the Process

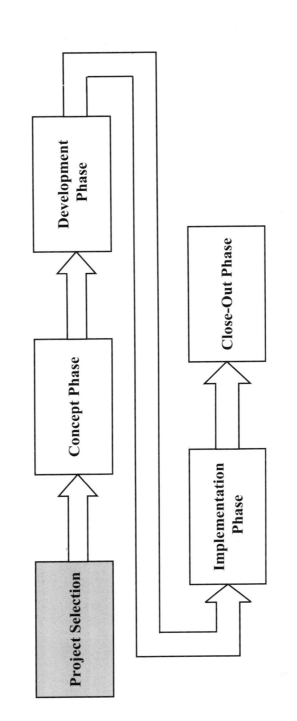

Project Selection Techniques

There are several project selection techniques. The most commonly used are:

- Payback or break-even point

- Return on Investment (ROI)

- Internal Rate of Return (IRR)

- Net Present Value (NPV)

- Benefit to Cost Ratio (B/C)

Payback or Break-Even Point

One of the most commonly used "hurdle" rates today is the Payback or Break-Even Point:

Payback: The point in a project when revenues equal costs.

How used:
- The payback period has to be equal to or less than target set by senior management. Often used as an early assessment of project viability.

Advantages:
- Fast
- Simple

Disadvantages:
- Assumes steady revenue stream
- Does not take into account the cost of money

Payback Period (*sample calculation*)

The estimated cost of a project is $10,000,000. The project is expected to yield $2,000,000 per year. What is the Payback Period?

Solution:

Payback = total cost/yearly revenues

= 10,000,000/2,000,000

= 5 years

Return on Investment (ROI)

Return on Investment (ROI), another very commonly used selection technique, is a financial measure of how much profit is likely from invested costs.

How used: Average profits are divided by the average costs expected over the period of the project's life. Hurdle rate is set by the senior management; product ROI must equal or exceed the hurdle rate

Advantages:
- Used by most companies as one viability measure
- Easily understood and calculated

Disadvantages:
- Does not take into account cost of money

ROI (*sample calculation*)

The average cost of a 6-year project is estimated to be $6,000,000 per year, and the estimated total returns are expected to be $12,000,000. What is the ROI?

Solution:

The average return is 12 million/6 = $2 million per year

$$ROI = (Average\ Returns/Average\ Costs) \times 100\%$$
$$= (2\ M/6\ M) \times 100\%$$
$$= 33\%$$

Internal Rate of Return (IRR)

Internal Rate of Return (IRR) is used to compare against other strategic financial Goals. It is the interest rate that makes the present value of all revenues equal to the present value of all costs.

How used:

- Usually measured against the IRR of the organization but may be an arbitrarily set "hurdle rate"
- Used by most organizations to determine project viability

Advantages:

- Takes into account the cost of money

Disadvantages:

- Can't be directly calculated; must be iterated from tables or by spreadsheet software

Preparing Data for an IRR Calculation

The IRR is much more accurate than the Payback or ROI methods because it accounts for the cost of money. It is used as a measure of a project's worth compared with the company's cost of capital rate.

Question: You have estimated the following revenues and costs for your project. If the corporate cost of capital is 18%, how does your project compare?

Years	Revenues	Costs
0	0	$10,000
1	$12,000	$10,000
2	$16,000	$10,000
3	$20,000	$15,000
4	$40,000	$15,000
5	$60,000	$20,000

(continued on next slide)

IRR Sample Calculation

Solution: Use the equation

$$PV = \sum_{t=0}^{n} \frac{PV}{(1+i)^t}$$

PV = present value of money
FV = future value of money
i = Internal rate of return
t = time period, i.e., 1st year, 2nd year
n = number of time periods

The PV of the revenues and costs are determined for the project's life cycle.

$$PV\,(\text{Revenues}) = \frac{12,000}{(1+i)^1} + \frac{16,000}{(1+i)^2} + \frac{20,000}{(1+i)^3} + \frac{40,000}{(1+i)^4} + \frac{60,000}{(1+i)^5}$$

$$PV\,(\text{Costs}) = \frac{10,000}{(1+i)^0} + \frac{10,000}{(1+i)^1} + \frac{10,000}{(1+i)^2} + \frac{15,000}{(1+i)^3} + \frac{15,000}{(1+i)^4} + \frac{20,000}{(1+i)^5}$$

(continued on next slide)

IRR Sample Calculation (*continued*)

Set the PV(Revenues) = PV(Costs)

$$\frac{12,000}{(1+i)^1} + \frac{16,000}{(1+i)^2} + \frac{20,000}{(1+i)^3} + \frac{40,000}{(1+i)^4} + \frac{60,000}{(1+i)^5} =$$

$$\frac{10,000}{(1+i)^0} + \frac{10,000}{(1+i)^1} + \frac{10,000}{(1+i)^2} + \frac{15,000}{(1+i)^3} + \frac{15,000}{(1+i)^4} + \frac{20,000}{(1+i)^5}$$

The computer iterates to determine value of *i* that makes the two sides of the equation equal. In this case,

$$i = 24\%$$

Project *i* (24%) > company cost of capital (18%). Therefore, pursue project.

Net Present Value

Net Present Value is the difference between the Present Value of the project revenues and costs.

How used:
- Uses the corporate IRR or another interest rate index
- "Goodness" is measured by whether NPV is positive or negative

  – NPV > 1, revenues greater than costs

  – NPV < 1, revenues less than costs

  – NPV = 0, revenues and costs the same

Advantages:
- Takes into account the cost of money
- Very accurate compared to other methods

Disadvantages:
- Not easily understood by everyone
- Costs and revenues not always easy to quantify

Set Up Data Table for NPV

Example: You have estimated the following revenues and costs for your project.
If the corporate IRR is 18%, what is the Net Present Value of your project?

Years	Revenues	Costs
0	0	$10,000
1	$12,000	$10,000
2	$16,000	$10,000
3	$20,000	$15,000
4	$40,000	$15,000
5	$60,000	$20,000

NPV Sample Calculation

Solution: Use the formula for Present Value to determine PV of revenues and costs.

$$PV = \sum_{t=0}^{n} \frac{PV}{(1+i)^t}$$

$$PV(\text{Revenues}) = \frac{12,000}{(1+.18)^1} + \frac{16,000}{(1+.18)^2} + \frac{20,000}{(1+.18)^3} + \frac{40,000}{(1+.18)^4} + \frac{60,000}{(1+.18)^5}$$

$$= 10,169 + 11,491 + 12,173 + 20,632 + 26,227 = \boxed{80,691}$$

$$PV(\text{Costs}) = \frac{10,000}{(1+i)^0} + \frac{10,000}{(1+i)^1} + \frac{10,000}{(1+i)^2} + \frac{15,000}{(1+i)^3} + \frac{15,000}{(1+i)^4} + \frac{20,000}{(1+i)^5}$$

$$= 10,000 + 8,475 + 7,182 + 9,129 + 7,737 + 8,742 = \boxed{51,265}$$

(continued on next slide)

2-14

Solution to Sample NPV Calculation

Net Present Value is the difference between the Present Value of the Revenues and Costs. Therefore,

NPV = PV (Revenues) – PV (Costs)

= 80,691 – 51,265

= 29,426

NPV is positive; pursue the project.

Benefit to Cost (B/C)

Benefit to cost is a useful measure of the worth of a project because it provides a comparison of the relative difference between benefits and costs.

To calculate B/C, the Present Value (PV) of the project's benefits (Revenues) is divided by the (PV) of the project's costs.

Revenues and costs are estimated from historical data or comparisons with similar projects and their PVs are calculated.

B/C Interpretation:

  B/C > 1; benefits greater than costs

  B/C < 1; benefits less than costs

  B/C = 1; break even (benefits and costs are equal)

Advantages and Disadvantages of B/C

Advantages:

- Takes into account the cost of money

- Very accurate compared to other methods

- Easier to interpret ratios or percentages than pure numbers

Disadvantages:

- Not easily understood by everyone

- Costs and revenues not always easy to quantify

Set Up Data Table for B/C

Question: You have estimated the following revenues and costs for your project. If the corporate IRR is 18%, what is the B/C ratio for your project?

Years	Revenues	Costs
0	0	$10,000
1	$12,000	$10,000
2	$16,000	$10,000
3	$20,000	$15,000
4	$40,000	$15,000
5	$60,000	$20,000

B/C Sample Calculation

Solution: The PV of the revenues and costs were calculated previously.

PV(Revenues) = $80,691

PV(Costs) = $51,265

B/C = 80,691/51,265
  or B/C = 1.57

Selection Techniques Exercise

Using the data in the table, determine:

1. The net present value of the project
2. The B/C ratio
3. The payback period

Assume IRR is 10%.

Years	Revenues	Costs
0	0	$10,000
1	$10,000	$25,000
2	$30,000	$20,000
3	$60,000	$50,000
4	$100,000	$50,000
5	$100,000	$50,000

Key Messages—Module 2

The key messages from this module are:

- Many project managers are involved in the project selection process or are asked for input into the analysis

- There are several techniques for determining a project's viability. The most common ones are:
  - Payback or break-even point
  - Return on Investment (ROI)
  - Internal Rate of Return (IRR)
  - Net Present Value (NPV)
  - Benefit to Cost Ratio (B/C)

Module 3: The Project Concept Phase

Defining and Organizing the Project

Objectives for Module 3

At the end of this module you will be able to:

- Describe the elements of a Statement of Work (SOW)

- Explain how to interpret a SOW

- Identify and describe project requirements

- Describe a Work Breakdown Structure (WBS)

Objectives for Module 3 (*continued*)

- Develop a high level WBS

- List project stakeholders and develop strategies for obtaining their support

- Describe the use and structure of a Project Charter

- Understand the elements of and conduct a kickoff meeting

Where We Are in the Process

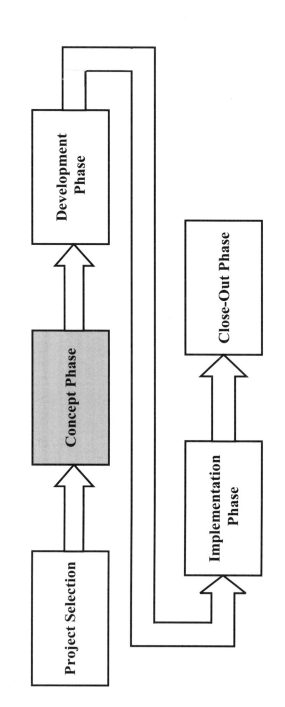

Activities in the Concept Phase

The project manager is chiefly concerned about understanding and organizing the project during this phase. The principal activities are:

- Interpreting the project requirements from:
    - Statement of Work (SOW)
    - Specifications
    - Contractual documents

- Developing a high level Work Breakdown Structure (WBS)

- Identifying project team skill requirements

- Providing input to the Project Charter

Statement of Work

The Statement of Work (SOW) is the principal document for trans-mitting the customer's project requirements. The characteristics of a SOW include:

- Written description of the project requirements

- High level schedule and milestones

- Occasionally a budget (usually for internal projects only)

- Acceptance criteria

Statement of Work (*continued*)

- Key personnel in the customer organization

- Technical or performance specifications

- Scope change process

- Communication requirements

SOW Outline

A typical SOW will have the following outline:

Section Number	Section Heading
1.0	Introduction
2.0	Key Assumptions
3.0	Seller/Provider Responsibilities
4.0	Buyer/Customer Responsibilities
5.0	Estimated Schedule
6.0	Project Acceptance Criteria
7.0	Type of Contract and Payment Schedule
8.0	Additional Terms and Conditions
9.0	Miscellaneous
10.0	Appendixes

Reasons That SOWs Are Misinterpreted

Projects fail most often because the project requirements are not fully understood or they are misinterpreted. Reasons include:

- Poorly written SOWs

- Use of ambiguous words and phrases

- Conflicting requirements

- Lack of communication between customer and project manager

- Unreasonable requirements, particularly in schedules

Reading the SOW

Reading the SOW critically helps to focus on and identify the requirements. A disciplined process for reading the SOW will follow this pattern:

- Summarize the project background and general purpose

- Describe the project goals and objectives

- Relate the project goals and objectives to the organization's strategic goals

- List all "shall" statements

- Identify and list all assumptions and constraints

Reading the SOW (*continued*)

- List all the project deliverables; data, services, hardware, software, documents
  - Decompose deliverables into component tasks
  - Identify required resources

- Gantt chart any imposed schedule dates or other key milestones

- List any risks

- Determine what the acceptance criteria are

Collecting the Requirements

Once the SOW has been thoroughly dissected, the requirements can be collected for interpretation and refining. They will be the:

- "Shall" statements

- Specific deliverables such as services, data, documentation, software, or hardware

- Tasks that are required to reach the customer's stated goals

- Ancillary tasks that support reaching the customer's goals, such as

  - Acquiring special equipment
  - Hiring specialists

- Reporting and communicating tasks to the customer and key internal personnel

Translating Requirements

Once the requirements are collected and generally understood, they can be interpreted and refined. The steps are:

1. List all the deliverables

2. Use an experienced initial team to help decompose and refine each of the task requirements

3. Develop a high level Work Breakdown Structure (WBS) for the project

4. Identify the resources that are needed to accomplish the task

5. Identify other project interdependencies

6. Identify risks because of project priorities and any constraints or assumptions that have been made

7. Develop strategies for completing the project

Initial Project Team

Initially, the project manager may be the only member of the project team. After analyzing the SOW, the project manager organizes an "initial" team to develop requirements and identify team skills. Initial team members:

- Are usually experienced, even supervisory level

- May not be a part of the final team composition

- Provide expertise on SOW interpretation and WBS development

- Are knowledgeable about identifying skill sets and team composition/organization

Work Breakdown Structure

The Work Breakdown Structure (WBS) is the most important project management tool and is the basis for all other project management planning. It is a structured way of decomposing a project into its various components. The WBS:

- Reduces the project into successively lower levels of detail

- Provides a way of identifying tasks and task resources

- Provides a structure for estimating costs

- Provides a structure for identifying project skill sets

Work Breakdown Structure (*continued*)

- Is used to develop network logic diagrams

- Is used to develop schedules

- Is used to identify risks

WBS Formats

The WBS can be represented in two ways:

1. Indented
   - Each lower level is indented as the project is decomposed
   - Resembles an outline format

2. Graphical or tree
   - Resembles a traditional organizational structure
   - Excellent for visual presentation of project tasks structure

Indented WBS

1.0 Project or Contract Name
  1.1 Major Project Subsystem A
    1.1.1 Task 1
      1.1.1.1 Subtask 1
      1.1.1.2 Subtask 2
    1.1.2 Task 2
      1.1.2.1 Subtask 1
      1.1.2.2 Subtask 2
  1.2 Major Project Subsystem B
    1.2.1 Task 1
    1.2.2 Task 2
      1.2.2.1 Subtask 1
      1.2.2.2 Subtask 2
        1.2.2.2.1 Work Package 1

Graphical WBS

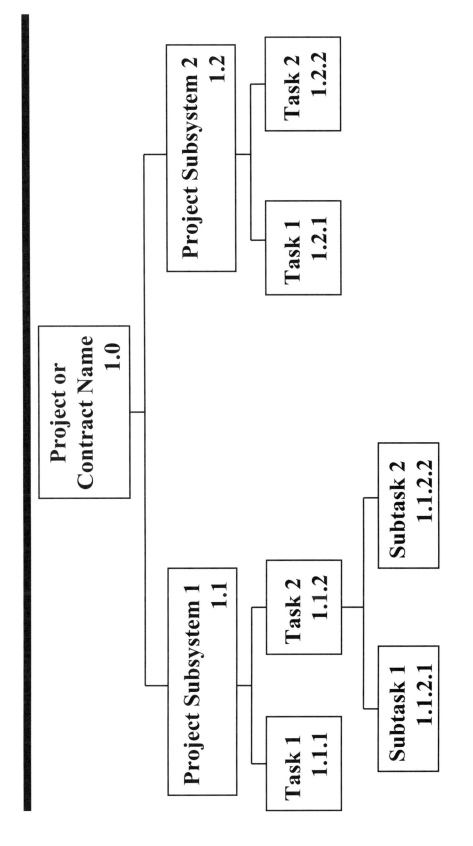

Developing High-Level WBS

Initially, there may not be enough information or understanding of the requirements to develop a complete WBS. The first task is to develop at least a high level WBS so that:

- Major project deliverables can be identified

- Project scope parameters are clear

- General requirements are understood enough to identify major tasks

- Team member composition can be established

- Top level cost, schedule, and resource estimates can be developed/confirmed

Stakeholders

Crucial to the project manager's success is the early identification and management of stakeholders.

Definition: A stakeholder is anyone with a vested interest in the project.

- — Customer

- — Sponsor

- — Project team members

- — Functional managers

The Stakeholder Analysis Worksheet

A stakeholder analysis includes identifying the stakeholder and determining how to sway them.

Stakeholder	+	0	−	Reason Against Project	Strengths & Weaknesses	Strategy

The Project Charter

The project charter is the major output of the Concept Phase of the project life cycle. It:

- Is an internal document signed by a senior executive who has functional authority over all the project's functional relationships

- Authorizes the project manager to begin work

- Is not a legal document

- Is a way to assign a project priority

- Is a way to obtain buy-in for the project

Major Elements of a Project Charter

A project charter identifies the project manager and gives him or her the authority to start the project. The major elements of a project charter are:

- Project Scope—Provides a short summary of the project scope and the deliverables.

- Assignment—Announces the project manager by name, the name of the project, and the customer's name.

- Responsibilities—Specifies the project manager's responsibilities in delivering the project, and the functional groups responsibilities in supporting it.

- Authority—Outlines the project manager's authority limits.

- Priority—Assigns a priority to the project relative to the other projects in the organization.

Kickoff Meetings

Kickoff meetings are excellent communication and team-building opportunities. The principal purpose is to get the project started on the right foot and should have all or most of the following objectives:

- Introduce team members to one another

- Establish working relationships and lines of communication

- Set team goals and objectives

- Review project status

Kickoff Meetings (*continued*)

- Review project plans

- Identify project problem areas

- Establish individual and group responsibilities and accountabilities

- Obtain individual and group commitments

The Kickoff Meeting Agenda

Kickoff meetings are important communication tools

1. Introductions
2. Vision
3. Scope and objectives
4. Risks, challenges, and project constraints
5. Project approach
6. Team members and project organization chart
7. Roles and responsibilities
8. Timeline
9. Major milestones
10. Process, standards, methods, and tools

The Kickoff Meeting Agenda (*continued*)

11. Quality plan
12. Project management and schedule planning standards and guidelines
13. Centralized documentation storage facility
14. Time collection and project status requirements
15. Training schedule
16. Lessons learned from previous post-project reviews
17. Success factors
18. Project expectations and next steps
19. Unresolved issues, responsibility assignments, and target dates
20. Adjournment

Key Messages—Module 3

- The SOW is the key document for transmitting the project requirements

- The SOW must be interpreted correctly to identify all the requirements

- The WBS is developed by an initial team once the requirements are identified

- The major output of the Concept Phase is the Project Charter

- The Project Charter identifies the project manager and gives him or her the authority to begin the project

- The kickoff meeting is critical for establishing communication channels and for team building

Module 4:   The Project Development Phase

Planning the Project

Objectives for Module 4

At the end of this module you will be able to:

- Develop project budget, schedule, and resource estimates from the WBS

- Develop a precedence table from the WBS

- Develop a network using the Precedence Diagramming Method (PDM)

- Develop a schedule using a Gantt chart

- Describe the elements of a project management plan

Where We Are in the Process

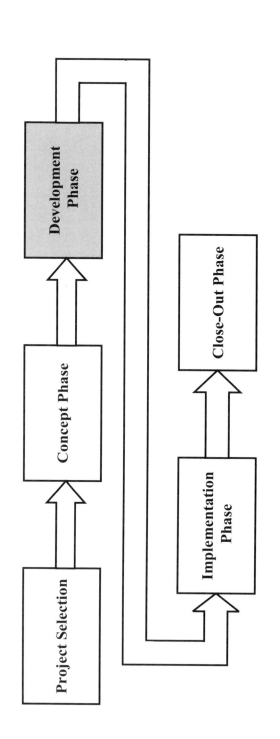

Activities in the Development Phase

The project manager is chiefly concerned about refining the requirements and developing the project plans during this phase. The principal activities are:

- Selecting and forming the project team

- Refining the requirements and clarifying the SOW

- Developing a complete WBS

- Developing budget, schedule, and resource estimates

- Developing a network analysis to determine critical tasks and the shortest time to complete the project

- Creating Gantt charts to describe the project schedules

- Performing a risk analysis

- Completing ancillary plans to support the project

Estimating Budgets

Project budgets are typically developed using one of the following methods:

- Rough order-of-magnitude (ROM)

- Top-down (analogous)

- Bottom-up (engineering or business)

Rough Order-of-Magnitude

Rough Order-of-Magnitude or ROM is the easiest and fastest estimating method, which provides an approximate figure for the project. It is useful as a general estimate of effort and:

- Is based on experience and some historical data, but is mostly based on intuition

- Gives a quick snapshot of the project costs or schedule

- Is usually done by one person

Disadvantages

- Is very inaccurate with estimates ranging between −25% and +75%

- It almost always sticks as the estimate when it is meant to provide an approximate guess for early planning purposes

Top-Down or Analogous Estimating

Top-down estimating is based on historical data and comparisons with other similar projects.

- Based on comparisons with similar projects within the group or company

- Parametric models are often used to extrapolate data from one project to fit another

- Relatively quick estimate and useful for obtaining reasonably good estimates

- Most appropriate technique for top level planning and decision making

Disadvantages
- Accurate to within −10% and +25%

- Good enough for planning, but not good enough for a final estimate

Bottom–Up or Definitive Estimating

The bottom–up estimating method is the most accurate of the three methods.

- Based upon the lowest level of the WBS

- Estimates are determined with the person who performs the task

- The project cost is "rolled-up" from the lowest WBS level to the highest WBS level

- This technique is used to update estimates for the final project budget

Disadvantages

- Takes time

- Within −5% and +10% accurate

Network Analysis

Network analysis is a scheduling tool developed from the WBS. It is used to:

- Show the interdependence of project tasks

- Determine the project duration

- Determine float or slack in a path

- Determine the project's critical path

- Expose risks

Steps in Developing a Network

Once the WBS is developed to the lowest desired level, the network can be developed and analyzed:

- The project team and other selected functional experts determine the interdependence of all the tasks

- Develop a precedence table after all task dependencies are established

- Construct the network

- Determine the duration, critical path, and float for each task

Precedence Tables

A precedence table is necessary for developing networks or logic diagrams. They usually have the following form:

Task Identifier	WBS Element	Predecessor	Task Duration
a	Task 1	—	5
b	Task 2	—	4
c	Task 3	a	4
d	Task 4	b	4
e	Task 5	b	3
f	Task 6	c	4
g	Task 7	d	5
h	Task 8	e	8
i	Task 9	f,g,h	8
j	Task 10	e	8

The Network Diagram

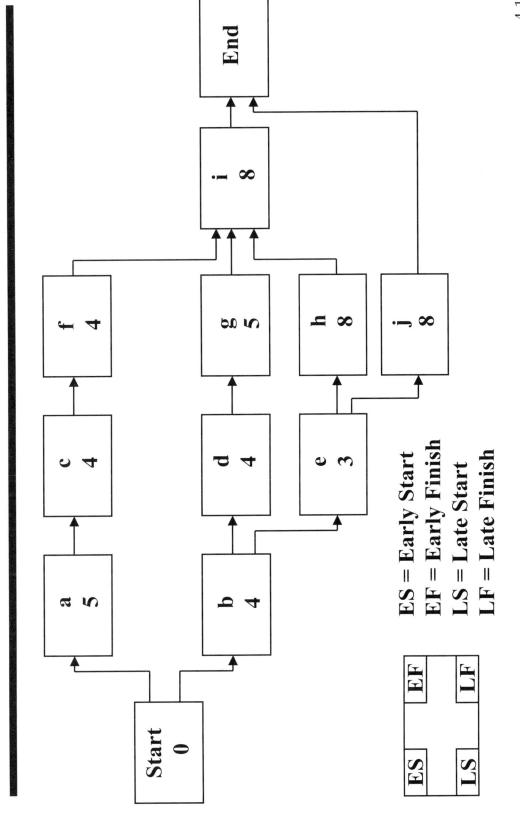

ES = Early Start
EF = Early Finish
LS = Late Start
LF = Late Finish

4-11

Early Schedule

In analyzing the network, the early schedule is determined first.

- Begin at the project start node and determine the earliest possible time each task can begin and finish

- The "Early Finish" of each task in succession is determined by adding the task duration to its "Early Start"

- The "Early Start" of a task is the "Early Finish" of the preceding task

- The process of determining the early schedule is referred to as the "Forward Pass"

Early Start

When two or more arrows enter a task, the "Early Start" is the LARGEST of the preceding task's "Early Finish"

Example:

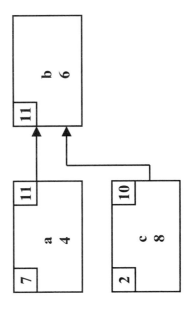

Forward Pass: The Early Schedule

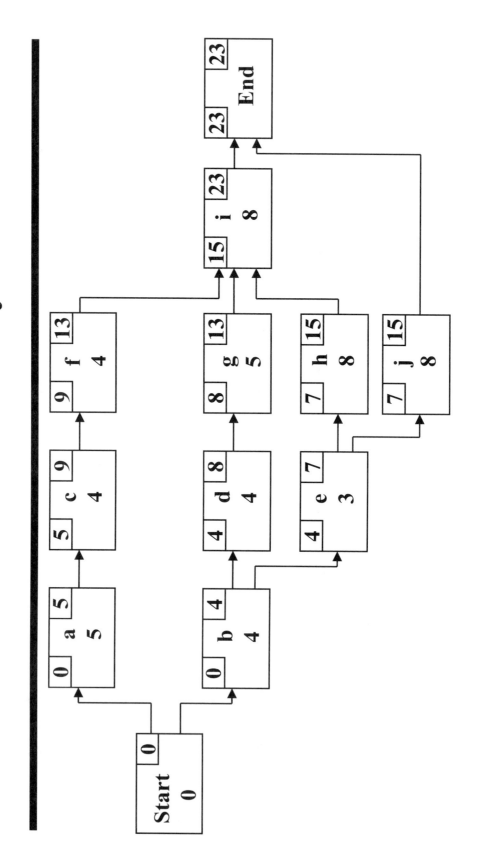

Late Schedule

The late schedule cannot be determined until after the early schedule is known.

- From the end of the project, work backwards through the network to determine the late schedule.

- Start with the duration determined by the Forward Pass as the beginning point

- The "Late Finish" of a task is the "Late Start" of the succeeding task

- The process of determining the late schedule is referred to as the Backward Pass.

Late Finish

When two or more arrows back into a task, the "Late Finish" is the SMALLEST of the succeeding task's "Late Start"

– Example:

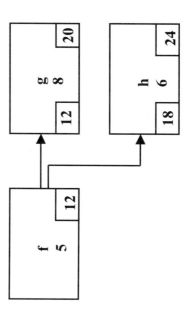

Backward Pass: The Late Schedule

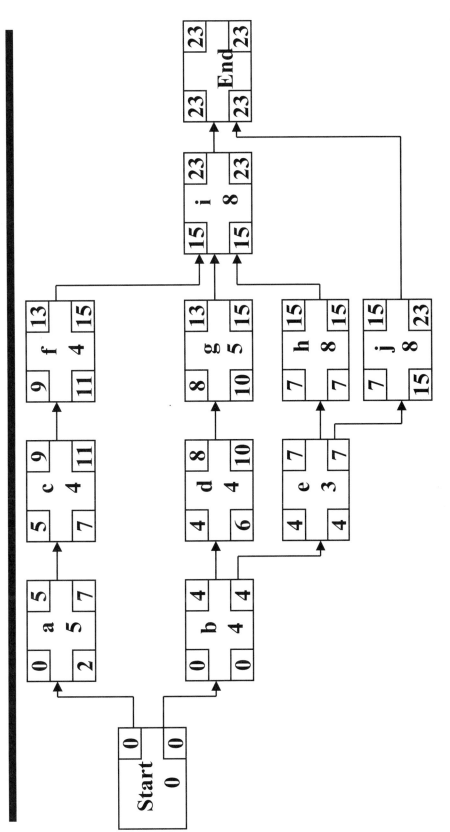

4-17

Project Duration, Float, and Critical Path

Three important pieces of information derived from network analyses are the duration, amount of float or slack in each path, and the project's critical path.

- Project duration: The shortest required time to complete the project.

- Float: The amount of time the start of a task can be delayed without impacting the schedule.

    Float = Latest Start – Earliest Start or Latest Finish – Earliest Finish

- Critical Path: The longest path through the network or the path with zero float. This path identifies the tasks that have to be managed closely so that no slips to the schedule occur.

The Critical Path

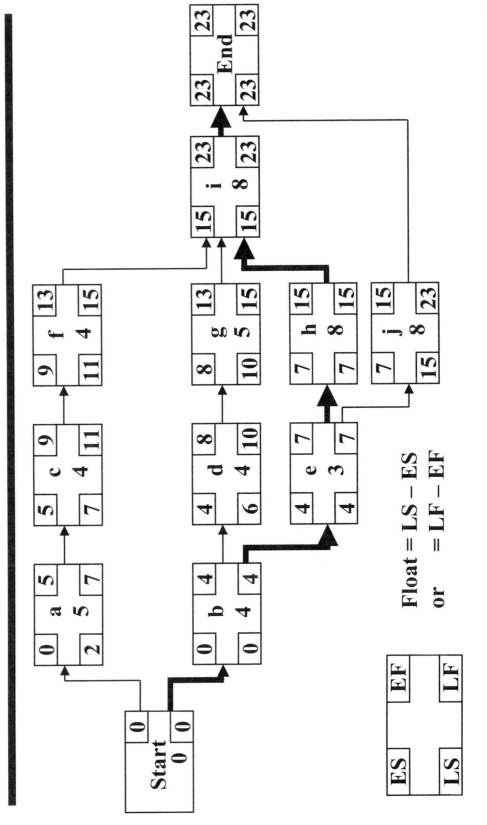

Float = LS – ES
or   = LF – EF

4-19

Exercise 4-1

Using the information from the precedence table, construct a
Network Diagram and answer the following questions:

1. What is the project duration?
2. What is the critical path?
3. How much float is in Task ....?

Task Identifier	WBS Element	Predecessor	Task Duration
a	Task 1	—	5
b	Task 2	—	6
c	Task 3	a	2
d	Task 4	a,b	5
e	Task 5	b	4
f	Task 6	c,d,e	4

Gantt Charts

Gantt charts are developed after the network analysis is completed.
They are used for:

- Showing beginning and ending points for each of the project tasks

- Graphically depicting project progress against the project baseline

- Communicating project progress to stakeholders

Sample Gantt Chart

The Gantt chart is a bar chart that shows each task and the beginning and ending dates. Other information can be added to the bars as desired

ID	❶	Task Name	December	January			February		March
			12/12	12/26	01/09	01/23	02/06	02/20	03/05
1	▦	Design Subsystem 1							
2		Develop Subsystem 1							
3		Manufacture Subsystem 1							
4		Test Subsystem 1							
5	▦	Install Subsystem 2							

The Project Management Plan

Once the schedule, budget, and resource estimates are completed, the project plan can be finalized. A format that will fit most projects will have these elements:

    I. Executive Summary
    II. Project Requirements and Objectives
    III. General Methodology or Technical Approach
    IV. Contractual Requirements
    V. Schedules
    VI. Resource Requirements
       A. Equipment
       B. Materials
       C. People
    VII. Potential Risks
    VIII. Performance Evaluations

Appendices
    Project Charter
    Supporting plans
    Drawings
    Specifications

Key Messages—Module 4

The key messages of this module are:

- There are three primary methods for estimating budgets, resources, and schedules. They are:
  - ROM
  - Top-down
  - Bottom-up

- The precedence diagramming method is a critical analysis tool. It provides the following information:
  - Project duration
  - Critical path
  - Float in each task

- The Gantt chart is a bar chart showing the beginning and ending of each task

- The project plan can be finalized once the budget, schedule, and resource estimates are completed

Module 5: The Project Implementation Phase

Monitoring and Controlling the Project

Objectives for Module 5

At the end of this module you will be able to:

- Develop a change management process

- Identify and prioritize project risks

- Develop a risk management plan

- Employ "earned value" concepts and formulas to track project progress

Where We Are in the Process

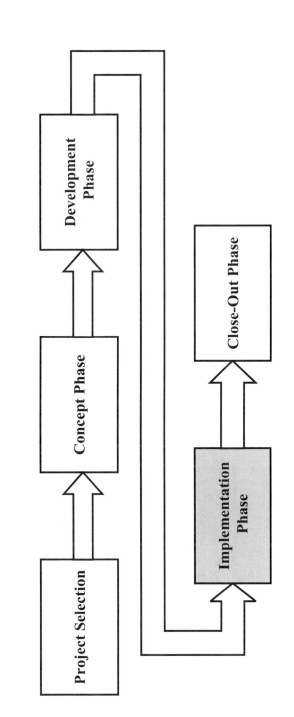

Activities in the Implementation Phase

The project manager is chiefly concerned about monitoring and controlling the project relative to the project baseline during this phase. The principal activities are:

- Setting up the project organization

- Securing the required resources

- Setting up and executing the work packages

- Directing, monitoring, and controlling the project

Goals of the Change-Control System

A well developed and documented change-control process is crucial to project management success. Change-control systems should:

- Continually identify changes, actual or proposed, as they occur

- Reveal the consequences of the proposed changes in terms of cost and schedule impacts

- Permit managerial analysis, investigation of alternatives, and an acceptance or rejection checkpoint

- Communicate changes to all stakeholders

- Insure that changes are implemented

The Change-Control Process

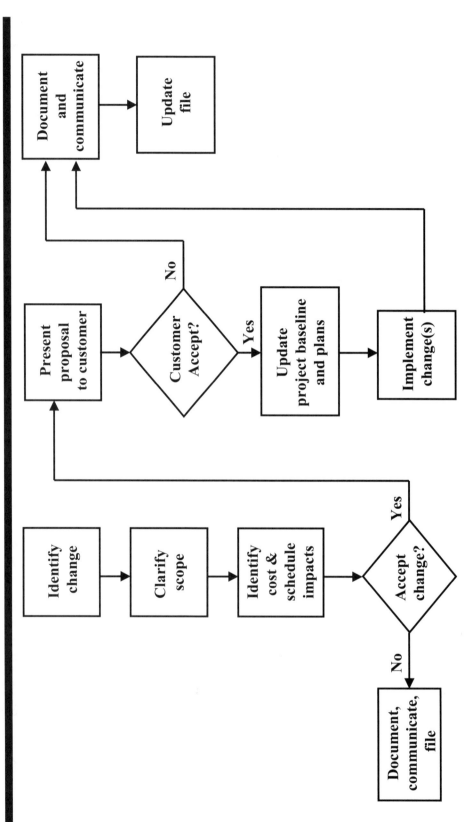

Why Risk Analysis?

The main objectives of a risk analysis are:

- Timeliness: A risk analysis must identify issues before they occur

- Priorities: Because of insufficient time or resources, a risk analysis must help assign realistic priorities

- Aggregation: The risk analysis must help aggregate all the individual risks into a measure of overall project risk

- Decision support: The risk analysis must produce information in a form that supports the decision makers

Types of Risk

There are two kinds of risk in a project. They are:

1. Business risks: Potential for loss but also an opportunity for gain

   – Example 1: Customer expands the project scope.

   – Example 2: A project task requires use or development of new technology. Successful completion of the development opens a new market to the company.

2. Pure or insurable risks: Potential only for loss

   – Example 1: Company is located in an area susceptible to hurricanes.

   – Example 2: Company has no expertise required by one of the project tasks.

Risk Assessment Methods

Methods for assessing risks fall into three broad groups:

1. Issue-based methods

2. Scoring techniques

3. Quantitative techniques

Risk Classifications for Issue-Based Risk Assessment

Issue-based methods usually start with the assertion that all risks can be classified under a set of headings, such as:

- Commercial
- Technical
- Programmatic
- Resource availability
- Project priorities

Advantages and Disadvantages of Issue–Based Risk Assessment

Advantages

- Provides a checklist, which helps in remembering to look at all project elements

- Checklists provide access to the experience of others

Disadvantages

- Checklists tend to be seen as exhaustive, giving a sense of false security

- Checklists don't help provide an overall level of risk in a project nor do they help determine realistic budget and schedule estimates

Scoring Techniques

Scoring techniques are natural extensions of checklists. They:

- Are based on a questionnaire

- Provide a checklist approach as memory joggers

- Ask for a numerical rating of a factor if it appears in the task or project

- Provide for a way to assess the overall project riskiness by adding the risk assessment points

Advantages and Disadvantages of Scoring Techniques

Advantages

- Combine the checklist approach with a numerical rating of the task riskiness

- Provide a way to measure overall project riskiness

- Valuable because they highlight separate issues and indicate which are the most important

Disadvantages

- Arbitrary scoring measures often are difficult to interpret

- Don't provide a clear insight into the risk's impact if it occurs

- The relationship between individual risks in a project and the risk to the whole project is more complicated than simple addition

Quantitative Techniques

Quantitative techniques are designed to identify the risk event and to determine the impact to the project if the event occurs. Quantitative techniques:

- Are based on the planning structures project managers use, i.e., cost breakdowns and schedules

- Identify the risk event

- Determine a probability of likelihood of occurrence

- Provide a way to prioritize the risks relative to the overall impact to the project

- Provide a basis for decision making

Advantages and Disadvantages of Quantitative Techniques

Advantages

- Provide a measure of the impact of a risk event on a project

- Provide a mechanism for decision making

- Easier to rank

Disadvantages

- Probabilities are not always easy to assign

- Using probabilities requires an understanding of how to apply "expected value" theory

Ranking Risks

Once the risks are identified, they can be prioritized. An easy-to-use technique involves comparing each identified risk with every other risk to determine which has the greatest impact on the project.

	A	B	C	D	E	F	G
A							
B							
C							
D							
E							
F							
G							

Six Major Sections of a Risk-Management Plan

1. Project summary and system description

2. Approach to risk management

3. Application issues and problems

4. Other relevant plans

5. Conclusions and recommendations

6. Approvals

A Risk-Management Plan Format—Part 1

I. Project summary and description
    1.1 Project summary
        1.1.1 Project and organizational objectives
        1.1.2 Operational and technical characteristics
        1.1.3 Key functions
    1.2 Project description
        1.2.1 Requirements
        1.2.2 Schedule
        1.2.3 Special contractual requirements

II. Approach to Risk Management
    2.1 Definitions
        2.1.1 Technical risk
        2.1.2 Programmatic risk
        2.1.3 Supportability risk
        2.1.4 Cost risk
        2.1.5 Schedule risk
    2.2 Risk assessment methods overview
        2.2.1 Techniques applied
        2.2.2 Implementation of assessment results

(continued on next slide)

A Risk–Management Plan Format—Part 2

III.   Application
       3.1 Risk Assessment
           3.1.1 Risk identification
           3.1.2 Risk quantification
           3.1.3 Risk prioritization
       3.2 Risk response development
       3.3 Risk response control
           3.3.1 Control evaluation
           3.3.2 Risk documentation

IV.   Other relevant plans

V.   Conclusions and Recommendations

VI.   Approvals

Important Earned-Value Terms

Earned value is the accepted technique for monitoring and tracking project progress. The concept of earned value revolves around these three measures:

BCWS: Budgeted Cost of Work Scheduled

- BCWS is the cumulative budget for the project.

ACWP: Actual Cost of Work Performed

- The cumulative costs actually expended during the project's life cycle.

BCWP: Budgeted Cost of Work Performed (Also called "Earned Value")

- The percentage of work actually performed measured against the budget for work scheduled or planned to be completed.

Cost and Schedule Variance

Cost and schedule variance are the two primary measures of the project progress. They can be determined by:

- Cost Variance (CV)

    CV = BCWP – ACWP

- Schedule Variance (SV)

    SV = BCWS – BCWS

If CV/SV = 0; then project is on track

If CV/SV = +; then project is under budget and ahead of schedule

If CV/SV = –; then project is over budget and behind schedule

Sample Calculation for
Cost and Schedule Variance

Example: You planned to be finished with Task A today. The scheduled cost of the task was $1,000. You have actually spent $900 to date but you are only 90% complete. What are the cost and schedule variances for Task A?

Solution: BCWS = $1,000 (Planned or scheduled cost of the task to date)

ACWP = $900 (Actual cost expended)

BCWP = BCWS x 90% = 1,000 x .90 = $900 (amount of work performed compared with amount scheduled)

CV = BCWP – ACWP

= 900 – 900

= 0

SV = BCWP – BCWS

= 900 – 1,000

= –100

Task is on budget but behind schedule.

Cost and Schedule Performance Indices

Two indices that are useful for communicating progress status are the Cost Performance Index and the Schedule Performance Index. They are determined by:

Cost Performance Index—The cost efficiency factor representing the relationship between the actual costs expended and the value of the physical work performed.

$$CPI = BCWP/ACWP$$

Schedule Performance Index—The planned schedule efficiency factor representing the relationship between the value of the initial planned schedule and the value of the physical work performed.

$$SPI = BCWP/BCWS$$

If CPI and SPI = 1, then the project is on budget and on schedule

    < 1, then the project is over budget and behind schedule

    > 1, then the project is under budget and ahead of schedule

Sample Calculations for CPI and SPI

Example: The BCWS for a task is $1,000, the ACWP is $900, and the BCWP is $900. What are the CPI and SPI for this task?

CPI = BCWP/ACWP

= 900/900

= 1.00

SPI = BCWP/BCWS

= 900/1,000

= .90

Project is on budget but behind schedule.

Estimate at Completion

The estimate at completion (EAC) is a projection of the final costs of work at project completion.

EAC = BAC/CPI

The project manager should recalculate the EAC each time project progress is measured.

Budget at completion (BAC) - Original estimate of completed project costs.

CPI = Cost Performance Index

Sample EAC Calculation

Example: The original estimate of the project costs is $100,000. If the BCWP for the project to date is $8,000 and the ACWP is $9,300, what is the new EAC for the project?

Solution: CPI = BCWP/ACWP

         = 8,000/9,300

         = .86

         EAC = BAC/CPI

         = 100,000/.86

         = 116,279.07

(Note: This will be the amount needed if no changes are made to the way the project is currently being managed.)

Estimate to Complete

Estimate to complete (ETC) or the amount of money needed to fund the project to completion is calculated by:

ETC = EAC – ACWP

Sample ETC Calculation

Example: If the estimate to complete for a project is $116,279.07 and the actual expenditures to date are $9,300, what is the estimate to complete the project?

Solution: ETC = EAC – ACWP

$$= 116,279.07 - 9,300$$

$$= 106,979.07$$

Exercise 5-1 Earned Value Life of Project

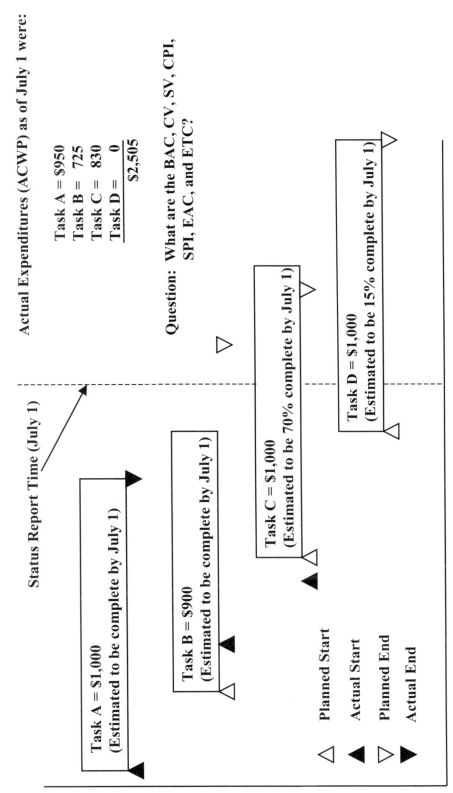

Status Report Time (July 1)

Task A = $1,000
(Estimated to be complete by July 1)

Task B = $900
(Estimated to be complete by July 1)

Task C = $1,000
(Estimated to be 70% complete by July 1)

Task D = $1,000
(Estimated to be 15% complete by July 1)

Actual Expenditures (ACWP) as of July 1 were:

Task A = $950
Task B = 725
Task C = 830
Task D = 0
            $2,505

Question: What are the BAC, CV, SV, CPI, SPI, EAC, and ETC?

△ Planned Start

◀ Actual Start

▽ Planned End

▶ Actual End

Earned Value Sample Solution

Solution:

1. BAC = Task A cost + Task B cost + Task C cost + Task D cost
   = 1,000 + 900 + 1,000 + 1,000 = $3,900

2. CV = BCWP − ACWP = 2,475 − 2,505 = −30

3. SV = BCWP − BCWS = 2,475 − 2,750 = −275

4. CPI = BCWP/ACWP = 2,475/2,505 = .99

5. SPI = BCWP/BCWS = 2,475/2,750 = .90

6. EAC = BAC/CPI = 3,900/.99 = 3,939.39

7. ETC = EAC − ACWP = 3,939.39 − 2,505 = 1,434.39

Exercise 5-2

You are working on a project that was estimated to be completed on May 5 for a cost of $150,000. Today is May 9 and the project is 85% complete. You have spent $145,000. Answer the following questions:

1. What is the BAC for this project?

2. What is the BCWS, BCWP, and ACWP for the project?

3. What is the CV?

4. What is the SV?

5. What is the CPI and the SPI?

6. What is the new EAC?

7. What is the ETC?

Key Messages—Module 5

The key messages of this module are:

- A well-structured and documented change-control system is crucial for project success

- Risk analysis begins with the interpretation of the SOW and continues throughout the project's life cycle

- There are two kinds of risk:
  - Business risk
  - Pure or insurable risk

- A risk management plan is required to be proactive rather than reactive to risks

(continued on next slide)

Key Messages—Module 5 (*continued*)

- Earned value is a concept that has been universally accepted as the best way to monitor and control project progress

- There are three basic definitions associated with earned value that have to be understood before the concept can be used:

  – Budgeted cost of work scheduled (BCWS)

  – Actual cost of work performed (ACWP)

  – Budgeted cost of work performed (BCWP)

- BCWP is known as the "earned-value" term

Module 6: The Project Close-Out Phase

Bringing the Project to a Successful Conclusion

Objectives for Module 6

At the end of this module you will be able to:

- Describe the project termination, or close-out process

- Determine and describe the project team's activities in completing the project requirements

- Describe the audit activities required to complete the project

- Describe and use a project close-out checklist

Where We Are in the Process

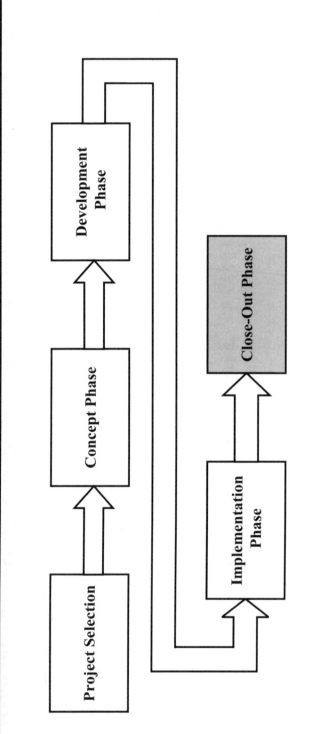

Plan, Schedule, and Monitor Activities

The project close-out phase is often the most difficult phase of the project's life cycle. To successfully close the project, the project manager must:

Plan, schedule, and monitor completion activities:

– Obtain and approve termination plans and schedules

– Prepare and coordinate termination plans and schedules

– Plan for reassignment of project team members and transfer resources to other projects

– Monitor termination activities and completion of all contractual agreements

– Monitor the disposition of any surplus materials or customer-supplied equipment

Administrative Activities

Complete administrative close-out activities:

- Close work orders and subcontracted work completion

- Notify all stakeholders of project completion

- Close project office and any other project facilities

- Close project books

- Archive project files and records

Customer Acceptance, Obligation, and Payment Activities

- Ensure deliverables are completed and accepted by customer

- Communicate to the customer completion of all contractual items

- Ensure all contract obligations and documentation are complete

- Transmit formal payment request to the customer

- Monitor customer payment and collection of payments

Project Audit Format—Part 1

The project manager and team must perform an audit of the project to ensure all the requirements are met and that the financial records are complete. A typical final audit format report includes:

I.   Executive summary

II.   Introduction

III. Project Review
    A. Project objectives
    B. Method or approach

IV.   Effectiveness of Planning

V.   Effectiveness of Project Management

VI.   Effectiveness of Technical Solution

VII. Project Deliverables
    A. Description
    B. Assessment against requirements

VIII. Quality
    A. Standards used
    B. Measurement
    C. Assessment against requirements

Project Audit—Part 2

IX. Schedule
    A. Delays
        1. Reasons
        2. Recovery actions
    B. Assessment against plan
X. Finances
    A. Problems
        1. Reasons
        2. Recovery actions
    B. Assessment against plan
XI. Resource Utilization
    A. Effectiveness
    B. Problems
        1. Reasons
        2. Recovery actions
XII. Lessons Learned
XIII. Individual Team-Member Assessment and Recommendations
    (submit as separate confidential report)
XIV.   Recommendations

Project Close-Out Checklist

☐ Prepare a close-out plan
☐ Verify scope
  – Contractual obligations
  – Administrative obligations
  – WBS (tasks and deliverables)
☐ Obtain customer acceptance of deliverables
☐ Document and archive files and records
☐ Document lessons learned
☐ Reassign resources
☐ Notify all stakeholders of project completion
☐ Celebrate success

Key Messages—Module 6

The key messages of this module are:

- The close-out phase is often the most difficult phase in a project

- The project manager has to complete numerous activities relating to
  - Technical and operational issues
  - Administrative issues
  - Customer approval and acceptance

- A formal project audit is necessary to ensure that all project requirements are complete

- The project manager and team should use a close-out checklist through the close-out process

Handouts

REQUIREMENTS RECORD

PROJECT TITLE: **DATE:**

PROJECT MANAGER:

REQUIREMENT:

ASSUMPTIONS:

CONSTRAINTS:

REQUIRED RESOURCES:

FUNCTIONAL GROUPS PARTICIPATING:

REQUIREMENTS RECORD

PROJECT TITLE: The Jacksonville Company Management Information System

PROJECT MANAGER: Michael James   **DATE:** May 14, 2002

REQUIREMENT: A Management Information System (MIS) to support a corporate office consisting of fifty people. The MIS will produce forms, reports, data, and analyses specified by the Information Systems Department's needs analysis (MIS Needs Analysis, dated January 30, 2002). The MIS will be operational no later than April 1, 2003.

ASSUMPTIONS: The following assumptions have been made in determining the resource requirements for this project:
*   Jack Smith will be assigned as the technical lead for the project
*   Jean Jordan and Bill Williams will be available 50% of their time to support the project manager with clerical and financial assistance
*   The IS department will complete their technology assessment by June 1, 2002
*   This project has priority 1 status

CONSTRAINTS:
*   Given the number of competing projects at Jacksonville, the schedule can be met only with complete functional area support of resources and materials
*   A budget of $200,000 may be insufficient to support IS's technology recommendations

REQUIRED RESOURCES:
*   Technical lead
*   Two full-time programmers
*   One part-time programmer
*   Two design engineers
*   One systems engineer

FUNCTIONAL GROUPS PARTICIPATING:
*   Engineering
*   Information Systems
*   Software Development

INITIAL PROJECT TEAM ANALYSIS WORKSHEET

PROJECT: _____

FUNCTIONAL REPRESENTATIVES

FUNCTIONAL REQUIREMENT DESCRIPTION	AREA	NAME	AREA	NAME	AREA	NAME	AREA	NAME	AREA	NAME	AREA	NAME

Stakeholder Analysis

Stakeholder Name	+	0	−	Reason for Position	Strengths & Weaknesses	Strategy

Project Charter Outline

I.   Purpose (Scope statement)

II.   Project Establishment (Business reason
       for the project)

III.   Project Manager Designation and Authority

IV.   Project Manager's Responsibility
       A.   Support organization's responsibilities
       B.   Project organization and structure
       C.   Project team composition

V.   Project Initiation
       A.   Formal project plan
       B.   Approved budgets
       C.   Approved plan

VI.   Project Personnel (By name if possible,
       but at least by skill area)
       A.   Assignments to projects
       B.   Reporting structure
       C.   Performance appraisals

VII.   Communication Plan

VIII. Definitions

IX.   Appendixes

Sample Project Charter

Project Title: Project Management Control System (PMCS)   Date: April 7, 2000

Scope and Objectives: The Jacksonville Information Systems Company is undergoing rapid change and growth resulting in an urgent need for a more efficient use of capital funds and for managing our many projects. To this end, we are implementing a new project management control system that will satisfy both these needs and will enhance our project teams' ability to better focus on our customers' requirements.

General Objectives:
1. Enable better communication among project, group, and corporate management with regard to progress of major projects.
2. Enable senior management to more closely monitor progress of major projects.
3. Provide project personnel the capability to manage and control their projects.

Specific Objectives:
1. Reporting and Control System
   (a) For communication of project activity within and between groups and senior management
   (b) Initially for high-cost projects, then for "critical," then for all projects
2. Computer Support Systems
   (a) Survey with recommendations to determine the amount and cost of computer support
3. Procedures Manuals
   (a) Document procedures and policies
   (b) Preliminary manual available by end of year for operator and user training
4. Project Management Training Course
   (a) Provide basic project planning and control skills to personnel directly involved in project management
   (b) Follow-on courses to provide software, financial, and contracting skills needed by project managers

Defining Conditions, Constraints, and Assumptions: The PMCS must be operational on the last day of this year. The first phase of this project is a technical survey and a feasibility study with a go/no-go decision point at the conclusion of the study. Implementation of the PMCS will commence on July 1 if the recommendation is to proceed.

Project Organization: The key members of the project organization are:

Sponsor: Dr. Jack Malloney, VP of IS
Project Manager: Mr. James Martin
User Representatives: Ms. Jean Matthews and Mr. John Collier
Technical Lead: Mr. Sean O'Reilly

Team Members: To be nominated by functional managers based upon the project manager's skill set requirements and his recommendations. Functional managers will provide team members for the project duration and they will be 100% dedicated to the project.

Project Manager Authority and Responsibilities
1. Staffing—the project manager will determine the skill requirements for the PMCS project and provide them, along with specific team member names, by June 1 to the appropriate functional managers. The project manager is authorized one clerical person and one cost analysis to assist him. Because of other project priorities, the project team is limited to no more than 10 technical members without specific authority from the President.
2. Budget—the initial estimate of the project cost is $500,000. This budget cannot be exceeded without authority from the President and the Chief Financial Officer.
3. Communications—status reports will be provided to the President, CFO, and the Sponsor bi-monthly.
4. Planning/Tracking—This project will be tracked using our in-house project management software. An earned value analysis will be provided in every other status report beginning with the second report.
5. Change Control—the project manager is authorized to make project changes provided they do not exceed $5,000 in additional cost and do not impact the schedule. Otherwise, any changes will be made through the Configuration Change Control Board.
6. Document/System Access—the project manager is authorized access to any company document or system in the pursuit of this project completion.
7. The project manager will provide a project plan to the Sponsor no later than May 12. The project plan will include a description of the work, schedules, budget, spending plan, resource utilization charts, risk management plans, and a quality plan.

Support Requirements from Other Organizations:
The PMCS project has the top priority in The Jacksonville Information Systems Company. Functional groups will provide all support possible to the project manager. Where conflicts in personnel assignments occur, the President will resolve them.

Approvals:

VP Project Management_____
VP Information Systems _____
Chief Financial Officer _____
VP Human Resources _____
President _____

Kickoff Meeting Agenda Format

1. Introductions

2. Vision

3. Scope and objectives

4. Risks, challenges, and project constraints

5. Project approach

6. Team members and project organization chart

7. Roles and responsibilities

8. Timeline

9. Major milestones

10. Process, standards, methods, and tools

11. Quality plan

12. Project management and schedule planning standards and guidelines

13. Centralized documentation storage facility

14. Time collection and project status requirements

15. Training schedule

16. Lessons learned from previous post-project reviews

17. Success factors

18. Project expectations and next steps

19. Unresolved issues, responsibility assignments, and target dates

20. Adjournment

TASK RESPONSIBILITY MATRIX

PROJECT: _____					
TASK ID(WBS #)	**TASK DESCRIPTION**	**TEAM MEMBER RESPONSIBLE/TASK DURATION**			

Legend: P = Primary   Note: Write the name of the person responsible
         S = Supporting   for the task and indicate whether they
                                 have a primary or supporting role.

TASK RESPONSIBILITY MATRIX

PROJECT:					
TASK ID(WBS #)	**TASK DESCRIPTION**	**TEAM MEMBER RESPONSIBLE/TASK DURATION**			

Legend: P = Primary
S = Supporting

Note: Write the name of the person responsible for the task and indicate whether they have a primary or supporting role.

PROJECT MANAGEMENT PLAN FORMAT

I. Executive Summary

II. Project Requirements and Objectives

III. General Methodology or Technical Approach

IV. Contractual Requirements

V. Schedules

VI. Resource Requirements
    A. Equipment
    B. Materials
    C. People

VII. Potential Risks

VIII. Performance Evaluations

Appendices
    Project Charter
    Supporting plans
    Drawings
    Specifications

RISK ASSESSMENT CHART

PROJECT PARAMETER	POTENTIAL PROBLEM	WHEN AND HOW IT COULD OCCUR	ALTERNATIVE ACTION
Quality			
Budget			
Schedule			

Comparative Risk Ranking Worksheet

A	A	B	C	D	E	F	G
B							
C							
D							
E							
F							
G							

A Risk-Management Plan Format

I.   Project summary and description
    1.1   Project summary
        1.1.1 Project and organizational objectives
        1.1.2 Operational and technical characteristics
        1.1.3 Key functions
    1.2   Project description
        1.2.1 Requirements
        1.2.2 Schedule
        1.2.3 Special contractual requirements

II. Approach to Risk Management
    2.1   Definitions
        2.1.1 Technical risk
        2.1.2 Programmatic risk
        2.1.3 Supportability risk
        2.1.4 Cost risk
        2.1.5 Schedule risk
    2.2   Risk assessment methods overview
        2.2.1 Techniques applied
        2.2.2 Implementation of assessment results

III. Application
    3.1   Risk Assessment
        3.1.1 Risk identification
        3.1.2 Risk quantification
        3.1.3 Risk prioritization
    3.2   Risk response development
    3.3   Risk response control
        3.3.1 Control evaluation
        3.3.2 Risk documentation

IV. Other relevant plans

V.   Conclusions and Recommendations

VI. Approvals

Earned Value Formulas

To Calculate	Use This Formula
Cost Variance	CV = BCWP – ACWP
Schedule Variance	SV = BCWP – BCWS
Cost Performance Index	CPI = BCWP/ACWP
Schedule Performance Index	SPI = BCWP/BCWS
Estimate at Completion	EAC = BAC/CPI
Estimate to Complete	ETC = EAC – ACWP

BCWP (budgeted cost of work performed) is the amount of work accomplished against the amount planned.

BCWP = BCWS x % of work completed

BCWS (budgeted cost of work scheduled) is the planned or estimated cost estimate of the task/project, i.e., the budgeted amount.

ACWP (actual cost of work performed) is the actual amount spent on the task/project.

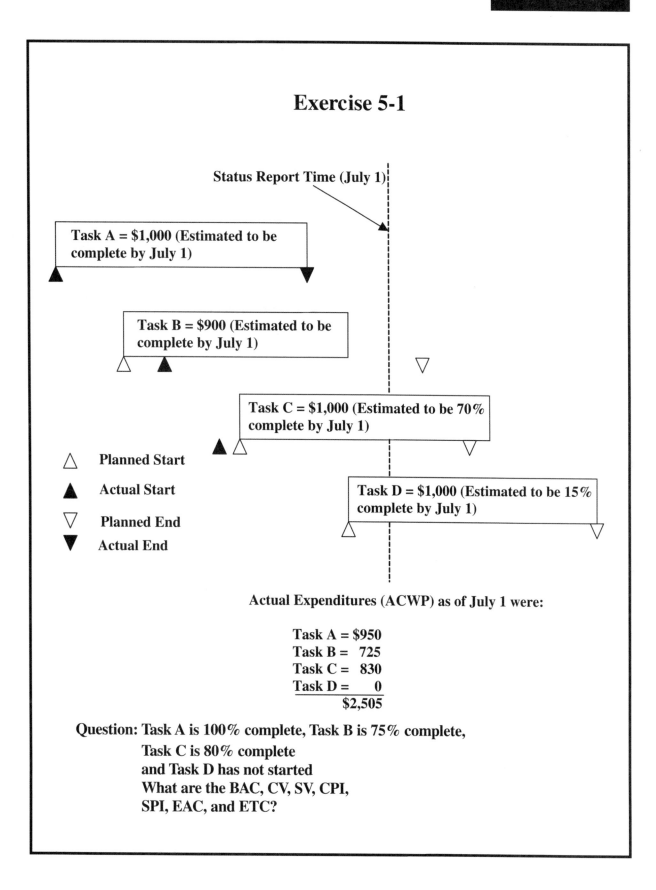

Exercise 5-1

Status Report Time (July 1)

Task A = $1,000 (Estimated to be complete by July 1)

Task B = $900 (Estimated to be complete by July 1)

Task C = $1,000 (Estimated to be 70% complete by July 1)

Task D = $1,000 (Estimated to be 15% complete by July 1)

△ Planned Start
▲ Actual Start
▽ Planned End
▼ Actual End

Actual Expenditures (ACWP) as of July 1 were:

Task A = $950
Task B = 725
Task C = 830
Task D =   0
$2,505

Question: Task A is 100% complete, Task B is 75% complete, Task C is 80% complete and Task D has not started. What are the BAC, CV, SV, CPI, SPI, EAC, and ETC?

Exercise 5-2

You are working on a project that was estimated to be completed on May 5 for a cost of $150,000. Today is May 9 and the project is 85% complete. You have spent $145,000. Answer the following questions.

1. What is the BAC for this project?

2. What are the BCWS, BCWP, and ACWP for the project?

3. What is the CV?

4. What is the SV?

5. What are the CPI and the SPI?

6. What is the new EAC?

7. What is the ETC?

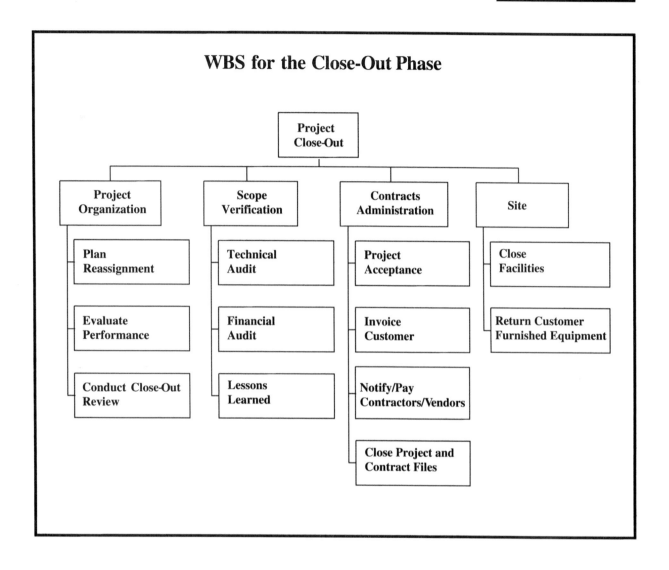

WBS for the Close-Out Phase

Project Close-Out

- Project Organization
  - Plan Reassignment
  - Evaluate Performance
  - Conduct Close-Out Review
- Scope Verification
  - Technical Audit
  - Financial Audit
  - Lessons Learned
- Contracts Administration
  - Project Acceptance
  - Invoice Customer
  - Notify/Pay Contractors/Vendors
  - Close Project and Contract Files
- Site
  - Close Facilities
  - Return Customer Furnished Equipment

Project Audit Format

The project manager and team must perform an audit of the project to ensure that all the requirements are met and that the financial records are complete. A typical final audit format report includes:

I. Executive summary
II. Introduction
III. Project Review
    A. Project objectives
    B. Method or approach
IV. Effectiveness of Planning
V. Effectiveness of Project Management
VI. Effectiveness of Technical Solutions
VII. Project Deliverables
    A. Description
    B. Assessment against requirements
VIII. Quality
    A. Standards used
    B. Measurement
    C. Assessment against requirements
IX. Schedule
    A. Delays
      1. Reasons
      2. Recovery actions
    B. Assessment against plan
X. Finances
    A. Problems
      1. Reasons
      2. Recovery actions
    B. Assessment against plan
XI. Resource Utilization
    A. Effectiveness
    B. Problems
      1. Reasons
      2. Recovery actions
XII. Lessons Learned
XIII. Individual Team-Member Assessment and Recommendations (submit as separate confidential report)
XIV. Recommendations

Project Close-Out Checklist

❏ Prepare a close-out plan

❏ Verify scope

    – Contractual obligations

    – Administrative obligations

    – WBS (tasks and deliverables)

❏ Obtain customer acceptance of deliverables

❏ Document and archive files and records

❏ Document lessons learned

❏ Reassign resources

❏ Notify all stakeholders of project completion

❏ Celebrate success

COURSE ASSESSMENT

Course Title: _____ Date: _____

For each of the five areas covered by the course, indicate:

— How much you knew about the areas before the course.

— How much you know now about the area.

— How valuable you think having the knowledge/skill in the area will be to you.

Assign a rating of 0 to 9 for each of the three questions, using the scale below.

0	1 2 3	4 5 6	7 8 9
Nothing/No Value	A Little	Some	A Lot

KNEW BEFORE	KNOW NOW	COURSE AREA	VALUE
		1. Project Selection Techniques — Payback Period — ROI — IRR — NPV — Benefit to Cost	
		2. Project Concept Phase — Defining Requirements — WBS — Project Charter	
		3. Project Development Phase — Network Analysis — Project Management Plan	
		4. Project Implementation Phase — Risk Management — Earned Value	
		5. Project Close-Out — Close-Out Procedures — Project Audits — Lessons Learned	

Welcome to *The Project Management Workshop*

- Emergency phone number
- Local emergency exit procedures
- Fax number
- Floor/facility layout
- Breaks
- Start and end expectations
- Attendance
  - Prerequisites
  - Maximum absence

Start on time = End on time

1-1

Workshop Objectives (*continued*)

- Develop a Work Breakdown Structure
- Perform a network analysis
- Develop schedules using the Gantt chart
- Develop a risk management plan
- Develop and use a change management process
- Control project budgets and schedules using Earned Value
- Close a project

1-2

Workshop Objectives (*continued*)

- Develop a Work Breakdown Structure
- Perform a network analysis
- Develop schedules using the Gantt chart
- Develop a risk management plan
- Develop and use a change management process
- Control project budgets and schedules using Earned Value
- Close a project

1-3

Project Management Model

LIFE-CYCLE PHASES OF A PROJECT

Selection	Concept	Development	Implementation	Close-out
Activities	**Activities**	**Activities**	**Activities**	**Activities**
•Financial analysis •Analyze strategic goals •Rank projects •Choose projects to pursue	•Gather data •Analyze requirements •Develop charter •Develop WBS •Organize project team •Kickoff meeting	•Refine WBS •Perform network analysis •Develop schedules •Develop plans	•Implement control process •Control project progress with earned value	•Scope verification •Technical audit •Financial audit •Contract close-out

1-4

Workshop Agenda

Time	Day 1
8:30	Module 1: Introduction to the Project Management Workshop
9:30	Module 2: Project Selection Techniques
10:30	↓
11:00	Module 3: Project Concept Phase
12:00	Lunch (1 hr.)
1:00	Module 3: Project Concept Phase (*cont.*)
2:00	Module 4: Project Development Phase
3:00	↓
4:00	Review Modules 2, 3, 4
4:30	Day 1 Ends

1-5

Workshop Agenda (*continued*)

Time	Day 2
8:30	Recap Day 1 Modules/Begin Case Study
9:30	Case Study
10:30	↓
11:00	
12:00	Lunch
1:00	Module 5: Project Implementation (*cont.*)
2:00	Module 6: Project Close-out
3:00	Module 7: Course Wrap-up
4:00	Day 2 Ends
4:30	

1-6

Module 2: The Project Selection Phase

How Projects Are Selected

2-0

Objectives for Module 2

At the end of this module you will be able to:

- Identify, define and apply various project selection techniques

- Describe the advantages and disadvantages of each selection technique

- Describe the use of project selection techniques

2-1

Project Selection Techniques

There are several project selection techniques. The most commonly used are:

- Payback or break-even point

- Return on Investment (ROI)

- Internal Rate of Return (IRR)

- Net Present Value (NPV)

- Benefit to Cost Ratio (B/C)

2-3

Payback or Break-Even Point

One of the most commonly used "hurdle" rates today is the Payback or Break-Even Point:

Payback: The point in a project when revenues equal costs.

How used:
  • The payback period has to be equal to or less than target set by senior management. Often used as an early assessment of project viability.

Advantages:
  • Fast
  • Simple

Disadvantages:
  • Assumes steady revenue stream
  • Does not take into account the cost of money

2-4

Payback Period (*sample calculation*)

The estimated cost of a project is $10,000,000. The project is expected to yield $2,000,000 per year. What is the Payback Period?

Solution:

Payback = total cost/yearly revenues
         = 10,000,000/2,000,000
         = 5 years

2-5

Return on Investment (ROI)

Return on Investment (ROI), another very commonly used selection technique, is a financial measure of how much profit is likely from invested costs.

How used: Average profits are divided by the average costs expected over the period of the project's life. Hurdle rate is set by the senior management; product ROI must equal or exceed the hurdle rate

Advantages:
  • Used by most companies as one viability measure
  • Easily understood and calculated

Disadvantages:
  • Does not take into account cost of money

2-6

ROI (*sample calculation*)

The average cost of a 6-year project is estimated to be $6,000,000 per year, and the estimated total returns are expected to be $12,000,000. What is the ROI?

Solution:

The average return is 12 million/6 = $2 million per year

ROI = (Average Returns/Average Costs) x 100%
   = (2 M/6 M) x 100%
   = 33%

2-7

Internal Rate of Return (IRR)

Internal Rate of Return (IRR) is used to compare against other strategic financial Goals. It is the interest rate that makes the present value of all revenues equal to the present value of all costs.

How used:
- Usually measured against the IRR of the organization but may be an arbitrarily set "hurdle rate"
- Used by most organizations to determine project viability

Advantages:
- Takes into account the cost of money

Disadvantages:
- Can't be directly calculated; must be iterated from tables or by spreadsheet software

2-8

Preparing Data for an IRR Calculation

The IRR is much more accurate than the Payback or ROI methods because it accounts for the cost of money. It is used as a measure of a project's worth compared with the company's cost of capital rate.

Question: You have estimated the following revenues and costs for your project. If the corporate cost of capital is 18%, how does your project compare?

Years	Revenues	Costs
0	0	$10,000
1	$12,000	$10,000
2	$16,000	$10,000
3	$20,000	$15,000
4	$40,000	$15,000
5	$60,000	$20,000

(continued on next slide)

2-9

IRR Sample Calculation

Solution: Use the equation

$$PV = \sum_{t=0}^{n} \frac{PV}{(1 + i)^t}$$

PV = present value of money
FV = future value of money
i = Internal rate of return
t = time period, i.e., 1st year, 2nd year
n = number of time periods

The PV of the revenues and costs are determined for the project's life cycle.

$$PV\ (Revenues) = \frac{12{,}000}{(1 + i)^1} + \frac{16{,}000}{(1 + i)^2} + \frac{20{,}000}{(1 + i)^3} + \frac{40{,}000}{(1 + i)^4} + \frac{60{,}000}{(1 + i)^5}$$

$$PV\ (Costs) = \frac{10{,}000}{(1 + i)^0} + \frac{10{,}000}{(1 + i)^1} + \frac{10{,}000}{(1 + i)^2} + \frac{15{,}000}{(1 + i)^3} + \frac{15{,}000}{(1 + i)^4} + \frac{20{,}000}{(1 + i)^5}$$

(continued on next slide)   2-10

IRR Sample Calculation (*continued*)

Set the PV(Revenues) = PV(Costs)

$$\frac{12{,}000}{(1 + i)^1} + \frac{16{,}000}{(1 + i)^2} + \frac{20{,}000}{(1 + i)^3} + \frac{40{,}000}{(1 + i)^4} + \frac{60{,}000}{(1 + i)^5} =$$

$$\frac{10{,}000}{(1 + i)^0} + \frac{10{,}000}{(1 + i)^1} + \frac{10{,}000}{(1 + i)^2} + \frac{15{,}000}{(1 + i)^3} + \frac{15{,}000}{(1 + i)^4} + \frac{20{,}000}{(1 + i)^5}$$

The computer iterates to determine value of i that makes the two sides of the equation equal. In this case,

$$i = 24\%$$

**Project i (24%) > company cost of capital (18%).
Therefore, pursue project.**

2-11

Net Present Value

Net Present Value is the difference between the Present Value of the project revenues and costs.

How used:
- Uses the corporate IRR or another interest rate index
- "Goodness" is measured by whether NPV is positive or negative
  - NPV > 1, revenues greater than costs
  - NPV < 1, revenues less than costs
  - NPV = 0, revenues and costs the same

Advantages:
- Takes into account the cost of money
- Very accurate compared to other methods

Disadvantages:
- Not easily understood by everyone
- Costs and revenues not always easy to quantify

2-12

Set Up Data Table for NPV

Example: You have estimated the following revenues and costs for your project. If the corporate IRR is 18%, what is the Net Present Value of your project?

Years	Revenues	Costs
0	0	$10,000
1	$12,000	$10,000
2	$16,000	$10,000
3	$20,000	$15,000
4	$40,000	$15,000
5	$60,000	$20,000

2-13

NPV Sample Calculation

Solution: Use the formula for Present Value to determine PV of revenues and costs.

$$PV = \sum_{t=0}^{n} \frac{PV}{(1 + i)^t}$$

$$PV(Revenues) = \frac{12,000}{(1 + .18)^1} + \frac{16,000}{(1 + .18)^2} + \frac{20,000}{(1 + .18)^3} + \frac{40,000}{(1 + .18)^4} + \frac{60,000}{(1 + .18)^5}$$

$$= 10,169 + 11,491 + 12,173 + 20,632 + 26,227 = \boxed{80,691}$$

$$PV(Costs) = \frac{10,000}{(1 + i)^0} + \frac{10,000}{(1 + i)^1} + \frac{10,000}{(1 + i)^2} + \frac{15,000}{(1 + i)^3} + \frac{15,000}{(1 + i)^4} + \frac{20,000}{(1 + i)^5}$$

$$= 10,000 + 8,475 + 7,182 + 9,129 + 7,737 + 8,742 = \boxed{51,265}$$

2-14

(continued on next slide)

Solution to Sample NPV Calculation

Net Present Value is the difference between the Present Value of the Revenues and Costs. Therefore,

NPV = PV (Revenues) – PV (Costs)
    = 80,691 – 51,265
    = 29,426

NPV is positive; pursue the project.

2-15

Benefit to Cost (B/C)

Benefit to cost is a useful measure of the worth of a project because it provides a comparison of the relative difference between benefits and costs.

To calculate B/C, the Present Value (PV) of the project's benefits (Revenues) is divided by the (PV) of the project's costs.

Revenues and costs are estimated from historical data or comparisons with similar projects and their PVs are calculated.

B/C Interpretation:

B/C > 1; benefits greater than costs

B/C < 1; benefits less than costs

B/C = 1; break even (benefits and costs are equal)

2-16

Advantages and Disadvantages of B/C

Advantages:

- Takes into account the cost of money
- Very accurate compared to other methods
- Easier to interpret ratios or percentages than pure numbers

Disadvantages:

- Not easily understood by everyone
- Costs and revenues not always easy to quantify

2-17

Set Up Data Table for B/C

Question: You have estimated the following revenues and costs for your project. If the corporate IRR is 18%, what is the B/C ratio for your project?

Years	Revenues	Costs
0	0	$10,000
1	$12,000	$10,000
2	$16,000	$10,000
3	$20,000	$15,000
4	$40,000	$15,000
5	$60,000	$20,000

2-18

B/C Sample Calculation

Solution: The PV of the revenues and costs were calculated previously.

PV(Revenues) = $80,691

PV(Costs) = $51,265

B/C = 80,691/51,265
or B/C = 1.57

2-19

Selection Techniques Exercise

Using the data in the table, determine:
      1. The net present value of the project
      2. The B/C ratio
      3. The payback period
Assume IRR is 10%.

Years	Revenues	Costs
0	0	$10,000
1	$10,000	$25,000
2	$30,000	$20,000
3	$60,000	$50,000
4	$100,000	$50,000
5	$100,000	$50,000

2-20

Key Messages—Module 2

The key messages from this module are:

- Many project managers are involved in the project selection process or are asked for input into the analysis

- There are several techniques for determining a project's viability. The most common ones are:
  – Payback or break-even point
  – Return on Investment (ROI)
  – Internal Rate of Return (IRR)
  – Net Present Value (NPV)
  – Benefit to Cost Ratio (B/C)

2-21

Module 3: The Project Concept Phase

Defining and Organizing the Project

3-0

Objectives for Module 3

At the end of this module you will be able to:

- Describe the elements of a Statement of Work (SOW)

- Explain how to interpret a SOW

- Identify and describe project requirements

- Describe a Work Breakdown Structure (WBS)

3-1

Objectives for Module 3 (*continued*)

- Develop a high level WBS

- List project stakeholders and develop strategies for obtaining their support

- Describe the use and structure of a Project Charter

- Understand the elements of and conduct a kickoff meeting

3-2

Activities in the Concept Phase

The project manager is chiefly concerned about understanding and organizing the project during this phase. The principal activities are:

- Interpreting the project requirements from:
  - Statement of Work (SOW)
  - Specifications
  - Contractual documents

- Developing a high level Work Breakdown Structure (WBS)

- Identifying project team skill requirements

- Providing input to the Project Charter

3-4

Statement of Work

The Statement of Work (SOW) is the principal document for transmitting the customer's project requirements. The characteristics of a SOW include:

- Written description of the project requirements

- High level schedule and milestones

- Occasionally a budget (usually for internal projects only)

- Acceptance criteria

3-5

Statement of Work (*continued*)

- Key personnel in the customer organization

- Technical or performance specifications

- Scope change process

- Communication requirements

3-6

SOW Outline

A typical SOW will have the following outline:

Section Number	Section Heading
1.0	Introduction
2.0	Key Assumptions
3.0	Seller/Provider Responsibilities
4.0	Buyer/Customer Responsibilities
5.0	Estimated Schedule
6.0	Project Acceptance Criteria
7.0	Type of Contract and Payment Schedule
8.0	Additional Terms and Conditions
9.0	Miscellaneous
10.0	Appendixes

3-7

Reasons That SOWs Are Misinterpreted

Projects fail most often because the project requirements are not fully understood or they are misinterpreted. Reasons include:

- Poorly written SOWs

- Use of ambiguous words and phrases

- Conflicting requirements

- Lack of communication between customer and project manager

- Unreasonable requirements, particularly in schedules

3-8

Reading the SOW

Reading the SOW critically helps to focus on and identify the requirements. A disciplined process for reading the SOW will follow this pattern:

- Summarize the project background and general purpose

- Describe the project goals and objectives

- Relate the project goals and objectives to the organization's strategic goals

- List all "shall" statements

- Identify and list all assumptions and constraints

3-9

Reading the SOW (*continued*)

- List all the project deliverables; data, services, hardware, software, documents
  - Decompose deliverables into component tasks
  - Identify required resources

- Gantt chart any imposed schedule dates or other key milestones

- List any risks

- Determine what the acceptance criteria are

3-10

Collecting the Requirements

Once the SOW has been thoroughly dissected, the requirements can be collected for interpretation and refining. They will be the:

- "Shall" statements

- Specific deliverables such as services, data, documentation, software, or hardware

- Tasks that are required to reach the customer's stated goals

- Ancillary tasks that support reaching the customer's goals, such as

  - Acquiring special equipment
  - Hiring specialists
- Reporting and communicating tasks to the customer and key internal personnel

3-11

Translating Requirements

Once the requirements are collected and generally understood, they can be interpreted and refined. The steps are:

1. List all the deliverables
2. Use an experienced initial team to help decompose and refine each of the task requirements
3. Develop a high level Work Breakdown Structure (WBS) for the project
4. Identify the resources that are needed to accomplish the task
5. Identify other project interdependencies
6. Identify risks because of project priorities and any constraints or assumptions that have been made
7. Develop strategies for completing the project

3-12

Initial Project Team

Initially, the project manager may be the only member of the project team. After analyzing the SOW, the project manager organizes an "initial" team to development requirements and identify team skills. Initial team members:

- Are usually experienced, even supervisory level

- May not be a part of the final team composition

- Provide expertise on SOW interpretation and WBS development

- Are knowledgeable about identifying skill sets and team composition/organization

3-13

Work Breakdown Structure

The Work Breakdown Structure (WBS) is the most important project management tool and is the basis for all other project management planning. It is a structured way of decomposing a project into its various components. The WBS:

- Reduces the project into successively lower levels of detail

- Provides a way of identifying tasks and task resources

- Provides a structure for estimating costs

- Provides a structure for identifying project skill sets

3-14

Work Breakdown Structure (*continued*)

- Is used to develop network logic diagrams

- Is used to develop schedules

- Is used to identify risks

3-15

WBS Formats

The WBS can be represented in two ways:

1. Indented
   - Each lower level is indented as the project is decomposed
   - Resembles an outline format

2. Graphical or tree
   - Resembles a traditional organizational structure
   - Excellent for visual presentation of project tasks structure

3-16

Indented WBS

```
1.0  Project or Contract Name
     1.1  Major Project Subsystem A
          1.1.1  Task 1
                 1.1.1.1  Subtask 1
                 1.1.1.2  Subtask 2
          1.1.2  Task 2
                 1.1.2.1  Subtask 1
                 1.1.2.2  Subtask 2
     1.2  Major Project Subsystem B
          1.2.1  Task 1
          1.2.2  Task 2
                 1.2.2.1  Subtask 1
                 1.2.2.2  Subtask 2
                          1.2.2.2.1  Work Package 1
```

3-17

Graphical WBS

3-18

Developing High-Level WBS

Initially, there may not be enough information or understanding of the require-ments to develop a complete WBS. The first task is to develop at least a high level WBS so that:

- Major project deliverables can be identified
- Project scope parameters are clear
- General requirements are understood enough to identify major tasks
- Team member composition can be established
- Top level cost, schedule, and resource estimates can be developed/confirmed

3-19

Stakeholders

Crucial to the project manager's success is the early identification and management of stakeholders.

Definition: A stakeholder is anyone with a vested interest in the project.
- Customer

- Sponsor

- Project team members

- Functional managers

3-20

The Stakeholder Analysis Worksheet

A stakeholder analysis includes identifying the stakeholder and determining how to sway them.

Stakeholder	+	0	−	Reason Against Project	Strengths & Weaknesses	Strategy

3-21

The Project Charter

The project charter is the major output of the Concept Phase of the project life cycle. It:

- Is an internal document signed by a senior executive who has functional authority over all the project's functional relationships
- Authorizes the project manager to begin work
- Is not a legal document
- Is a way to assign a project priority
- Is a way to obtain buy-in for the project

3-22

Major Elements of a Project Charter

A project charter identifies the project manager and gives him or her the authority to start the project. The major elements of a project charter are:

- Project Scope—Provides a short summary of the project scope and the deliverables.
- Assignment—Announces the project manager by name, the name of the project, and the customer's name.
- Responsibilities—Specifies the project manager's responsibilities in delivering the project, and the functional groups responsibilities in supporting it.
- Authority—Outlines the project manager's authority limits.
- Priority—Assigns a priority to the project relative to the other projects in the organization.

3-23

Kickoff Meetings

Kickoff meetings are excellent communication and team-building opportunities. The principal purpose is to get the project started on the right foot and should have all or most of the following objectives:

- Introduce team members to one another
- Establish working relationships and lines of communication
- Set team goals and objectives
- Review project status

3-24

Kickoff Meetings (*continued*)

- Review project plans

- Identify project problem areas

- Establish individual and group responsibilities and accountabilities

- Obtain individual and group commitments

3-25

The Kickoff Meeting Agenda

Kickoff meetings are important communication tools

1. Introductions
2. Vision
3. Scope and objectives
4. Risks, challenges, and project constraints
5. Project approach
6. Team members and project organization chart
7. Roles and responsibilities
8. Timeline
9. Major milestones
10. Process, standards, methods, and tools

3-26

The Kickoff Meeting Agenda (*continued*)

11. Quality plan
12. Project management and schedule planning standards and guidelines
13. Centralized documentation storage facility
14. Time collection and project status requirements
15. Training schedule
16. Lessons learned from previous post-project reviews
17. Success factors
18. Project expectations and next steps
19. Unresolved issues, responsibility assignments, and target dates
20. Adjournment

3-27

Key Messages—Module 3

- The SOW is the key document for transmitting the project requirements
- The SOW must be interpreted correctly to identify all the requirements
- The WBS is developed by an initial team once the requirements are identified
- The major output of the Concept Phase is the Project Charter
- The Project Charter identifies the project manager and gives him or her the authority to begin the project
- The kickoff meeting is critical for establishing communication channels and for team building

3-28

Module 4: The Project Development Phase

Planning the Project

4-0

Objectives for Module 4

At the end of this module you will be able to:

- Develop project budget, schedule, and resource estimates from the WBS
- Develop a precedence table from the WBS
- Develop a network using the Precedence Diagramming Method (PDM)
- Develop a schedule using a Gantt chart
- Describe the elements of a project management plan

4-1

Activities in the Development Phase

The project manager is chiefly concerned about refining the
requirements and developing the project plans during this phase.
The principal activities are:

- Selecting and forming the project team
- Refining the requirements and clarifying the SOW
- Developing a complete WBS
- Developing budget, schedule, and resource estimates
- Developing a network analysis to determine critical tasks and the shortest time to complete the project
- Creating Gantt charts to describe the project schedules
- Performing a risk analysis
- Completing ancillary plans to support the project

4-3

Estimating Budgets

Project budgets are typically developed using one of the following methods:

- Rough order-of-magnitude (ROM)
- Top-down (analogous)
- Bottom-up (engineering or business)

4-4

Rough Order-of-Magnitude

Rough Order-of-Magnitude or ROM is the easiest and fastest estimating method,
which provides an approximate figure for the project. It is useful as a general
estimate of effort and:

- Is based on experience and some historical data, but is mostly based on intuition
- Gives a quick snapshot of the project costs or schedule
- Is usually done by one person

Disadvantages

- Is very inaccurate with estimates ranging between −25% and +75%
- It almost always sticks as the estimate when it is meant to provide an approximate guess for early planning purposes

4-5

Top-Down or Analogous Estimating

Top-down estimating is based on historical data and comparisons with other similar projects.

- Based on comparisons with similar projects within the group or company

- Parametric models are often used to extrapolate data from one project to fit another

- Relatively quick estimate and useful for obtaining reasonably good estimates

- Most appropriate technique for top level planning and decision making

Disadvantages
- Accurate to within –10% and +25%

- Good enough for planning, but not good enough for a final estimate

4-6

Bottom-Up or Definitive Estimating

The bottom-up estimating method is the most accurate of the three methods.

- Based upon the lowest level of the WBS

- Estimates are determined with the person who performs the task

- The project cost is "rolled-up" from the lowest WBS level to the highest WBS level

- This technique is used to update estimates for the final project budget

Disadvantages

- Takes time

- Within –5% and +10% accurate

4-7

Network Analysis

Network analysis is a scheduling tool developed from the WBS. It is used to:

- Show the interdependence of project tasks

- Determine the project duration

- Determine float or slack in a path

- Determine the project's critical path

- Expose risks

4-8

Steps in Developing a Network

Once the WBS is developed to the lowest desired level, the network can be developed and analyzed:

- The project team and other selected functional experts determine the interdependence of all the tasks
- Develop a precedence table after all task dependencies are established
- Construct the network
- Determine the duration, critical path, and float for each task

4-9

Precedence Tables

A precedence table is necessary for developing networks or logic diagrams. They usually have the following form:

Task Identifier	WBS Element	Predecessor	Task Duration
a	Task 1	—	5
b	Task 2	—	4
c	Task 3	a	4
d	Task 4	b	4
e	Task 5	b	3
f	Task 6	c	4
g	Task 7	d	5
h	Task 8	e	8
i	Task 9	f,g,h	8
j	Task 10	e	8

4-10

The Network Diagram

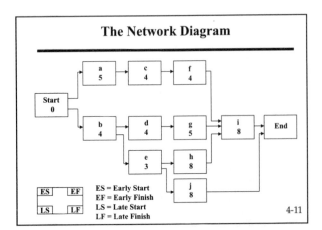

| ES | EF |
| LS | LF |

ES = Early Start
EF = Early Finish
LS = Late Start
LF = Late Finish

4-11

Early Schedule

In analyzing the network, the early schedule is determined first.

- Begin at the project start node and determine the earliest possible time each task can begin and finish

- The "Early Finish" of each task in succession is determined by adding the task duration to its "Early Start"

- The "Early Start" of a task is the "Early Finish" of the preceding task

- The process of determining the early schedule is referred to as the "Forward Pass"

4-12

Early Start

When two or more arrows enter a task, the "Early Start" is the LARGEST of the preceding task's "Early Finish"

Example:

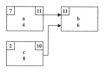

4-13

Forward Pass: The Early Schedule

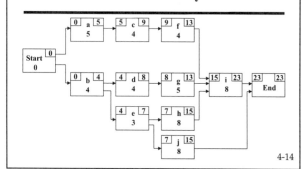

4-14

Late Schedule

The late schedule cannot be determined until after the early schedule is known.

- From the end of the project, work backwards through the network to determine the late schedule.

- Start with the duration determined by the Forward Pass as the beginning point

- The "Late Finish" of a task is the "Late Start" of the succeeding task

- The process of determining the late schedule is referred to as the Backward Pass.

4-15

Late Finish

When two or more arrows back into a task, the "Late Finish" is the SMALLEST of the succeeding task's "Late Start"
- Example:

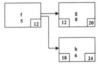

4-16

Backward Pass: The Late Schedule

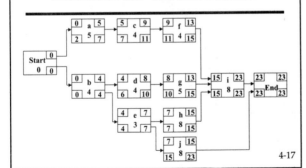

4-17

Project Duration, Float, and Critical Path

Three important pieces of information derived from network analyses are the duration, amount of float or slack in each path, and the project's critical path.

- Project duration: The shortest required time to complete the project.

- Float: The amount of time the start of a task can be delayed without impacting the schedule.

    Float = Latest Start – Earliest Start or Latest Finish – Earliest Finish

- Critical Path: The longest path through the network or the path with zero float. This path identifies the tasks that have to be managed closely so that no slips to the schedule occur.

4-18

The Critical Path

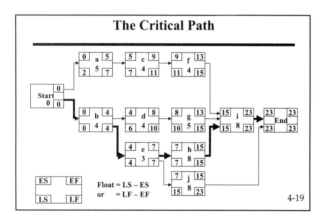

ES	EF
LS	LF

Float = LS – ES
or   = LF – EF

4-19

Exercise 4-1

Using the information from the precedence table, construct a Network Diagram and answer the following questions:
1. What is the project duration?
2. What is the critical path?
3. How much float is in Task ....?

Task Identifier	WBS Element	Predecessor	Task Duration
a	Task 1	—	5
b	Task 2	—	6
c	Task 3	a	2
d	Task 4	a,b	5
e	Task 5	b	4
f	Task 6	c,d,e	4

4-20

Gantt Charts

Gantt charts are developed after the network analysis is completed.
They are used for:

- Showing beginning and ending points for each of the project tasks

- Graphically depicting project progress against the project baseline

- Communicating project progress to stakeholders

4-21

Sample Gantt Chart

The Gantt chart is a bar chart that shows each task and the beginning
and ending dates. Other information can be added to the bars as
desired

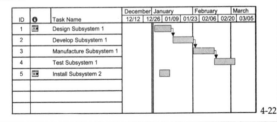

ID	❶	Task Name	December	January		February		March
			12/12	12/26	01/09	01/23	02/06	02/20	03/05
1	▦	Design Subsystem 1							
2		Develop Subsystem 1							
3		Manufacture Subsystem 1							
4		Test Subsystem 1							
5	▦	Install Subsystem 2							

4-22

The Project Management Plan

Once the schedule, budget, and resource estimates are completed, the project
plan can be finalized. A format that will fit most projects will have these elements:

    I. Executive Summary
    II. Project Requirements and Objectives
    III. General Methodology or Technical Approach
    IV. Contractual Requirements
    V. Schedules
    VI. Resource Requirements
        A. Equipment
        B. Materials
        C. People
    VII. Potential Risks
    VIII. Performance Evaluations

    Appendices
        Project Charter
        Supporting plans
        Drawings
        Specifications

4-23

Top 10 Signs, cont'd from page 1

5. Your project team is too small.

Maybe it's just you and one other person who meet behind closed doors.

Solution. Projects should be collaborative efforts of many, or the results won't be trusted. Get out and see the processes that will be affected, and enroll others in your team. Build consensus among all stakeholders.

4. Everyone is working off a different schedule.

Solution. Use a master plan. Your schedule must be updated on a regular basis by the one person who has been given that authority. Then the schedule should be distributed weekly. A software tool may provide help in this area.

3. People are exiting in droves; the team dynamic is changing on a regular basis.

It's not uncommon for team members to leave for a better job as soon as they have some of this project installation experience under their belt.

Solution. Assess morale and risk upfront. You may want to commit to match job offers for team members for the duration of the project. Or you may provide for contingencies by double stacking the team.

2. Nobody is looking at company processes or culture issues.

Solution. The team must examine how business is currently being carried out. Adding new systems and technologies isn't enough. The processes and procedures need to be reviewed, and may need to change to support the technology. Work flow should be defined.

1. Project is due at the end of the week and you haven't started.

This means you have an unreasonable project, and something must give.

Solution. You can start by adding a dedicated senior project manager to the project, and then provide incentives for top talent to join the team. Remove competing projects, barriers to communication and actions, non-essential scope, and resource and cost barriers. ∎

HOW EFFICIENT IS YOUR AUDITOR?

In a recent article, William C. Balhof, a partner at Postle-thwaite & Netterville, A.P.A.C., discussed the best practices of auditors. His purpose was to advise auditors on how to operate more efficiently and profitably. But by turning the tables a bit, you—as a client—can look at these best practices to see if your auditor is operating efficiently on your behalf; that is, making the best use of your time, and enlisting assistance from your company in appropriate ways.

Obtaining information. Auditors need information, which you, as the client, must prepare. Do they give you a list in advance of what prepared-by-client (PBC) data is needed? Balhoff suggests that auditors also provide examples, checklists and due dates to make the process easier for you as well as them. The data your company is expected to provide can be written into the engagement letter.

Providing education. The auditors should try to educate you, the client, says Balhof. He recommends that the auditor communicate the purpose and value of the audit to the directors. The directors, in turn, should communicate this message to staff. Balhoff suggests that auditors offer advice throughout the process whenever improvements can be pointed out. He also recommends an exit conference where the auditor shows how the audit time could be decreased for the next go-round. Of course, the client could also offer their suggestions at the conference.

Financial incentives. Auditors will often charge more if the client doesn't have data ready, and prepared correctly, at the time specified, and Balhof agrees with this. As the client, you'll want to be sure the charges are reasonable and conform to the engagement letter.

Providing the right staff. Balhoff notes that "a stable and dedicated staff means continuity and familiarity with clients." Do you find the auditor's staff dedicated? Do the same people come year after year? Such familiarly breeds efficiency.

Proper planning. The required amount of planning will vary from one audit to another. An experienced auditor visiting a long-time client may not do much planning other than reviewing last year's audit and considering ways to improve it. But where there's less familiarly, it may behoove the auditor to do some planning to prevent inefficiency and over-auditing. This may include learning about the client's operations, business and industry, and considering client risks.

Using risk assessment. Good auditors will correlate their efforts to levels of risk and materiality. Balhoff recommends use of analytical procedures, finding them more efficient than transaction testing in low- to moderate-risk situations. You want your auditors to devote more of their efforts to high-risk areas. ∎

Accountants as Project Managers

Some of the recognized strengths of accountants are very useful in project management, while some weaknesses can hurt a project.

Useful Traits	Less-than-Useful Traits
Attention to detail	Looking for the last penny
Deadline driven	Operating solo
Able to translate technical information	Poor in verbal communications
Good at using checklists	Slow to change
Knowledgeable about setting up repeatable processes	Unable to think out of the box

You might understandably reject some of the stereotyped portrayals above. Still, there's probably enough truth there for accountants to look closely at themselves and see if they can improve what they bring to the project management table. This exercise also helps in choosing, as other members of your team, those who can fill in the gaps.

Controllers *Update*

Published by the Controllers Council of the IMA

November 2001 ■ *Issue No. 196*

TOP 10 SIGNS YOUR SOFTWARE IMPLEMENTATION IS IN TROUBLE

At the IMA Annual Conference in New Orleans last June, two directors from Navision Damgaard US gave a presentation with the above title. But their program could just as easily have been called, "How Accounting and Finance Professionals Can Ace the Job of Project Manager." Judging from the many questions and comments from the enthusiastic audience, accountants and finance people are often taking the lead role in software implementation and other projects these days.

The two speakers represented the ying and yang of accounting software implementation. That is, Geni G. Whitehouse, CPA, carried the banner for accountants, while Greg Hunt, PMP (Project Management Professional) represented the project management troops. And while they directed some good-natured jibes at each other, in actuality they have a history of working together on teams, where each one's strengths complement the other's.

The two agreed on some key differences between accounting and project management. Accounting always has something to balance back to, Whitehouse observed. It involves repetitive processes, historical tracking, and measurement, and is basically two dimensional: debit and credit, red and black. By comparison, project management has many dimensions, including schedule, cost and scope. Repetitive processes are often involved, but project management is basically about change. The project manager needs to find where the company can go in a certain area. "We try to measure," says Hunt, "but our key issue is time rather than balancing things."

Below are the ten signs that a software implementation—or any other project, for that matter—is in trouble, together with some solutions to prevent or cure the problems. We present them here, as Whitehouse and Hunt did, in reverse order of impact.

10. The scope of the project is not well defined. People keep adding to the dimensions of the project, causing the dreaded "scope creep."

Solution. You need to define the scope at the onset of the project. After all, says Hunt, you "can't hit a moving target." Prepare a statement setting forth the project's scope early on, and have all participants agree to it.

9. You have no project plan. As a result, activities are failing to follow a critical path.

Solution. Bring all the players together, and break the scope into tasks. Then make sure the players are committed to the tasks and the schedule. You want everyone to understand the interdependencies between tasks. Project management software can help here.

8. Project management is not an enterprise priority. It's not uncommon for a company to have 50 priorities at one time. Yet companies can deal with only so many priorities. When there are too many, ample time won't be allotted to your project.

Solution. Break the project into small wins. This is a way to keep attention on your project. By demonstrating success, you keep executive support high.

7. The executive sponsor of the project is invisible. He/she is not vocal and vigilant in support of your project.

Solution. Meet with the sponsor and ask directly for the support you need. If necessary, explain the whole process you're engaged in and get the sponsor's buy-in for the schedule. Coach him/her to be out there in front.

6. You've invested all of the intellectual capital in your consultants.

Solution. Remember that when the consultant leaves, you own what's left. Get involved. Have the end-user do a set-up of the system. Then have him or her teach and coach the staff. Demand documentation from consultants, and be sure the vendor has time with staff to train them. In addition, it's a good idea to have someone other than the consultant write down what's being done, step by step.

As a preliminary move, Hunt and Whitehouse advised that you carefully choose the people from the consultant's group who will work on your team. Your contract with the consultant should give you that authority.

continues on page 2

Inside

Your Auditors:
How efficient are they? 2
Q&A's from the Internet:
Delays in entering invoices 3
M&E Policy:
Limits for the sales force 4

Key Messages—Module 4

The key messages of this module are:

- There are three primary methods for estimating budgets, resources, and schedules. They are:
  - ROM
  - Top-down
  - Bottom-up

- The precedence diagramming method is a critical analysis tool. It provides the following information:
  - Project duration
  - Critical path
  - Float in each task

- The Gantt chart is a bar chart showing the beginning and ending of each task

- The project plan can be finalized once the budget, schedule, and resource estimates are completed

4-24

Module 5: The Project Implementation Phase

Monitoring and Controlling the Project

5-0

Objectives for Module 5

At the end of this module you will be able to:

- Develop a change management process

- Identify and prioritize project risks

- Develop a risk management plan

- Employ "earned value" concepts and formulas to track project progress

5-1

Activities in the Implementation Phase

The project manager is chiefly concerned about monitoring and controlling the project relative to the project baseline during this phase. The principal activities are:

- Setting up the project organization
- Securing the required resources
- Setting up and executing the work packages
- Directing, monitoring, and controlling the project

5-3

Goals of the Change-Control System

A well developed and documented change-control process is crucial to project management success. Change-control systems should:

- Continually identify changes, actual or proposed, as they occur
- Reveal the consequences of the proposed changes in terms of cost and schedule impacts
- Permit managerial analysis, investigation of alternatives, and an acceptance or rejection checkpoint
- Communicate changes to all stakeholders
- Insure that changes are implemented

5-4

The Change-Control Process

5-5

Why Risk Analysis?

The main objectives of a risk analysis are:

- Timeliness: A risk analysis must identify issues before they occur

- Priorities: Because of insufficient time or resources, a risk analysis must help assign realistic priorities

- Aggregation: The risk analysis must help aggregate all the individual risks into a measure of overall project risk

- Decision support: The risk analysis must produce information in a form that supports the decision makers

5-6

Types of Risk

There are two kinds of risk in a project. They are:

1. Business risks: Potential for loss but also an opportunity for gain
   - Example 1: Customer expands the project scope.
   - Example 2: A project task requires use or development of new technology. Successful completion of the development opens a new market to the company.

2. Pure or insurable risks: Potential only for loss
   - Example 1: Company is located in an area susceptible to hurricanes.
   - Example 2: Company has no expertise required by one of the project tasks.

5-7

Risk Assessment Methods

Methods for assessing risks fall into three broad groups:

1. Issue-based methods

2. Scoring techniques

3. Quantitative techniques

5-8

Risk Classifications for
Issue-Based Risk Assessment

Issue-based methods usually start with the assertion that all risks can be classified under a set of headings, such as:

- Commercial
- Technical
- Programmatic
- Resource availability
- Project priorities

5-9

Advantages and Disadvantages of
Issue-Based Risk Assessment

Advantages
- Provides a checklist, which helps in remembering to look at all project elements
- Checklists provide access to the experience of others

Disadvantages
- Checklists tend to be seen as exhaustive, giving a sense of false security
- Checklists don't help provide an overall level of risk in a project nor do they help determine realistic budget and schedule estimates

5-10

Scoring Techniques

Scoring techniques are natural extensions of checklists. They:

- Are based on a questionnaire
- Provide a checklist approach as memory joggers
- Ask for a numerical rating of a factor if it appears in the task or project
- Provide for a way to assess the overall project riskiness by adding the risk assessment points

5-11

Advantages and Disadvantages of Scoring Techniques

Advantages

- Combine the checklist approach with a numerical rating of the task riskiness
- Provide a way to measure overall project riskiness
- Valuable because they highlight separate issues and indicate which are the most important

Disadvantages

- Arbitrary scoring measures often are difficult to interpret
- Don't provide a clear insight into the risk's impact if it occurs
- The relationship between individual risks in a project and the risk to the whole project is more complicated than simple addition

5-12

Quantitative Techniques

Quantitative techniques are designed to identify the risk event and to determine the impact to the project if the event occurs. Quantitative techniques:

- Are based on the planning structures project managers use, i.e., cost breakdowns and schedules
- Identify the risk event
- Determine a probability of likelihood of occurrence
- Provide a way to prioritize the risks relative to the overall impact to the project
- Provide a basis for decision making

5-13

Advantages and Disadvantages of Quantitative Techniques

Advantages

- Provide a measure of the impact of a risk event on a project
- Provide a mechanism for decision making
- Easier to rank

Disadvantages

- Probabilities are not always easy to assign
- Using probabilities requires an understanding of how to apply "expected value" theory

5-14

Ranking Risks

Once the risks are identified, they can be prioritized. An easy-to-use technique involves comparing each identified risk with every other risk to determine which has the greatest impact on the project.

A	A	B	C	D	E	F	G
B			X	X	X	X	X
C				X	X	X	X
D					X	X	X
E						X	X
F							X
G							

5-15

Six Major Sections of a Risk-Management Plan

1. Project summary and system description

2. Approach to risk management

3. Application issues and problems

4. Other relevant plans

5. Conclusions and recommendations

6. Approvals

5-16

A Risk-Management Plan Format—Part 1

I. Project summary and description
   1.1 Project summary
      1.1.1 Project and organizational objectives
      1.1.2 Operational and technical characteristics
      1.1.3 Key functions
   1.2 Project description
      1.2.1 Requirements
      1.2.2 Schedule
      1.2.3 Special contractual requirements

II. Approach to Risk Management
   2.1 Definitions
      2.1.1 Technical risk
      2.1.2 Programmatic risk
      2.1.3 Supportability risk
      2.1.4 Cost risk
      2.1.5 Schedule risk
   2.2 Risk assessment methods overview
      2.2.1 Techniques applied
      2.2.2 Implementation of assessment results *(continued on next slide)*

5-17

A Risk-Management Plan Format—Part 2

III. Application
    3.1 Risk Assessment
        3.1.1 Risk identification
        3.1.2 Risk quantification
        3.1.3 Risk prioritization
    3.2 Risk response development
    3.3 Risk response control
        3.3.1 Control evaluation
        3.3.2 Risk documentation

IV. Other relevant plans

V. Conclusions and Recommendations

VI. Approvals

5-18

Important Earned-Value Terms

Earned value is the accepted technique for monitoring and tracking project progress. The concept of earned value revolves around these three measures:

BCWS: Budgeted Cost of Work Scheduled
- BCWS is the cumulative budget for the project.

ACWP: Actual Cost of Work Performed
- The cumulative costs actually expended during the project's life cycle.

BCWP: Budgeted Cost of Work Performed (Also called "Earned Value")
- The percentage of work actually performed measured against the budget for work scheduled or planned to be completed.

5-19

Cost and Schedule Variance

Cost and schedule variance are the two primary measures of the project progress. They can be determined by:

- Cost Variance (CV)

$$CV = BCWP - ACWP$$

- Schedule Variance (SV)

$$SV = BCWP - BCWS$$

If CV/SV = 0; then project is on track
If CV/SV = +; then project is under budget and ahead of schedule
If CV/SV = –; then project is over budget and behind schedule

5-20

Sample Calculation for
Cost and Schedule Variance

Example: You planned to be finished with Task A today. The scheduled cost of the task was $1,000. You have actually spent $900 to date but you are only 90% complete. What are the cost and schedule variances for Task A?

Solution: BCWS = $1,000 (Planned or scheduled cost of the task to date)
ACWP = $900 (Actual cost expended)
BCWP = BCWS x 90% = 1,000 x .90 = $900 (amount of work performed compared with amount scheduled)

$$CV = BCWP - ACWP$$
$$= 900 - 900$$
$$= 0$$
$$SV = BCWP - BCWS$$
$$= 900 - 1,000$$
$$= -100$$

Task is on budget but behind schedule.

5-21

Cost and Schedule Performance Indices

Two indices that are useful for communicating progress status are the Cost Performance Index and the Schedule Performance Index. They are determined by:

Cost Performance Index—The cost efficiency factor representing the relationship between the actual costs expended and the value of the physical work performed.

CPI = BCWP/ACWP

Schedule Performance Index—The planned schedule efficiency factor representing the relationship between the value of the initial planned schedule and the value of the physical work performed.

SPI = BCWP/BCWS

If CPI and SPI = 1, then the project is on budget and on schedule
< 1, then the project is over budget and behind schedule
> 1, then the project is under budget and ahead of schedule

5-22

Sample Calculations for CPI and SPI

Example: The BCWS for a task is $1,000, the ACWP is $900, and the BCWP is $900. What are the CPI and SPI for this task?

$$CPI = BCWP/ACWP$$
$$= 900/900$$
$$= 1.00$$

$$SPI = BCWP/BCWS$$
$$= 900/1,000$$
$$= .90$$

Project is on budget but behind schedule.

5-23

Estimate at Completion

The estimate at completion (EAC) is a projection of the final costs of work at project completion.

$$EAC = BAC/CPI$$

The project manager should recalculate the EAC each time project progress is measured.

Budget at completion (BAC) - Original estimate of completed project costs.

CPI = Cost Performance Index

5-24

Sample EAC Calculation

Example: The original estimate of the project costs is $100,000. If the BCWP for the project to date is $8,000 and the ACWP is $9,300, what is the new EAC for the project?

Solution: CPI = BCWP/ACWP
            = 8,000/9,300
            = .86

    EAC = BAC/CPI
            = 100,000/.86
            = 116,279.07

(Note: This will be the amount needed if no changes are made to the way the project is currently being managed.) 5-25

Estimate to Complete

Estimate to complete (ETC) or the amount of money needed to fund the project to completion is calculated by:

$$ETC = EAC - ACWP$$

5-26

Sample ETC Calculation

Example: If the estimate to complete for a project is $116,279.07 and the actual expenditures to date are $9,300, what is the estimate to complete the project?

Solution: ETC = EAC – ACWP
= 116,279.07 – 9,300
= 106,979.07

5-27

Exercise 5-1 Earned Value Life of Project

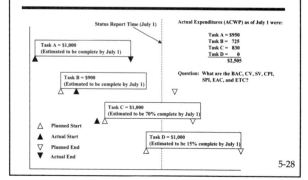

Status Report Time (July 1)

Actual Expenditures (ACWP) as of July 1 were:

Task A = $950
Task B = 725
Task C = 830
Task D = 0
$2,505

Task A = $1,000
(Estimated to be complete by July 1)

Question: What are the BAC, CV, SV, CPI, SPI, EAC, and ETC?

Task B = $900
(Estimated to be complete by July 1)

Task C = $1,000
(Estimated to be 70% complete by July 1)

△ Planned Start
▲ Actual Start
▽ Planned End
▼ Actual End

Task D = $1,000
(Estimated to be 15% complete by July 1)

5-28

Earned Value Sample Solution

Solution:

1. BAC = Task A cost + Task B cost + Task C cost + Task D cost
= 1,000 + 900 + 1,000 + 1,000 = $3,900
2. CV = BCWP – ACWP = 2,475 – 2,505 = –30
3. SV = BCWP – BCWS = 2,475 – 2,750 = –275
4. CPI = BCWP/ACWP = 2,475/2,505 = .99
5. SPI = BCWP/BCWS = 2,475/2,750 = .90
6. EAC = BAC/CPI = 3,900/.99 = 3,939.39
7. ETC = EAC – ACWP = 3,939.39 – 2,505 = 1,434.39

5-29

Exercise 5-2

You are working on a project that was estimated to be completed on May 5 for a cost of $150,000. Today is May 9 and the project is 85% complete. You have spent $145,000. Answer the following questions:

1. What is the BAC for this project?

2. What is the BCWS, BCWP, and ACWP for the project?

3. What is the CV?

4. What is the SV?

5. What is the CPI and the SPI?

6. What is the new EAC?

7. What is the ETC?

5-30

Key Messages—Module 5

The key messages of this module are:

- A well-structured and documented change-control system is crucial for project success

- Risk analysis begins with the interpretation of the SOW and continues throughout the project's life cycle

- There are two kinds of risk:
  - Business risk
  - Pure or insurable risk

- A risk management plan is required to be proactive rather than reactive to risks

5-31
(continued on next slide)

Key Messages—Module 5 (*continued*)

- Earned value is a concept that has been universally accepted as the best way to monitor and control project progress

- There are three basic definitions associated with earned value that have to be understood before the concept can be used:
  - Budgeted cost of work scheduled (BCWS)
  - Actual cost of work performed (ACWP)
  - Budgeted cost of work performed (BCWP)

- BCWP is known as the "earned-value" term

5-32

Module 6: The Project Close-Out Phase

Bringing the Project to a Successful Conclusion

6-0

Objectives for Module 6

At the end of this module you will be able to:

- Describe the project termination, or close-out process

- Determine and describe the project team's activities in completing the project requirements

- Describe the audit activities required to complete the project

- Describe and use a project close-out checklist

6-1

Plan, Schedule, and Monitor Activities

The project close-out phase is often the most difficult phase of the project's life cycle. To successfully close the project, the project manager must:

Plan, schedule, and monitor completion activities:

- Obtain and approve termination plans and schedules

- Prepare and coordinate termination plans and schedules

- Plan for reassignment of project team members and transfer resources to other projects

- Monitor termination activities and completion of all contractual agreements

- Monitor the disposition of any surplus materials or customer-supplied equipment

6-3

Administrative Activities

Complete administrative close-out activities:

- Close work orders and subcontracted work completion
- Notify all stakeholders of project completion
- Close project office and any other project facilities
- Close project books
- Archive project files and records

6-4

Customer Acceptance, Obligation, and Payment Activities

- Ensure deliverables are completed and accepted by customer

- Communicate to the customer completion of all contractual items

- Ensure all contract obligations and documentation are complete

- Transmit formal payment request to the customer

- Monitor customer payment and collection of payments

6-5

Project Audit Format—Part 1

The project manager and team must perform an audit of the project to ensure all the requirements are met and that the financial records are complete. A typical final audit format report includes:

    I.   Executive summary
   II. Introduction
  III. Project Review
      A. Project objectives
      B. Method or approach
  IV. Effectiveness of Planning
   V. Effectiveness of Project Management
  VI. Effectiveness of Technical Solution
 VII. Project Deliverables
      A. Description
      B. Assessment against requirements
VIII. Quality
      A. Standards used
      B. Measurement
      C. Assessment against requirements

6-6

Project Audit—Part 2

IX. Schedule
    A. Delays
       1. Reasons
       2. Recovery actions
    B. Assessment against plan
X. Finances
    A. Problems
       1. Reasons
       2. Recovery actions
    B. Assessment against plan
XI. Resource Utilization
    A. Effectiveness
    B. Problems
       1. Reasons
       2. Recovery actions
XII. Lessons Learned
XIII. Individual Team-Member Assessment and Recommendations
    (submit as separate confidential report)
XIV. Recommendations

Project Close-Out Checklist

❑ Prepare a close-out plan
❑ Verify scope
   – Contractual obligations
   – Administrative obligations
   – WBS (tasks and deliverables)
❑ Obtain customer acceptance of deliverables
❑ Document and archive files and records
❑ Document lessons learned
❑ Reassign resources
❑ Notify all stakeholders of project completion
❑ Celebrate success

Key Messages—Module 6

The key messages of this module are:

• The close-out phase is often the most difficult phase in a project

• The project manager has to complete numerous activities relating to
   – Technical and operational issues
   – Administrative issues
   – Customer approval and acceptance

• A formal project audit is necessary to ensure that all project requirements are complete

• The project manager and team should use a close-out checklist through the close-out process

Index

actual cost of work performed (ACWP), 173-175
   in cost/schedule performance indices, 214-216
   in cost/schedule variance, 211-213
   definition of, 207, 208
   in earned value formulas, 210
   and estimate at completion, 219
   and estimate to complete, 220-221
agenda
   for Introduction Module, 5
   for kickoff meetings, 115-117
   workshop, 13-14
analogous (top-down) estimating, 139, 142
audits, project, 248-252
average net cash flow, 21

BAC, *see* budget at completion
Backward Pass, 157
B/C, *see* benefit-to-cost ratio
BCWP, *see* budgeted cost of work performed
BCWS, *see* budgeted cost of work scheduled
benefit-to-cost ratio (B/C)
   advantages/disadvantages, 52
   content notes on, 25
   data table, 53
   sample calculation of, 54
   training notes on, 50-51
bidding
   "shotgun" approach to, 18
bottom-up (definitive) estimating, 139, 143
break-even point, *see* payback
budget at completion (BAC), 217, 219
budgeted cost of work performed (BCWP), 173-175

   in cost/schedule performance indices, 214-216
   in cost/schedule variance, 211-213
   definition of, 207, 208
   in earned value formulas, 210
   in estimate at completion, 219
budgeted cost of work scheduled (BCWS), 173-174
   in cost/schedule performance indices, 214-216
   in cost/schedule variance, 211-213
   definition of, 207, 208
   in earned value formulas, 210
budget/schedule estimating technique(s), 122-123
   bottom-up technique as, 122-123, 139, 143
   in Development Phase, 139-143
   rough order-of-magnitude as, 122-123, 139-141
   XXtop-down technique as, 122-123, 139, 142
capability (of company), 18
cash flow
   average net, 21
   projected, 18-19
CCB, *see* configuration control board
change control, 171, 172, 182-185
   authority for, 183
   goals of, 182-183
   process of, 184-185
choosing projects, 18, *see also* Selection Phase.
Close-Out Phase, 231-257
   administrative activities in, 244-245
   content theory for, 233-234
   customer acceptance/obligation/payment
      activities in, 246-247
   key messages in, 256-257
   objectives of, 232-233, 238

Close-Out Phase (*continued*)
  plan/schedule/monitor activities in, 241-242
  process of, 4
  project audit in, 248-251
  project checklist for, 253-254
  and project management process, 240
  summary of, 235
  training agenda for, 236
  training notes on, 238-257
  training objectives of, 234
Concept Phase, 59-119
  activities in, 4, 73-74
  content notes on, 61-65
  graphical WBS in, 98
  high-level WBS in, 99
  identification of stakeholders during, 100-105
  indented WBS in, 97
  key messages in, 119
  kick-off meetings in, 112-117
  objectives of, 59-61
  and organizing initial project team, 90-92
  project charter in, 63, 105-111
  in project management process, 72
  stakeholder analysis/management technique
      for, 63-65
  Statement of Work document in, 75-89
  training agenda for, 67
  training objectives of, 65, 69-71
  Work Breakdown Structure in, 61-63, 93-99
configuration control board (CCB), 171, 179, 183
cost performance index (CPI), 214-216
  in estimate at completion, 217-219
  formula for, 210
cost variance (CV), 210-213
CPI, *see* cost performance index
critical path, 158-160
customers, and Statement of Work, 78
CV, *see* cost variance

decision making, 18, 19
definitive (bottom-up) estimating, 139, 143
Department of Defense (DOD), 172
Development Phase, 121-168
  activities in, 4, 135-137
  budget/schedule estimates in, 122-123,
      139-143
  content notes on, 122-128
  exercise for analysis of, 161-162
  Gantt charts in, 163-164
  key messages in, 168
  management plan in, 125-128

  network analysis in, 123-125, 144-145, 151-152
  network diagram in, 149-150
  objectives of, 121-122
  precedence tables in, 148
  project-management plan in, 165-167
  in project management process, 134
  summary of, 129
  training agenda for, 129-130
  training objectives of, 128-129, 132-133
discount rate, *see* internal rate of return
DOD (Department of Defense), 172
duration, project, 159

EAC, *see* estimate at completion
Early Schedule, 151
Early Start, 153
earned value, 172-173, 207-227
  and actual cost of work performed, 173-175,
      207, 208, 210-216, 219-221
  and budgeted cost of work performed, 173-175,
      207, 208, 210-216, 219
  and budgeted cost of work scheduled, 173-174,
      207, 208, 210-216
  cost/schedule performance indices for,
      214-216
  cost/schedule variances for, 211-213
  data collection for, 209
  and estimate at completion, 217-219
  and estimate to complete, 220-221
  exercises for analysis of, 222-227
  formulas for, 175, 210
  over life of project, 222-227
  terms related to, 207-208
estimate at completion (EAC), 217-219
  in estimate to complete, 220-221
  formula for, 210
estimate to complete (ETC), 210, 220-221

float, 159-160
Forward Pass, 154

Gantt charts, 136, 163-164
Graphical WBS, 98
high-level WBS, 99
"hurdle rate," 41

Implementation Phase, 169-229
  activities in, 4, 181
  change control in, 171, 172, 182-185
  content theory for, 170-175
  earned value in, 172-173, 207-227

key messages in, 222-229
objectives of, 170
in project management process, 180
risk identification and analysis in, 171, 173, 186-206
training agenda for, 176
training objectives of, 175, 178-179
indented WBS
content notes on, 62-63
training notes on, 97
initial project team, 90-91
internal rate of return (IRR)
content notes on, 22-24
preparation of data, 42
sample calculation of, 43-44
training notes on, 40-41
Introduction Module, 1-16
and project life cycle model, 3, 4, 11-12
student introductions in, 15-16
training agenda for, 5
welcome time in, 7-8
and workshop agenda, 13-14
and workshop objectives, 9-10
introductions, student, 15-16
IRR, *see* internal rate of return
issue-based risk assessment, 192-193

key messages
in Close-Out Phase, 256-257
in Concept Phase, 119
in Development Phase, 168
in Implementation Phase, 222-229
in Selection Phase, 58
kickoff meetings
agenda for, 115-117
training notes on, 112-117

Late Finish, 156
Late Schedule, 155
life cycle, project, 3, 4, 11-12

management information system (MIS), 20
meetings, kickoff, see kickoff meetings
MIS (management information system), 20

net present value (NPV)
content notes on, 24-25
data table for, 47
sample calculation of, 48-49
training notes on, 45-46
net returns, 21

network analysis (Development Phase), 144-145, 151-152
Backward Pass in, 157
critical path in, 158-160
Early Schedule in, 151
Early Start in, 153
float in, 158-159
Forward Pass in, 154
Late Finish in, 156
Late Schedule in, 155
precedence diagramming method in, 123-125
project duration in, 158
network development, 146-147
NPV, *see* net present value

objectives, *see also* training objectives.
of Close-Out Phase, 232-233, 238
of Concept Phase, 59-61
of Development Phase, 121-122
of Implementation Phase, 170
of Selection Phase, 18-19
workshop, 9-10
opportunity costs, 42

payback
content notes on, 20-21
sample calculation of, 35
training notes on, 33-34
PDM, *see* precedence diagramming method
PERT (project evaluation research technique), 60
PMI, *see* Project Management Institute
PMPs, *see* project management professionals
precedence diagramming method (PDM), 123-125
precedence tables, 148
present value (PV), 40, *see also* net present value.
profit, projected, 19
project audits, 248-252
Project Charter
content notes on, 63
major elements of, 107-108
outline of, 109
sample, 110-111
training notes on, 105-111
project duration, 159
project evaluation research technique (PERT), 60
project life cycle model, 3, 4, 11-12
project management, growth of, as field, 2
Project Management Institute (PMI)
certification of PMPs by, 18, 39
on number of certified project management professionals, 1

project-management plan, 125-128, 165-167
project management professionals (PMPs), 18, 39
project managers
    and decision-making process, 19
    and project selection process, 29
    and Statement of Work, 78
project team, initial, 90-91
PV, *see* present value

quantitative techniques, risk assessment, 196-198

ranking, risk, 199-201
return on investment (ROI)
    content notes on, 21
    sample calculation of, 38-39
    software for, 38
    training notes on, 36-37
risk identification and analysis, 171, 173,
        186-206
    assessment chart for, 190
    assessment methods for, 191190
    issue-based assessment for, 192-193
    quantitative techniques for, 196-198
    ranking risks in, 199-201
    responsibility for, 187
    and risk-management plans, 202-206
    scoring techniques for, 194-195
    and types of risk, 188-189
risk-management plans, 202-206
risks
    accounting for, in budget, 209
    ranking, 199-201
ROI, *see* return on investment
rough order-of-magnitude (ROM), 122-123,
        139-141

schedule estimating techniques, *see* budget/
        schedule estimating technique(s)
schedule performance index (SPI), 210, 214-216
schedule variance (SV), 210-213
scoring techniques, risk assessment, 194-195
Selection Phase, 17-58
    activities in, 4
    benefit-to-cost ratio technique for, 25, 50-54
    content notes for, 19-25
    discussion in, 29
    exercise for analysis of, 55
    internal rate of return technique for, 22-24, 40-44
    key messages in, 58
    net present value technique for, 24-25, 45-49
    objectives of, 18-19

payback (break-even point) technique for, 20-21,
        33-35
    in project management process, 30
    project managers' inclusion in, 29
    project selection techniques for, 31-32
    return on investment technique for, 21, 36-39
    training agenda for, 26
    training objectives of, 25, 28-29
"shotgun" approach to bidding, 18
SOW, *see* Statement of Work
SPI, *see* schedule performance index
spreadsheet software, 38
stakeholders
    content notes on, 63-65
    training notes on, 100-105
Statement of Work (SOW)
    collection of requirements in, 84-87
    critical reading of, 81-83
    outline of, 79
    reasons for misinterpretation of, 80
    training notes on, 75-89
    translation of requirements in, 88-89
student introductions, 15-16
A Survival Guide for Project Managers, 2
SV, *see* schedule variance

top-down (analogous) estimating, 139, 142
training agenda
    for Close-Out Phase, 236
    for Concept Phase, 67
    for Development Phase, 129-130
    for Implementation Phase, 176
    for Introduction Module, 5
    for Selection Phase, 26
training notes (Close-Out Phase), 238-257
training objectives
    of Close-Out Phase, 234
    of Concept Phase, 65, 69-71
    of Development Phase, 128-129, 132-133
    of Implementation Phase, 175, 178-179
    of Selection Phase, 25, 28-29

WBS, *see* Work Breakdown Structure
welcome (Introduction Module), 7-8
Work Breakdown Structure (WBS)
    for Close-Out Phase, 232, 243
    content notes on, 61-63
    graphical format for, 98
    high level, 99
    indented format for, 62-63, 97
    training notes on, 93-99